HER NAME WAS ELIZABETH

Her Name Was Elizabeth

The Life of Elizabeth Fisher Brewster
Christian Missionary to China 1884–1950

Eva M. Brewster

Red Hart Press
Mount Shasta, California

Red Hart Press
Mount Shasta, California
cpreus@finestplanet.com

Printed in the United States of America
First printing October 2018

Paintings on cover and on Title pages by Karis Manton,
granddaughter of Elizabeth Brewster
Catherine Preus *Cover Design, Interior Design*
www.FourWildGeeseDesign.com
Maria Hirano *Copy Editor*
marialodes.wixsite.com/lotus
Frances Buran *Indexer*

Photographs:
Center for Southeast Louisiana Studies, China Collection—
pages 161, 163, 164
Barbara B. Ward—pages 164–168

ISBN 978-1-7324373-0-2
Library of Congress Control Number: 2018950746

HER NAME WAS ELIZABETH The Life of Elizabeth Fisher Brewster
Christian Missionary to China 1884-1950 / Eva M. Brewster

1. Biography. 2. Christian Missions. 3. China. 4. Women's Education.

Table of Contents

Acknowledgements *vii*

Map *viii*

Editor's Preface *ix*

Preface *xiii*

1 Buckeye Days *1*

2 Child of the King *15*

3 Miss Star of China *33*

4 All Things Work Together for Good *55*

5 Elizabeth and Will *77*

6 As the Apple Tree Among the Trees of the World *99*

7 So Was My Beloved *123*

8 Part of the Answer *169*

9 A Daughter-in-law for Elizabeth *179*

10 The Legend of Elizabeth *199*

11 Elizabeth and Her Children *241*

12 Our Priceless Dower *283*

Index *313*

Photographs follow Chapter Seven, on pages 161–168

Acknowledgments

As the loving granddaughter of Elizabeth Fisher Brewster, it is with gratitude and humility that I wish to acknowledge the faithful contributions of many friends who have read the original copies of the unpublished draft of the book, *HER NAME WAS ELIZABETH*, written by Eva M. Brewster during the years 1950-1954.

Many of my friends and colleagues have encouraged me to pursue publishing so as to allow scholars and others to have access to information regarding the powerful and inspired labors of the early Christian Mission work in China during the late 19th and early 20th centuries.

I wish to especially thank and acknowledge Catherine Preus, who has carefully edited and presented the book in its present format. Her enthusiasm, technical expertise, and belief in the value of this project have been key to the accomplishment of a long held dream of mine to make this manuscript available to the public.

Barbara Brewster Ward

I wish to thank Maria Hirano for her editing expertise. Her contribution has made all the difference—not only did she ensure the correct placement of hundreds of commas and dashes, but her subtle and sensitive edits transformed Eva's 70-year-old manuscript into a smoothly readable form for today's reader. I also wish to thank Valerie Lashbaugh for her insightful comments on design, and Frances Buran for her excellent index and helpful editorial input. I thank Ana Daniel for recommending me for the job and introducing me to Barbara Ward. It has been a delight working on this project with Barbara and sharing in the glow of a spiritual legacy continuing through the generations.

Catherine M. Preus

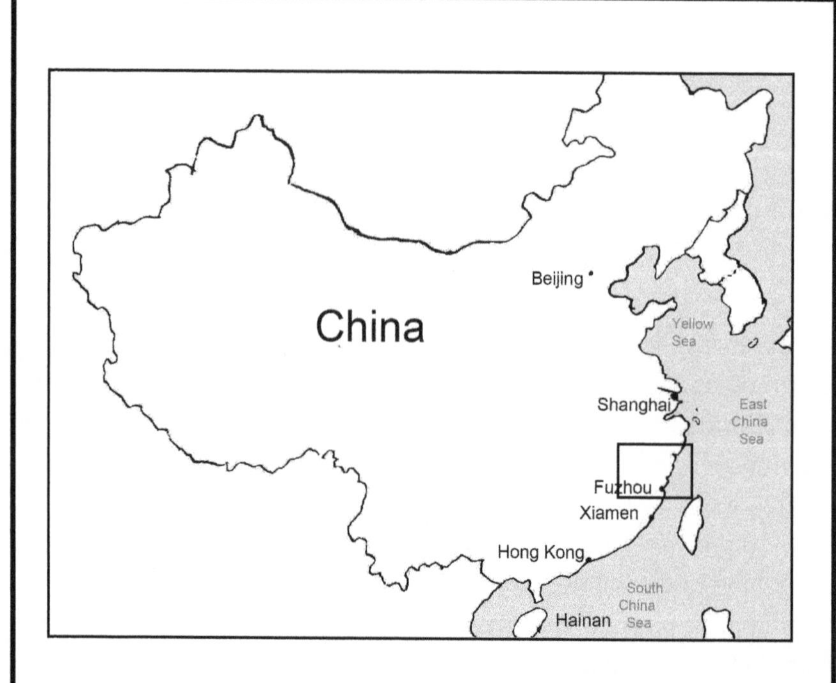

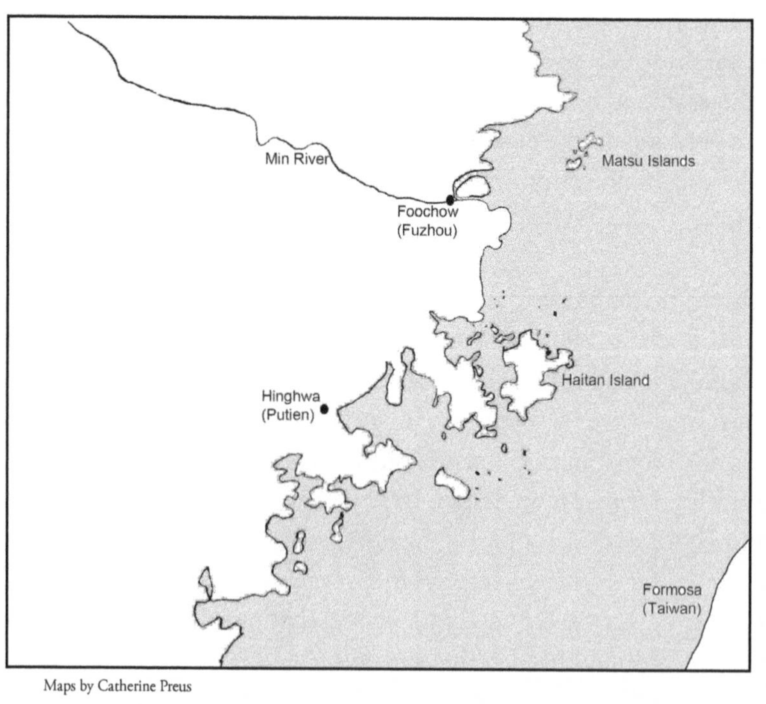

Maps by Catherine Preus

Editor's Preface

Elizabeth Fisher Brewster was one of the multitudes of single-women missionaries who in the late 19th and early 20th centuries left their homes and sailed to far-off exotic places, living lives of dedicated Christian service. In a time when women's roles were largely circumscribed by home and family, single women missionaries with few professional credentials and no special status thrust themselves into adventurous and sometimes heart-breaking lives of great toil and achievement.

The 67 years of Elizabeth's missionary service spanned an era of revolution, war and unprecedented change in China. When Elizabeth first arrived in 1884, the Imperial banners of the dying Manchu Dynasty still flew high across the land. The Chinese masses lived lives of crushing toil in rural poverty with little hope of a better life. Among her many duties, it was the downtrodden women, who were considered unworthy of being educated, that were Elizabeth's strong concern.

Travelling to country villages, she was paraded before the populace, who wished to see the "big heavenly feet" of the foreign lady missionary. Elizabeth labored mightily to change the cruel practice of foot-binding and the attitudes and customs that literally hobbled women, seeking to instill an ideal of education as the way forward for women. When she was asked to speak at a convention on the topic: "How Much Education Should We Give Our Girls?" her words were short and to the point, "Exactly as much as we give our boys." This was a vision for the fulfillment of women's potential that surpassed even the most liberal-minded of those days. The Hwa Nan College for Women was founded in 1908 by the Methodist mission and is still going strong today.

In 1890, Elizabeth married fellow Methodist missionary and

minister, William Nesbitt Brewster. They settled in Hinghwa (Putien) on the Min River near the coastal city of Foochow (Fuzhou) in the southeast of China. They raised a family of seven children and carried on the work of the mission—preaching and teaching; founding schools and hospitals; supervising an orphanage; building churches for the leper colony; improving agricultural methods; and even founding a colony in Borneo, offering the impoverished farmers a way to make a new life. The essence of their mission was "Christ made visible through deeds." Material things are holy, too, they believed, and they made every effort to improve the lot of their adopted countrymen. They persisted in the face of criticism from the mission board, some of whom felt that missionaries should limit their efforts to evangelism.

"Dealing with war and armies was not my special ability," said Elizabeth, in her matter-of-fact manner. Yet she endured almost constant war and revolution. For decades the self-aggrandizing Western nations had been competing to divide up China for their own benefit and consequently, China's anger was taken out on all foreigners. There was the Hwa Sang (Kucheng) massacre in 1895, in which 11 missionaries were brutally killed. In June of 1900, the Empress Dowager ordered that all foreigners be killed. Elizabeth and William escaped that fate, thanks to the heroism of two Chinese officials, who were later martyred. The Boxer Rebellion, the defection of the Imperial army, war with Japan, civil war, the establishment of the communist regime...throughout Elizabeth's years in China, the chaos and unrest continued unabated.

Many missionaries were killed, many more fled the country. Elizabeth and her husband stayed. When William died in 1916, Elizabeth stayed on another 34 years, entrusting her life and work into God's hands. Like the story of Ruth in the Bible, she had made the Chinese people her own people. When China was plunged into civil war, Elizabeth strove to keep the mission's schools, hospitals and churches oases of neutrality. Under bombardment and imminent danger of total destruction, she kept her equilibrium, saying, "It is often necessary to go quietly on with work in hand, knowing the spirit will speak when it is necessary." Her "outsider" status as a missionary and her spirit-led decisions were, on several occasions, crucial in saving lives and averting catastrophes.

The local Chinese people found much to admire in this woman of enduring selfless service. They called her "Miss Star" when she was young; a spirited woman, freshly arrived in their country. Later they called her "Mother Shepherdess" and even "Friend of the Bandits." Elizabeth traveled safely in rural areas between feuding factions, displaying a white flag. All of the involved parties knew her as the kindly foreign missionary woman who had taught their countrymen and cared for them when they were children.

Years later when asked about the sacrifices she had made, Elizabeth said, "God doesn't want sacrifice. He wants us to surrender our will in obedience." It was this that made her life one of extraordinary accomplishment and fulfillment. Hers was not a life of dreary slavery, but one of adventure and joyous service. Some questioned if anything of lasting value had been achieved during this era of revolution and war, especially since China embraced a communist regime of atheist conviction. Ultimately, this question was not the issue. "We plant beside all waters," Elizabeth maintained. The important thing was to keep on adapting to changing circumstances, tackling great problems with cheerful practicality, and continuing to carry out the daily tasks God put before her.

She stood firm in her God-directed work in the face of war, revolution, disease, natural disaster, near starvation, political instability and economic collapse. The Chinese villagers needed her courage and message of spiritual hope even more than the material help and vision, and begged her to stay. It was never her desire to leave, but in 1950 the Communists forced all missionaries out of China. Thus it was that Elizabeth ended her 67 years in China, not with her being buried there as she wished, but with her return to the United States for the last years of her life.

There seems to be a hidden motive to God's ways in this sudden reversal of Elizabeth's dwelling place in her late eighties. Elizabeth's inspiring life is the stuff of legends, and yet her story might have been lost forever had she not been forcibly returned to her native country, and were it not for the dedication of Eva Brewster, also a missionary and a talented writer, who took up the task of recording the stories and preserving the memory of her beloved mother–in-law.

An adept storyteller, Eva fashioned *Her Name Was Elizabeth* into an engrossing tale of spiritual devotion and adventure. We learn first-hand how daily life was lived; the cultural exchanges that took place; where strangers became friends and hearts touched hearts in a foreign land. We learn how the two women's lives intertwined, when they were both missionaries in China; and even after Eva returned to the U.S. during the depression and WWII, while Elizabeth continued her work in China; and later when Eva was in post-WWII Germany with her husband, who took part in the U.S.-led restoration efforts to aid a devastated people and country.

Eva's talent in catching and distilling the timeless lessons of faith in the stories she recounts makes this book a treasure. The narrative unfolds in the context of conversations between the two women—one an artist by temperament, the other a seasoned missionary and revered family elder. The tenderness of their relationship gives this book, written almost 70 years ago, a freshness and warmth which shines through and imparts courage and hope to today's reader.

Catherine M. Preus

Preface

"Just a wink of an eye from heaven..."

There was no escaping the noise that invaded our sleeping farmhouse. It wasn't the wild buffeting of wind; it wasn't the awesome crash of thunder. Even as I cowered in my cavern of sleep, I knew it for something alien and infinitely menacing. It came again—a scrabbling, a thud, ending in a final fleshly thump and un-echoing silence. My husband and I arrived simultaneously at the bedroom door, brought there by my terrified screaming.

As we fumbled for the doorknob and then the light switch, we knew what we would find. At the foot of the stairs, her limp feet on the bottom step, her head resting on the thick Chinese rug, lay my husband's ninety-one year old mother. As my husband knelt beside her, I stood at the head of the stairs wailing. A vast regret filled me, for that was no ordinary little lady lying there so quietly. That was Elizabeth Fisher Brewster, a missionary to China for sixty-seven years and beloved mother to tens of thousands. Guilt sharpened my grief for I had an unfulfilled contract with her.

For twenty years we had planned, she and I, that someday, when I had time, I would put down on paper what had made life wonderful for her, and there was so much to tell. Even the chartreuse pajamas which clothed her so decently had a story. Elizabeth had told it to me just that afternoon, as she stood ironing and I rolled out a pie for dinner. Noticing the gay garment she was working on, I asked,

"Mother, when did you start wearing pajamas? I distinctly remember the embroidered nighties you used to wear."

She nodded, pleased at the invitation to visit. "It must be about twenty years since I decided to change over," she said, enlivening our work by telling me why.

It seems that she made her decision one summer when two of her friends had been vacationing in Kuling, a mountain resort in central China. When it was time for them to go back to work, there was fighting in Shanghai, and all shipping was tied up. The women decided to travel by rail south to Canton, and take a coastal steamer up to Hinghwa. Their plans proceeded with no more than usual discomfort and inconvenience until, on their way up the coast, they ran into a typhoon. Typhoons are not unusual to China travelers, but this one was so violent that it overwhelmed their little ship, driving it aground near a rocky island. The alarmed passengers were routed out of their bunks and hurried on deck without opportunity to dress. Life boats were launched, and everyone had to climb down a ladder and jump for his life. Miraculously, all passengers were landed safely on the shelter-less island, where they huddled until the storm subsided and they were rescued.

As Elizabeth talked, I pictured, from the delicious safety of or our home, the terror of that night: the solid wind driving chill spray into bodies still warm from bed, the vicious waves crashing down the sloping deck, sucking and tearing at the legs of the passengers, the two elderly women clutching at anything solid for support, as the wind whipped clouds and sea and night into chaos around them. I pictured them clambering down the unsteady ladder, and held my breath as they made the jump—that could have just as well been a leap into the water, as into the careening life boat.

"How awful," I shuddered. "How did they ever manage?"

"That's what I asked them, too," replied Elizabeth. "They said they were wearing pajamas made like a suit of Chinese clothes, so though they were wet and cold, they were well-dressed through it all. I decided right then and there, the world being what it is, I would have the tailor make me several suits of pajamas, and I have worn them ever since."

She was startled by my burst of laughter.

"Did I say something funny?"

"It's just that I had never thought of pajamas as the answer to typhoons, Mother dear," I explained. I considered suggesting to her that the world being what it is, a lady her age might better settle down somewhere outside the sphere of expected violence; but I didn't want to ruffle her feelings. She is not ready to retire nor is she looking for safety. No, adequately prepared with a suit of pajamas in her bag, she will continue to risk war, earthquake, typhoon or an atom bomb, if they cross the path God has chosen for her to travel. At best these will furnish the excitement she loves; at most they will cost her life on earth—but what is that to Elizabeth who has always lived just a wink of an eye from heaven?

Now the emergency for which the pajamas were planned had arrived, not a typhoon or a bomb, but a fall in the night down the stairs of our farmhouse in Wisconsin. The silk net still held her silver curls in place; the night cream still shone on her face. How alive and gay she had been just two hours earlier, when I sat watching her careful evening-beauty ritual!

"She's dead," I mourned. "Mother's been killed."

"No, she isn't," snapped her oldest son, my husband. "She's breathing. Her head is cut badly, and all her front teeth are knocked out, but she isn't dead. Stop acting like a banshee and get me a wet towel to wipe away all this blood."

Unbelievably, as he sponged her face, she rose to her hands and knees, and began to look around. My husband picked her up, deaf to my protests that it wasn't good first-aid practice to do so, and laid her on the davenport. Her upper lip was split to her nose; her front teeth were indeed knocked out, and scattered on the stairs. Her one good eye was already puffed up from an ugly cut on the ridge of the socket.

Pointing to her ear, she demanded as clearly as her damaged mouth would allow,

"My hearing aid; get me my hearing aid."

When I put it in her hands she adjusted the earpiece and turned on the switch.

"What happened?" she demanded.

She couldn't hear what I was saying, and I wondered sadly if the fall had destroyed the last vestige of hearing. But the keen mind was still alert. "Oh, it's the battery. I took it out when I went to bed." It was a nightly ritual I had forgotten about.

When the battery was replaced, she asked again, "What did I do?"

"You fell down the stairs, head over heels, judging from the noise you made, and the marks on the steps."

She made a sound of exasperation and began manipulating her arms, wrists and legs.

"Well, nothing's broken, anyway," she announced with satisfaction to her son who had been calling the ambulance.

"How exactly alike they are," I thought, "she wants no sympathy and he offers none."

Neither in the ambulance, nor at the hospital was there any hysteria. After an hour of stitching and patching, the doctor emerged, shaking his head and laughing.

"She'll be all right. What a woman! She's bruised all over, but broke only a little finger. She isn't even suffering from shock. I wouldn't blame anyone for getting hysterical after such a fall, blood running down her throat, and me stitching her mouth and eye, but all she said was, 'I hope you don't spoil my Jeffersonian nose.' What did she mean by that?"

This time it was I who laughed and shook my head, for Elizabeth's one sin is pride in family. Not even her battered mouth could prevent her from telling the doctor that she had inherited that proud little nose with the flaring nostrils from her Field Jefferson ancestor, kin to Thomas Jefferson himself.

I went into her room, still laughing, and asked, "How are you, darling?" She answered with the old spirit,

"Well, the doctor has just finished with me, so I guess I must be all right." Then a little wistfully, "I suppose this is the end of my beauty, though."

That question I couldn't answer immediately, for she was by then a horrifying sight, puffed and discolored beyond recognition. She remained calm and poised through the whole ordeal, however.

"The lady in the next bed had an operation," she confided to me the second morning. "She had a bad night. She can't seem to get ahold of herself."

But Elizabeth had ahold of herself, and I knew why. She had told me once, that years ago when she was still a very young girl, the peerless experience of the presence of God had come to her.

"From that time to this I have never been without the knowledge of His presence except for a few bitter hours when I heard that Will (her husband) had died. For a while my grief was so great that it shut God out, but not for long."

She was just twenty-two when she went to China as a missionary. In November of 1884 she had sailed up the Min River to Foochow for the first time. She was dressed in her best, hoping to please both God and man. She wore a light weight suit of beige wool, her size-three shoes just showing beneath the ankle length skirt three-yards in width. Her bright brown hair was combed into a high pompadour on top of which perched a hat of fine cream-colored straw lined with canary velvet. Her eyes, a deep and lively blue, were wide with excitement as the Chinese tapestry of old mountains, tawny river, pagodas and sampans unrolled before her.

But it was the naked children, the toiling women, the sweating men that Elizabeth saw with her heart. It was for this she had left her home; for this she had embarked on the old *City of New York* to sail across a wide and stormy ocean. She had come to bring them the good news of God's love—and not all the enchantment of China ever made her forget it.

"Why did you go to China," I questioned one day. "Was it to make Methodists of the people, to raise their standards of living, or what?"

She gazed at me in disbelief. "I went to China in obedience to the will of God, relying on Him to lead me every step of the way. I preached Jesus and His good news to people who had never heard of Him before. Many of them became Christians and most of those became Methodists, to be sure. Certainly their standard of living was raised; that naturally follows becoming a follower of Jesus. I taught and fed and comforted and did whatever else He put before me to do.

Whatever did you think I went for?"

Surely no one, not even the confident Elizabeth, could foresee the decades of time and the variety of service those God-led steps would cover. Sixty-six years later, in 1950, she toured the fields of her labor for the last time. Bombing planes flew overhead, armies clashed around her, but everywhere she went, carried in a chair on the shoulders of Chinese coolies, the people of the villages ignored the planes and armies alike, and came out to meet her with banners waving and firecrackers popping.

Her eldest daughter accompanied her on that trip, for Mother Brewster's eyes were almost blind then and she was almost deaf.

But her love sped ahead to greet the welcoming crowds. Her memory searched among them, and sorted them out by names and families.

Of her arrival at the beloved seashore community of Bing Hai, her daughter Mary wrote:

"In one place two former Orphanage young people, both with nurse's training, which mother had made possible, and doing their work in a former Station House which they had been able to purchase through her efforts, came out to see her. They brought their children with them. The husband knelt to get on a level with her hearing aid, and said:

'More than to the mother who bore me, I owe to you, Shepherdess Mother. We dare not think where we would have been without your concern and help. Every day, we speak of our debt of gratitude to you and ask the Heavenly Father to help us repay you by helping others.'

"Every church we visited, she delighted the Christians assembled by inquiring for their absent members, whose very names she remembered."

How often I have heard Elizabeth ask God to bless each and every one of her loved ones, near and far: "Thou knowest each by name and the need of each." Tears fill my eyes as her faith brushes doubt from my heart. Surely her own incredible memory for countless individuals is but a reflection of God's own infinite capacity to know us each by name.

Elizabeth's faith has changed over the years into knowing, and God has literally become her source of living on earth, and her confident hope of life after death and in the land of "everlasting clearness."

For that reason hers is a story worth telling. May it light your path as it has mine.

CHAPTER ONE

Buckeye Days

There was nothing remarkable about Elizabeth's childhood except that she had a father who knew God. Her mother knew Him, too, but not so well, Elizabeth thought. Her father always beamed with joy when he spoke of God, but her mother always choked up and cried, especially when she was witnessing in church. This made Elizabeth want to hide under the pew. She was determined that when she grew up and got to know God, she would beam like her father and not cry like her mother when she talked about Him.

Her father was William Henry Raper Fisher, and so long as Elizabeth knew him, he was a Methodist preacher. He hadn't always wanted to preach. In fact, he was definitely opposed to following this vocation of his grandfather. Neither was he inclined to operate the big farm which his father owned just outside of Midway, Ohio. He was frail in body, but inquiring of mind and eager in spirit.

So his father, puzzled as to the boy's future, bought a perpetual scholarship at Ohio Wesleyan Academy and sent William, then 17, to be its first beneficiary. At the end of one year, he was home again. Something had been spoken which he was unwilling to hear. Perhaps a Billy Graham of that day conducting a revival meeting at college had tossed the burning word. Perhaps God Himself in some unexpected moment had spoken it. At any rate, William Fisher had received the call to preach, even though he didn't want to do it. His answer was flight.

"I knew if I stayed on at college, I couldn't avoid the call to preach," he confided later. "I couldn't face the thought, so I left school."

In 1856 at the age of twenty, he married Mary Jane Minshall, who lived on a neighboring farm. One can almost hear him saying, "Surely, raising a family is enough of a responsibility for any man, and a fine contribution to society, as well."

But the Hound of Heaven is not so easily thrown off the scent.

For some years the little Fisher family lived on one or another of the family farms. The going was hard. William was not strong enough for the lifting and digging and long hours of manual labor required on a farm. Neither was his heart in the work, which subconsciously he recognized as evasion. Children were born, Pitzer in 1858, named for the beloved evangelist, Richard Pitzer; Addie in 1860, Elizabeth in 1862, Carrie in l864, and Will in 1866.

Meanwhile, the Word burned deeper into William's soul, until he could bear it no longer. Humbly he bowed to a Will that was stronger than his own, and began to witness at prayer meetings about God's intensely personal dealings with him.

Soon, nearby churches and those far away by horse-buggy travel invited him to help in the two-week revivals, then an annual event in the Ohio Methodist Churches. Years later, Elizabeth, visiting these same churches on behalf of her work in China, rejoiced to meet many people who not only remembered her father, but gave him the credit for their own vital Christian experience. They especially remembered him for his radiant faith, which caused his face to shine as if from an inner sun.

Elizabeth still speaks of him as a man like Moses, "who wist not that his face shone." He was always so kind, so loving and yet, so sternly just upon occasion that he became for her on earth what she thought God must be in Heaven.

During all her life she knew him, too, as a man with a book in hand. For now her father had to do not only his own will, but God's too, as he explained to her. He had his fine family to support, and also his lessons to prepare, since he was studying for the ministry. In those days, candidates for the ministry in the Methodist church had to take a course of study prescribed by "conference," which is the governing body for designated areas for the Methodist churches.

One summer stands out vividly in Elizabeth's mind. Her father had found a job as road supervisor near a little town called Bethel in Ohio. In order to be near him, the family made one of their frequent moves to a farm home in the neighborhood. All summer long and into the sunny fall, her father weighed loads of gravel and supervised its spreading. His delighted little children played in the dusty woods, gathering the shining buckeyes in baskets along the new road, and he played quiet games with them when he sat down between loads.

"Sh! Father is studying now," they would caution each other when he picked up his book.

Last summer, when Elizabeth, then ninety-one, came to us from Ohio, she carried in her pocket a buckeye.

"I wondered if you had ever seen one," she asked, stroking its glossy brown surface, lovingly. "There were so many when we were children. How we loved to play with them! Now they have become very scarce."[1]

If all Elizabeth's childhood days could be wrapped up like the kernel of a buckeye into a shining brown shell with a dazzling white eye, that eye would be the day her father passed his examinations, became a minister, and had a church of his own. How they had longed for that day! They were tired of moving from one job to another, sad to see their adored father always working, always studying, and

---

1 The buckeye is familiar to most of us as the horse chestnut. Ohio Indians named it Hetuk, which means "eye of a buck" because of its resemblance to the eyes of the spirited animals which used to roam the Ohio hills. There is a story that on September 2, 1788, Indian braves gathered at Marietta, Ohio, to make peace treaties with the white men. In order to impress them, all the white officers paraded in what regalia they could muster. The Indians were delighted with the display, especially with one officer, a Colonel Ebenezer Sproat. This gentleman was over six feet tall and carried himself and his sword with such gallantry that the Indians commented admiringly, "Heap big Hetuk." And so the name "Heap Big Buckeye" stuck to the colonel, and was gradually passed on to all Ohio residents.

becoming frailer.

In the golden September of 1864, that longed for day arrived. Her father went to conference and passed his examinations: "I stood higher on the list than some who had four years of college preparation," he told them in joyous confidence.

This was a matter of intense pride for them all, especially for small Elizabeth, who loved him with a single devotion. It was the complete justification of fourteen years of sacrifice and poverty.

William Fisher became a pastor on trial and was assigned as junior preacher in a distant corner of the conference in Mount Pleasant, in Vinton County, where the Appalachian Mountains subside into rolling hills.

Then came the best time of all for the children—moving day. Two wagons were borrowed from relatives. Their own spring wagon, a kind of surrey without a top, was rolled out. Before the children's delighted eyes, beds were knocked down and piled into the wagons. Clothes were taken down from the wall pegs and packed into iron strapped trunks. Bureaus and tables and chairs were piled between and on top of barrels of dishes and pots and pans with feather beds filling up the crannies. And then everything was roped snugly to the wagon box.

All machinery, tools and animals had been sold. The Fishers were through with farming. Father was at last a minister.

Uncle Newt and Aunt Leora were there to drive one wagon; Uncle Theodore and Aunt Ella had charge of the other. The aunts weren't really necessary, but they wanted to visit Aunt Rhoda in Circleville, and besides, they had never seen the hill country. No doubt the children looked longingly at the chairs perched high on the loads, wishing to be seated on them, but luckily for them, they were tucked snugly in between the adults on the hard wagon seats.

The trip began. Down the narrow rutted roads the wagons bumped and rolled toward the Scioto Trail. Everywhere there was activity. The Civil War was over, and Ohio people were happy and hopeful once more. The Fishers saw log cabins being torn down along the way, and the piles of sawed lumber which would build new houses. They met land owners like their own Uncle Quinn, driving fine horses as they carried on their dealings in land and cattle. Everywhere men were chopping down the forests for larger fields. The Fishers were seeing a new world in the making.

The first night was spent at Aunt Rhoda's in Circleville. They could have driven ten thousand miles and not found a spot more mysterious. The first white men to venture up the Scioto Trail had come upon a clearing chopped out of the dim forests. In it, open to the sun, they found an altar surrounded by earthen walls forming a perfect circle. No one knows who built it or when. The Indians who lived under the mighty umbrella of trees which covered Ohio in those days had no memory of the builders. Their legends had no explanation for it. One thing was certain; whoever had built it knew enough of the principles of mathematics and engineering to build a perfect circle.

The white men, grateful that there were no trees to be chopped, settled there. They built a courthouse on the large altar, and when the area within the walls began to grow crowded, they tore the walls down. So, Aunt Rhoda told them that the only thing circular about the town now was its name, Circleville.

Early the next day, the rattling cavalcade was on its way again. Now they were almost 20 miles from home and all the sights were new. They crossed a stream on a bridge that looked like a house set across the water. They drove along roads where the black forest pressed so close that the branches raked the furniture on the wagons and would have swept the chairs right off except for the stout rope that tied them down. Sometimes they passed lonely clearings where old apple trees and lilacs guarded a few tumbled logs or there was nothing at all. At such times, the adults would fall silent as they gazed, perhaps remembering the words of the Psalmist, "Man goeth to his long rest, and his place knoweth him no more."

Was it Indians? Or fire? Had children like theirs once romped over the grass catching the sun in their tangled curls, and shattering the quiet forest with their laughter?

And the thoughts of the women raced swiftly to the Western

prairies where even then, other women watched the ocean of waving grass for fire or for movements not made by wind.

There was the moment at once solemn and exciting when the wagons reached Zane's Trace, the road which had opened up the whole Western wilderness.[2] But the Fishers could not linger on the edge of history. They had to hurry on to the future awaiting them in Vinton County.

The real excitement, Elizabeth remembers, was the hill country. Never had she imagined such a sight! The hills were like the teeth of a gigantic saw, rising and falling one after the other. The horses labored until sweat streaked their shining coats as they dragged the wagons up the steep, rough roads.

At first they laughed and leaned forward to ease the upward pull. Before long, however, the women and children were clambering out over the high wheels and walking up the hills. At the top, the weary horses rested, their heads hanging, while the erstwhile passengers, breathless and red-faced, caught up and climbed back into the wagons.

Then, the real fun began. The wagons were made for flat country and had no brakes; the horses were unaccustomed to digging-in in order to hold back on the load. So when the rattling, swaying wagons began to push against their tails, the frightened animals let go and ran. Elizabeth, who has never in all her life known fear, still laughs at the memory. The aunts screamed in terror, and hung on to the children and the wagon frame. Branches slapped them as the top-heavy wagons lurched from side to side. The children shouted in pure excitement. Underneath the clamor, the voices of the men called reassuringly to the horses. The scene is so vivid in Elizabeth's memory,

---

2 Up to 1796, the forests of Ohio stood like a living wall across the path of westward travel. People could travel westward by boat on the Great Lakes or on the Ohio River, but for settlers in the heart of the territory, and for the caravans of great freight wagons wanting to go West, the mighty forest was as impenetrable as stone. In that year, Congress authorized Ebenezer Zane to clear a road from Wheeling, West Virginia, to Maysvilie, Kentucky. This road was used so much that Ohio settlers used to say about it, "Ruts deep enuf to bury a horse." By 1838, a northern branch carried the road from Zanesville to Columbus and Springfield; and beyond, the land lay open to the Pacific Ocean.

she can remember the names of the horses.

"Whoa, Loll! Steady Boy! Whoa there, Fan. Pony, steady!"

But the horses ran until the next hill rose to slow them to a trembling walk. Elizabeth has forgotten how many hills were left behind before the horses became accustomed to the terror of the wagons hitting their tails, but admits there were too many for comfort. Everyone was scratched and bruised, but strangely enough, no real harm was done.

At the end of a long day, the weary travelers arrived at a crossroads. The sun had set, and gloom spilled out of the pressing forest. As they rested, wondering which way to go, the yellow light of a lamp flickered through the night. There was a farm house in the woods across the road. This time it was Will Fisher who stiffly climbed over the wheel, and went to ask directions. He came back running, calling joyously that their journey was over. The farmer, Mr. Johnson, belonged to their church and had invited them to stay overnight.

The daughter of the house was especially kind to the battered travelers, carrying hot water for washing up, frying potatoes and salt pork for their supper, and finally, lamp in hand, leading them up to rag-carpeted rooms and cloud-soft feather beds.

Forty years later, Elizabeth was exchanging Ohio memories with a group of women in California. She told of her exciting first journey into Vinton County and of the lovely young woman who had been so kind at the end of that strenuous day. A woman in the group gasped and exclaimed, "Why, I remember that night, perfectly. That was my father's house, and I was that young lady!"

The next morning Mr. Johnson took them to their new home. The children were out of the wagons before they stopped, rapturously investigating their new domain. The home was snuggled between two towering hills which sloped smooth, and green to its very walls. There was a barn for Fan and Pony; a well with a bucket and a wooden water trough for the horses, like the one on Uncle Quinn's farm back home. Behind the house, an orchard climbed the slope. The children never walked down those slopes when it was dry enough to roll, and all they needed for winter coasting was a smooth board on which to come spinning downhill.

The first thing William Fisher did was to take his spring wagon to a blacksmith for possible repairs and the addition of brakes. There were six churches scattered through the county for him to serve and he had no desire to risk himself and his horses on those hills again with a brakeless wagon.

Then began a year of most joyous service. William Fisher was not a spectacular preacher, but one who knew the God of whom he spoke. This had an irresistible appeal wherever he went, and many new members were added to his church rolls; many old ones learned to know God for the first time from him.

In the late autumn of that first year, the pastor in charge left for the West to look for a more prosperous circuit. William Fisher and his family rejoiced in this new responsibility and the added prestige of being the pastor in charge. That winter was very cold. A large group of new Christians asked to be baptized by immersion, a somewhat unusual request from Methodists. But William respected their desire and had blocks of ice cut out of a stream nearby and, in spite of the cold and his own frail health, immersed them all. Elizabeth says that he caught a very bad cold and was never really well again.

Meanwhile the children rollicked through the days. All Elizabeth's happiest childhood memories are of those days on the Mount Pleasant circuit.

There were forests all around—it was a heavenly place to play or even to work. One day, a parishioner who was clearing land for farming invited Pitzer to drive over and fill the family spring wagon with the big chips of firewood left by the tree choppers. Preachers' cash salaries were so small that gifts of food and fuel were necessary to keep their families alive. Of course Elizabeth and Carrie wanted to go along. They helped pile the wagon high, and then climbed up and sat on top of the pile for the ride home. Pitzer guided the horses as best he could between the stumps, but a wheel ran over one of them. Out went little Carrie along with the chips with Elizabeth in close pursuit. Carrie landed on her back and Elizabeth fell face down, her head cushioned on Carrie's stomach, as the rear wheel of the wagon ran over her head. Carrie was unhurt and Elizabeth suffered only a bruised and aching head.

Their favorite game was to fly through the air on saplings which Pitzer would bend down for them and then release, or romp through the sweet hay in the big barn. Once Elizabeth fell through the open trapdoor and hung by her armpits until her father came running to rescue her. Another time, in a game of hide-and-seek, she was in too much of a hurry to go back through a gate, so she climbed a fence and jumped into the long grass where a rusty pitchfork pierced through her bare foot. Sister Ada pulled the fork out and Elizabeth's mother bound a piece of salt pork on the ugly wound. Everyone waited for lockjaw to set in, but nothing happened. The foot healed.

"You see, I am still here," chuckled Elizabeth as I squirmed over the story, "but as long as I wore that salt-pork poultice, the neighborhood dogs followed me around sniffing, hungrily."

These are all experiences common to children of those days. They are important only because they indicate that Elizabeth's childhood was normal, and that she was an unusually active, outgoing child.

One experience that could happen only to the child of God-conscious parents has lighted her whole life. The country school the children attended was far enough away so that they had to carry their noon lunch. Beyond the rail-fenced schoolyard were woods and pastures, in one of which stood a great shed where the patient sheep huddled out of the winter wind.

June had come, and the sheep were on pasture. The vacant shed became the favorite play spot during the long lunch period. Sometimes it was a blockhouse, sometimes a castle, but always Elizabeth's sister, Ada, was the heart of the game. Ada was two-years-older than Elizabeth; with a mass of auburn curls perfect for scalping or holding a princess' crown. She sang like an angel and was always the star of church and school programs.

Vacation was only a few days off, and the children were tired and excited. The great event of the whole year, the family Sunday school picnic was to be the next day. The noon game was reaching its shrieking, bloodcurdling climax, and Ada was struggling heroically to escape her fate for the day, aided by the loyal and sweating, Elizabeth.

Suddenly two men from the church appeared, they called Ada from her captors. The game fell apart as the disappointed children watched her walk away. They were important men, part of the Sunday School picnic committee, and the children knew that Ada was being taken away to a rehearsal. But just the same, they felt cheated and outraged at the interruption. Elizabeth was all but speechless with indignation. She began to jump up and down, fists clenched, and then she began to yell after them using language that made even the roughest boys in the group gape in astonishment.

"Now, you'll catch it, Liz," was the prediction of the horrified children.

For the rest of that hot afternoon, Elizabeth sat at her desk and repented. When school was out, she dragged her feet along the country road, raising a cloud of dust. She was ashamed to face her sisters and Pitzer at home. Supper passed without incident.

That night there was a prayer meeting and her beloved father asked if anyone cared to attend with him.

Gratefully, Elizabeth put her hand in his and trudged off through the summer dusk. At church, she poured out her sorrow and shame in silent prayer and felt that God had heard and forgiven her. Once more her heart lifted and she skipped gaily alongside her father on the way home, chattering about the picnic and all the goodies her mother and Grandmother Fisher had prepared for it.

But when she came into the room where her mother sat mending by the lamp, she knew what had happened.

Little Carrie had told her mother the dreadful words Liz had yelled at the committee men.

Sorrowfully, her mother sent her to her room. Later, her father came to talk to her about her naughtiness.

"I could whip you," he said, "that would help you to remember never to use such foul language again. But that would be just half of the punishment you deserve. As a minister I have a responsibility to the children who heard you, as you do, too. They must know that we are terribly ashamed and sorry for what happened, and that you have been punished. So your mother and I have decided that you may not go to the picnic. Everyone will notice your absence, and will know you are being punished. In addition, you will have nothing but bread and water, and will stay in your room all day."

Poor Elizabeth! The house was fragrant with the preparation of food. Pies and cakes and buns, pickles and preserves and jelly, chicken and ham and baked beans had been prepared and set on the swinging shelves in the cellar to keep cool and safe from two-legged mice. Now none of it was for Elizabeth.

The next morning the household was up early. The day was perfect. Carrie, Ada and Pitzer were dressed in their Sunday clothes as befitted children of the minister in charge. Just before leaving, her father came in to say how sorry he was, and to report that Grandmother Fisher had changed her mind about going. She, too, was staying at home.

Dear Grandmother Fisher! Elizabeth says she was as lovely as a rose and white cameo; gentle, loving and quick to understand a little girl's troubles. But even little Elizabeth was not deceived. Everyone knew how Grandmother wanted to hear father preach, and that she was staying at home only for Elizabeth's sake. This added an almost unbearable remorse to Elizabeth's already sorrowful heart.

The long morning wore on! The room was hot and the flies buzzed drearily against the window. The whitewashed walls were bare of interest. Elizabeth had a treasure box containing a little jug from the Crook's Pottery nearby, and other trifles now forgotten. There were, no doubt, colored stones, her beloved buckeyes, and pretty buttons. These she fondled for comfort and tried not to think of the picnic. At noon, grandmother opened the door. She brought to Elizabeth some bread and water. That was the law to the letter. But in addition, as a special gift of love, understanding and forgiveness, she brought a piece of rhubarb pie. That made Elizabeth cry.

Throughout her long life, she has never seen a piece of rhubarb pie without remembering Grandmother Fisher's gift of love. To her it has always been the perfect illustration of the meaning of grace—the undeserved goodness and love of God for His erring children.

Without warning, the happy times at Mt. Pleasant came to a close. The West had not offered a more desirable circuit, and the former minister in charge returned and once again took up his duties. William Fisher, worn from overwork and the cold which would not leave him, heard at conference that he was to be transferred to Berlin Crossroads in the cool hills of Hocking County.

Once again, Mary Jane packed, this time, sadly. She sensed that the year at Mt. Pleasant was the happiest her family would ever know. Anxiously, she watched her husband as he took over the new circuit. Here again he rejoiced in being in charge, but the responsibility for six churches scattered through the hills was more than a well man could carry alone. Between him and his people, there was quick fellowship. But the task that so warmed his spirit, wore out his body. The cold that had racked him so long grew steadily worse. Finally, Mary Jane wrote to London for someone to come for Will. She hoped that rest and care in his old home would restore his health. She and the children lived in the parsonage at Berlin Cross Roads waiting for his return. Several months later, a letter came urging her and the family to come at once. This time there was no roller-coaster ride across country. Instead the children had their first train ride.

Beautiful Ada was ailing and feverish when they reached London. To protect the other children from possible contagion one of the aunts took her home. But in those days there was not much one could do for meningitis and, several days later, the stunned family learned that Ada had died.

Deep in sorrow, they moved back to their old home in Midway, taking their father with them. There a few months later, he died, too, at the age of 36. He had spent ten years preparing to become a member of the conference of the Methodist church, and missed achieving this goal of his life by two months. In spite of this disappointment, he died happy. His faith was not the kind that demanded reward, or the realization of personal ambitions as the payment for serving God. He believed quite simply, that for those who truly love Him, whatever comes is right and good. So he accepted disappointed hopes and early death serenely, and the confident faith that had lent radiance to his life was fulfilled in his death.

That morning the family gathered around his bed to be with him during his last moments on earth. Slowly, light faded from his face, and when the stillness of death had crept into the farthest corners of the room, his youngest sister begun to sob uncontrollably, calling his name.

The closed eyes opened, reluctantly. Calmly, they sought her out, and almost reproachfully, he addressed her.

"Why did you call me back, Ella? I was in heaven. Oh, why did you call me back?"

Elizabeth was only ten at the time, but even now, after eighty years, that triumphant day glows in her memory. Her beloved father had nothing to give her, but he took forever from her the fear of death. She remembers that he spoke joyfully of meeting a younger brother in that brief excursion Beyond, and of other wonders that left all those present awestricken, but grateful.

Serenely he waited through the afternoon. When once again the radiance that was William Fisher faded from his face, someone led Ella out into the garden where her grief could not re-call her brother.

So in the dusk of that long ago day, no one had to explain to Elizabeth that her father had gone to heaven. She was sure of it. She had seen him leave, and knew that he went gladly.

She stood in the road watching men lift his coffin into the wagon that was to carry him to the cemetery in London, Ohio. Something small and bright fell from it and dropped at her feet, as if her father were sending her a secret shining message of love. Searching in the dust she found a diamond-shaped head of a coffin nail. Pondering, Elizabeth put it in her box of treasures, and cherished it as the most precious one of them all. But the wonder of her father's love and faith she kept in her heart, where it flourished unseen until the day when it should bear much fruit.

CHAPTER TWO

Child of the King

Yesterday Elizabeth sat by the window in our sunny kitchen visiting as I worked. Our conversation had been swinging in great circles around the world as we discussed the affairs of her other children in New York, Ohio, California and Burma. The spiral gradually narrowed and retreated until we were back in Ohio looking in on her Mother, Mary Jane, in the weeks that followed her husband's funeral. Pityingly, she shook her head.

"Poor Mother! Imagine being a widow for fifty-five years!" She stared unseeing out our window as she re-lived those days long ago. Her delicate fingers moving aimlessly across the red and white cloth on the kitchen table found a sharp dry crumb and she pursued it until it was ground to powder. Returning to the present, Elizabeth brushed the cloth smooth.

"I haven't seen a table cloth like this for years," she mused. "Our kitchen in Midway had a sunny window, too, with a red-and-white cloth covering the table standing by it. Mother used to sit there watching for us when we came home from school after father died and after Pitzer went away to work. That was a hard time for us all."

The week after Will's death there had been a family conference in Midway. The London aunts and uncles, knowing that Will had left her only two village lots and less than a hundred dollars in cash, had offered to adopt the children. Mary Jane could see them happily at home in their comfortable wide-porched houses, but she could not let them go. She sat overwhelmed by the good intentions of her husband's family, miserably determined to keep her children. Inarticulate as always, she nervously pleated her apron between her fingers until fifteen-year-old Pitzer, seeing her distress, spoke up.

"I will help mother support the children," he promised. "I will go to work on a farm."

Not to be outdone, ten-year-old Elizabeth volunteered, "I will do the housework so mother can work and earn money. We don't want to go to London." And so it had been decided. Mary Jane had been saved from total destitution by her children.

In answer to the troubled question of what she could do to earn money, Mary Jane had no ready answer. Anxiously the family explored possibilities. She could cook, wash and iron, and sew; in fact, she had a real flair for sewing. So it was arranged that the family would move to London where Mary Jane would take lessons from the best seamstress. Heaven knows, sewing was better than taking in washing, the family agreed.

It was this future that Mary Jane stared into from her place by her kitchen window. Instead of a position of honor in the community as the wife of the beloved pastor, she was now to support her family as a seamstress. The cottage in London was rented. Pitzer had already gone to work on a farm to earn that rent. It hurt Mary Jane that this gifted boy could not go to school, but he had promised to make up in the three-month winter term what the others did in nine months, and his mother knew he would do it.

Elizabeth, too, was true to her promise. As a symbol of her position as her mother's helper, she stood every morning before the mottled mirror over the kitchen wash basin braiding her hair. Her big sister had always done it for her. After Ada's death, her mother had laid the shining brown strands in place. Now Elizabeth resolutely struggled with the task herself while her mother smiled at her middle child. And both of them knew that for the first time she was seeing Elizabeth as she really was, sturdy and dependable, standing loyally by mother.

Fortunately for Mary Jane there was not much time for melancholy or daydreaming. There were still hungry children to feed, and clothes to mend; there was sorting to do and all the wearisome details of packing to plan. The good neighbors did what they could to help. Today Elizabeth's memory of that last week in Midway, Ohio, is a kaleidoscope of dusty hot sunlight, bouquets of wilting asters and mottled dahlias, good food in unheard of quantities and her mother's tears. By the end of September the Fishers were settled in the cottage in London. It was a very modest home, Elizabeth recalls, close to the tracks, but, fortunately for her proud spirit, on the right side of them.

For the next eight years she lived a busy life. There was little time for play. Every night she hurried home to do the housework and prepare supper; every Friday afternoon she did the family washing; every Saturday, the ironing and cleaning.

Tucked in between all these duties she acted as receptionist and consultant for her mother, who never overcame her shyness in the presence of strangers. Sometimes now, when Elizabeth has talked more than usual, she laughingly apologizes,

"I guess I talk too much because I always had to talk for two as a child. Those were the days of fancy clothes and it took lots of talking to get everything as the ladies wanted it.

"And, oh, the pleating they asked for! In those days dresses were three-yards-wide at the bottom, and were covered with pleated flounces. After I had the dishes done, the beds made and the supper started, I had to sit at the pleating frame and fold and dampen and press those pleated flounces. I must have made miles of the stuff."

"Was your mother able to make a living for you as she hoped?"

"Yes, although it was sometimes very skimpy. There were times when we had cornmeal mush for breakfast, fried mush for dinner, and baked mush for supper. Often we were hungry, but no one ever knew it. Sometimes when I had only a nickel to spend for food, I would buy liver. I could get enough to feed us all day for that amount. We didn't like it, but it was filling. I can't abide the stuff to this day.

"When the Fayette County Jeffersons came to town they brought us eggs and crocks of home-churned butter. In the summer they laid grape leaves over it to keep the dust out. Around butchering time they brought us spare ribs and back meat. It was wonderful to have rich relatives! Most of our clothes came from the London aunts, and mother would make them over for us. My favorite dress was a brown-and-blue-wool-plaid with diamond-shaped insets of blue velvet around the hem. I never had a new dress until my high school graduation when Pitzer gave me a new silk one. That was wonderful!"

"Did you ever have any fun?" I wondered.

"Oh, my yes! Uncle Quinn had beautiful horses which I was allowed to drive. My favorite was Blackie. He was an 'also ran' race horse but plenty fast on the road. I could drive him anywhere alone, even ten miles out in the country at night. All I had to do was to shake the reins and say, 'Come Blackie,' and no one could get near me.

"People used to pull off the road when they saw us coming. I guess I was as much of a terror on the road then as teenagers are today with their hot rods.

"Uncle Wyatt's contribution was not so much fun, but it was useful to me in China. He was the choir director in the Methodist Church and a stern taskmaster. Every child in the family had to learn to read music, to sing in pitch and to keep accurate time. He was so proud of Ada and her voice, and the rest of us felt that he never forgave us for being alive when she died. He tried to teach me to play the organ, too, but I was kept too busy at home to do much practicing. I learned to play with three fingers, and even that was very useful in China. God used every bit of ability I had; even the hours over the pleating frame weren't wasted.

"But you asked about fun. Did I ever tell you about the cowboy episode? We thought that was fun. One of my classmates answered a newspaper advertisement from a Texas cowboy looking for a wife. Letters traveled back and forth, and one day all the girls in our class were invited to go down to the depot to meet the train that was bringing him to town.

"He arrived in full regalia—boots, spurs, wide hat, bowed legs and narrow hips. Hat in hand he swept poor Clara into his arms. Oh, dear me, how shocked we were, and yet every one of us was envious too. We stood there giggling and whispering while Clara introduced us. His western approach was too much for London folk, I guess, so he took the next train home.

"Does that give you some idea of fun when I was a girl? I hope so. I can't seem to think of anything else," she announced, concluding the interview. "Is it time for the news yet?" Even the delights of the past cannot hold Elizabeth from the stirring events that blare from her radio a dozen times a day.

* * *

She was fourteen when romance of another kind trailed dreams of glory across her pleating frame. A notice which appeared in the newspapers of all important American cities was relayed to the Minshalls of London, Ohio. The last Earl of Minshall had died without heirs in England. It was known that an earlier Minshall had gone to the American colonies. If he had living descendants, there was a vast fortune being held in he chancery in London, waiting for proof of their right to the title.

It was family tradition that the Minshalls were descended from an English earl, a source of some of the pride which Elizabeth later would have to confess as a minor sin. But had anyone kept records to substantiate the tradition?

Mary Jane was too poor and too busy sewing for a living to begin a search for records. The other Minshalls were wealthy enough to be rather indifferent, but not Elizabeth. Life was now charged with exciting possibilities. Perhaps she was really a Marchioness or even a Duchess, and on wash days, when the boiling water dripped from the wad at the end of her clothes stick, she heard the fountains splashing in the great park of Minshall castle and saw the white clouds billowing over her ancestral home. To her joy one of the Minshalls in Cincinnati undertook the investigation, and the young people in all the families concerned lived in happy anticipation of splendor ahead. For years the search continued. Records were found in abundance to establish the male line, but in those early days wives were recorded by given names only, and since both direct descent and lateral line Minshalls had wives with identical names, the records were not considered sufficient proof of right to title. At last a courthouse was pinpointed where the all important key papers should be. However, when the eager searchers arrived, they learned that the original building and all its contents had burned years before. So, as far as we know, that fortune was never claimed.

Elizabeth chuckled at the memory of those exciting years, and added, "Not that I needed a fortune to build up my ego. You see, I was a child of the King."

As I looked up inquiringly, she began to sing, tapping out the time on the checkered cloth:

My Father is rich in houses and lands,
He holdeth the wealth of the world in His hands!
Of rubies and diamonds, of silver and gold,
His coffers are full; He has riches untold.

My Father's own son, the Savior of Men,
Once wandered o'er earth as the poorest of them;
But now he is reigning forever on high,
And will, give me a home in heaven by and by.

I once was an outcast, stranger on earth,
A sinner by choice, an alien by Birth!
But I've been adopted, my name's written down,
An heir to a mansion, a robe, and a crown.
A tent or a cottage, why should I care?

They're building a palace for me over there.
Tho' exiled from home, yet still I may sing
All glory to God, I'm the child of the King.

Chorus: I'm the child of a King,
I'm the child of the King,
With Jesus, my Savior,
I'm the child of the King.

"That was our favorite song while I was growing up."

Perhaps Andrew Fletcher knew what he was talking about when

he said, "Give me the making of the songs of a nation, and I care not who makes its laws." For an exultant lifetime Elizabeth has been a child of the King, and now, at an age when most people are apathetic, she is alert and eager. Her failing faculties hamper her keen mind, but cannot dim her spirit. She is like the tree in the Book of Revelation whose leaves have been given for the healing of the nations, and now in her winter she waits confident of Spring. Not that she is happy to have lost her beauty, her sight and hearing. She hates that, and is not at all patient about it. Sometimes even a little asperity creeps in when she wonders why she is kept waiting so long.

"We don't live longer than 92 in our family; and here I am almost 93," she said reprovingly, the other day. It reminded me of another child of God, St. Theresa, who, wet and scared by a fall into a raging river, chided Him, saying, "If this is the way you treat your friends, it's no wonder you have so many enemies."

Almost wistfully now, I repeated the last line of the chorus she had just finished:

"With Jesus my Savior, I'm the child of a King."

"How do you know you are, Mother Brewster? Multitudes of us would like to share your certainty. Can you remember how it came to you?"

The fingers started on another search across the table cloth as she stared at me, smiling, incredulously.

"Surely you know, my dear?"

"Not the way you do," I replied. She began, then, with the first spiritual crisis of her life, and through the long afternoon we sorted out the experiences that have made her one of the great Christians of our day.

"I was ten when my father died. There was no one I loved so much, as I have told you before. Through all my life I have remembered how his face shone, and his remarkable smile. It was the memory of that smile that helped me through troubles, and his faith that kept me on the way to God when doubts bothered me. I was thirteen when I joined the church. I didn't understand what I was doing; I only knew I felt close to my father there. I was conforming, too, to the customs of those days. Every young person was expected to make public confession of his sins in order to be saved from everlasting death. So I did what was expected of me.

"But my church had no program for an active youngster and I needed counseling and work to do. I was no goody-goody. I never have been. When Pitzer brought home complaints from people about the way I drove Blackie, I used to laugh and say, 'I always have him under perfect control,' just like teenagers today.

"Of course, we were a family of church goers. Mother would never allow me to miss worship or Sunday school, and Uncle Wyatt saw to it that I sang at every service.

"But all through high school I was restless. I had seen my father live and die as one destined for glory, and I felt drab in comparison. I discovered that I could inherit a religion, but not a religious experience. What my father had was not mine just for going to church. Although I knew I would have to win what he had for myself, the memory of him kept me steady until I knew his God as my own.

"Somewhere during those early days I belonged to a mission study group. One of our projects was to make potholders and sell them from door to door to raise money for missionaries. But after several doors were slammed in my face, I resigned from the group, and washed my hands of missions, or so I thought.

"We had a pastor from Appleton, Wisconsin. He was my first contact with your state. A fine pastor and a good speaker, but when I consulted him on my search for God, I found that he was seeking to brush the dimness of his own faith away. He was unhappily aware that his first transforming experience of God was long past, its richness used up by years of serving people with little time left over for loving God. They are not one and the same thing, you know. In the humility of his spiritual poverty he attended a preaching mission, and like a miracle, there came to him his second vivid experience of the reality and presence of God. Like my father, he was aflame with joy. Now he, too, spoke with authority, and I was unhappier than ever. These two strode far ahead where the sun shone on them always, and I couldn't catch up.

"I was eighteen, a senior in high school, when a Quaker came to our town to conduct meetings. I made up my mind that I would follow the formula of earnest prayer, admission of my shortcomings, and responding to the altar call, if one was made. I would do everything in my power to clear the way for God. Kneeling at the altar, the moment came for me, too. There is no describing that joy if you haven't had the experience yourself.

"As a good Methodist I knew the definition of salvation, the clear witness of the Holy Spirit in my heart that my sins had been forgiven and I had been accepted as a child of God. Now the words had become fact for me. God had put His arms around me, and made me His own."

She sat lost in that heavenly memory while I pursued troubled thoughts.

"What about all of us who have never had such an experience, Mother? Don't you think it's possible that we, too, are children of God? My favorite modern saint, Thomas Kelly, says that for us it must be a matter of will and faith. What do you think?"

Elizabeth considered this. "It would never occur to me that you weren't a child of God, my dear. As for becoming one by will and faith, I think that is possible. But pray to be shown if something is separating you from Him, and wait always for His appearing to you. When I was a young missionary I used to explain it like this. If one of my girls came to me asking how she could become a child of God, I would take a pin or a book or anything handy, and say to her:

"Whose book is this?"

"Yours," she would reply.

"Very well, Now I give it to you. Take it." When she held the object in her hand, I would ask, "Whose is it?"

"Mine," she would reply.

"Then don't go around sighing that you wish you had a book. You have. Rejoice in it. Use it. Profit by what it says. If you leave it here and walk away from it, it is still yours, but it won't do you any good.

"Becoming a child of God can be like that, too. First you have to want to be one, then believe that you are, and act like one with all your heart and will. Only now the gift is not a book or a pin, but a personality, and joy and light will come—but it always seems to me it must be like the light of the moon, not the sun when it comes this way."

As I prepare this manuscript for typing two years after the above conversation, I rejoice to record my first lovely illumination. On a morning last week, I awakened early. My mind immediately returned to my manuscript and my constant concern as to how I could share what I had not experienced. Without any logical reason, I became absorbed in the Parable of the Prodigal Son which I had read during my quiet time the previous day. As I meditated, it occurred to me, "Why, in one respect Elizabeth was like the younger son. When she rose up and went to her Father's house, He came to meet her, put His arms around her, and kissed her." Enviously I surveyed the scene. Suddenly, it was as if I were enveloped in love, at once pitying and approving. Within me a voice spoke:

"My child, you have been with me all the time, and everything I have is yours."

With amazement I recognized the words. They were spoken by the father to the envious older son, who I had never given any attention. For me the important character had always been the younger son and I could never identify myself with him. But the envious elder son, who had been enjoying the love and hospitality of his father through the years without appreciation or gratitude—so this is me! I gladly accept the reproof for the joy of the acknowledgement, "My child," and wait, as Elizabeth bade me, in gratitude and patience, for further illumination.

Elizabeth's words that afternoon called to my mind two roads in Germany. One was a super highway with no traffic hazards or lights. But sometimes I got mixed up in the clover leaf entrance to it, and came out on another road which twisted through a dozen villages where cows and geese and children and narrow right-angle turns made driving a torment. But both roads took me to Bayeuth and the PX, where, I suddenly remembered, my most important purchase was always coffee. Here we were, so carried away into the realm of the sublime that I had forgotten what for us both was the big event of the day. Reaching into the cupboard for two cups, I dropped powdered coffee in each, and added boiling water. Elizabeth's head turned as the fragrance reached her.

"If you're having coffee, I'll join you in a cup." she offered, "but none of that nerve stuff for me, please." This was daily ritual.

Laughing, I set a cup in front of her, "Oh, never," I assured her. "This is your favorite brand, dear." I watched her spooning the hot brown liquid, appraisingly, and waited for her customary joke.

"Ah, yes, what Mr. Chase doesn't know about coffee, Mr. Sanborn does!"

Revived by her favorite drink, Elizabeth was ready to go on.

"Now let me see. Where were we when we got sidetracked by coffee?" she wanted to know.

"You were eighteen and had just discovered what it means to be a child of God."

"Yes—well, that summer I went to camp meeting and met there some of the great evangelists of the day. They rejoiced with me in my new life, but warned me that I could not live on a memory. There was no standing still they said, and suggested that I go on in faith to the next step which was to give myself and my life to God.

"This wasn't easy. I had hoped to go far in the educational world. I wanted to be the best teacher in the state. I wanted to write, too.

"But those men of blessed memory warned me that if I wanted to have the continuing presence of God I would have to give Him my plans and my ambitions, yes, even life itself. 'Self-surrender' and 'obedience unto death' were the words they used. That is a very different thing from making your own plans and asking God's blessing on them. This was a hard decision for me. I was very proud and strong-willed. I had made my own life plans and knew that I could carry them out. But to do so at the risk of losing the new life that had come to me--this I couldn't face. After days of prayer and thought, I went again to the altar. This time the heavens did not open for me, although I gave everything—myself and my life—into God's hands. Instead, a great peace came upon me, and the certainty of the companionship of God.

"I couldn't wait to tell my family. What a shock I had then. Except for my little sister, Carrie, everyone was unhappy.

"They felt that I had disgraced them by confessing to sin, and deserted them by giving my life away. Being a church member and conforming to accepted standards of right and wrong were enough, they were certain. I went to church and taught Sunday school, didn't play cards or go to theater and dances. I didn't lie or cheat or steal. I kept all the commandments and that was all that could be expected of anyone they said. They were embarrassed by my new found joy. Their reaction was not peculiar to them, I discovered. Dr. Jackson's experience of "perfect love," too, was an embarrassment to so many in his congregation that he was soon moved to another church and replaced by a man not so "spiritual."

Elizabeth was frankly nodding now, leaving me to consider the situation which had confronted her so long ago. The people she loved best were content where they were. After all, it had taken a heavenly visitor to turn her to periods of prayer, earnest study of the Bible, meticulous tithing and a joyous yielding to the will of God, and they had received no such visitation.

There came to my mind a day at the farm when a winter ice storm had bewitched the countryside. Late in the afternoon I went for a walk, the better to see the crystal landscape. Crunching through the frozen grass I climbed to the top of a hill where I turned to look into the sunset. I was in the Book of Revelations looking at a world of gold and jewels. The ice had turned every blade of grass, every twig, the utility wires and the outline of our farm building into prisms capturing the gold and coral of the sky. I stood enthralled, until I realized that in all the countryside I alone was seeing this magic. I hurried home and asked the family to come out to the highway to see beauty such as they never imagined. They looked out the window agreeing that the crystal world was beautiful, but as for going to a high place where they could look into the sunset, they laughed. "Go out and risk breaking a leg? I should say not. We can see from here that it's beautiful."

They will never know what they missed that day.

But there was more I wanted to know, and Elizabeth was glad to wake up and talk.

"I can't help but wonder, dear, what sins you had to confess. What possible wrong could you have done?"

Elizabeth shook her head in mock despair. "My dear, you remind me of one of my best friends. I knelt beside her one day when she was searching for the joy and peace I had found. The evangelist in charge came to her asking if she felt the witness of the Holy Spirit that her sins were forgiven.

"I can't think of any sins I have to be forgiven," she complained.

"I'll never forget how that man roared at her, 'No sins? Then your sin is pride and your heart is black as hell with it. And it was, too. As soon as she realized that, she asked to be forgiven, and then joy broke over her, and she, too, was a transformed person.

"But you want to know what my sins were? Well, first, I had a terrible temper. I guess I inherited it from some of my redheaded Minshall relatives. I would go into blind furies and scream and even say vile things as I did that time at school when I disgraced the family reputation.

"I had a fierce will. I wanted to have my own way always. I was overbearingly proud of my ancestry. I wanted to be King of my own life without yielding to anyone. I was not easy to live with, I am sure. When I realized how I must look to God I was ashamed. I asked for a new kind of life and it was given."

"Wise Elizabeth," I reflected. She had inherited the sins of her fathers, but had accepted as her own responsibility the decision to hold or discard them.

"When you say a new life was given, what do you mean, Mother?"

"After that I always felt like a child of God and full of joy, unafraid always. Do you remember Paul's words, 'People who all their lives live captive to the fear of death?' Well, I was completely free of that. As a child I had seen father die happy and unafraid, and that had left me unafraid, too. But now there was a joyous expectancy in me that I had not known before. I always expected wonderful things to happen, and they always did. I never felt poor. I began giving away a tenth of my income, a practice I follow to this day. I set aside a definite time for prayer and devotional reading every day and soon my whole life was interlaced and undergirded with prayer. Before long I reached the place where I made no decisions until I had guidance from God. For this self-yielding, self-discipline and sharing I have been given perfect freedom and abounding joy throughout my life."

"But I was lonesome for human companionship. My family was unsympathetic. My best friend who had shared my experience died within the year, and Dr. Jackson, my minister, as I told you, proved too spiritual for his congregation and was moved to another city.

"There was a group of older people in Ohio then whose aim was holiness. I joined them hoping to find fellowship, but I found them singularly lacking in love and understanding. They took me sternly to task for vanity, especially for all the pleating on my dresses! So I had mother make me some absolutely plain ones. But they turned out to be much more becoming than the fancy ones, and my Holiness friends were more displeased than ever. When our hours together degenerated into pointing out each other's sins, I resigned from the group."

From Elizabeth's diaries I continue the story.

For the next four years she taught school, attending religious camps every summer, waiting to be shown what her next step was to be. She met missionaries from Mexico, South America, home missionaries from the deep South, deaconesses who worked in city parishes. All of them thought Elizabeth ideally adapted for their fields, and, although she considered each suggestion prayerfully, none of them seemed the will of God for her.

One day an invitation arrived inviting her to go to China. She was asked to be one of two young women to take over a school for women and girls in Foochow.

She said she felt as if a door was opened before her, and hedging her around and urging her on were the words from Isaiah which have guided her ever since:

This is the way; walk in it.
Even though the Lord may have given you
Bread in short measure and water in scanty allowance

Your teacher will no more hide himself
But you will behold your Teacher,
And when you turn to the right or to left
Your ears will hear a voice behind you saying:
This is the way; walk in it.

Joyously she went home to report to her family that she was going to be a missionary to China. Again they were dismayed and almost unanimously disapproving. Even the townspeople were startled and indignant. Such a plan was so unusual and daring as to be almost improper for a young girl, they thought. Besides, her family needed her, they remonstrated.

Mary Jane was overwhelmed. What would she do without this daughter who had been her comfort and support for so long? Who would do the housework? Who would receive the customers and beguile them with cheerful chatter through the tedium of fitting and pinning? To lose Elizabeth was second only to the loss of Will.

Pitzer thought she was very foolish to give up a good job and future in teaching for anything as risky as going to China. She might as well be going to the moon. Without bitterness, but a little weary, he wondered how his own life would be affected.

Only Carrie and Grandmother Fisher approved.

"I knew one of my Will's children would take up his work, my dear," confided her grandmother, but Elizabeth sensed the unspoken wish that even she wished a less daring form of serving God had been chosen.

At home the plans for departure were undertaken in silence. Mary Jane set about sewing an outfit for her daughter fine enough for a trousseau, and wished fervently it were. Elizabeth respected the feelings of her family and talked little of her plans. She hated to leave them and was concerned for their welfare. She was committed to obedience to God, however, and knew that He would care for her family too. Elsewhere she became a heroine, and was invited to many churches and feted in many towns and cities. In those days a trip to China was something to talk about, and for a girl of twenty—almost unheard of. Since she was going out as a missionary from the Baltimore area she was invited there for her commissioning. The kindness of the people who entertained her and the gracious beauty of their homes is something for which Elizabeth still gives thanks.

On a September day in 1884, she stood at the railroad station in London, Ohio, her family and friends gathered round her. They saw a tiny girl of twenty-two, dressed in the most modish costume her mother's loving fingers could fashion—a beige suit of fine wool, ankle length and three-yards-wide at the hem. On her bright brown pompadour sat a hat of finest panama straw, its turned up brim lined with canary yellow velvet. She seemed so very young and inexperienced, they thought—high school and four years of primary teaching! Was that sufficient to face the terrors of unknown China? Only faintly they perceived her spiritual armor—the companionship of God, and a joyous conviction of His power for good in her life. That was the Presence that was to confound the learning of many Chinese scholars who could match religions with her miracle for miracle, precept for precept, virtue for virtue, but who finally had to admit:

"There is not much new in this story that you bring us. It is an Oriental story, and its tales of wonder are old to us. But the Love you bring us, and the Power to make people do what they know is right and good and true, this we have never seen before."

This is, of course, the genius of Christianity.

* * *

The engine bell was ringing. People were crowding close around her, Uncle Wyatt pressed a five-dollar gold piece into her hand; an admirer pinned a gold watch on her lapel. Her mother was crying. Her always dependable, beloved brother, Pitzer, was patting her shoulder, whispering,

"Don't worry, Liz. I'll take care of mother."

Carrie suddenly called out, "I'll join you in two years, Lizzie!"

The faces around her suddenly became blurs partially covered with white handkerchiefs. The conductor came up, announcing with quiet apology,

"All aboard, please!"

Everyone strained for a last look as Elizabeth climbed the steps of the train. From the platform her eyes swept up and down the familiar street, then came back to her mother.

"Good-by, Mother!"

"Good-by, Elizabeth!"

Then everyone was shouting and waving, "Good-by!" And China lay ahead.

CHAPTER THREE

Miss Star of China

On the 17th of November, a Blue Funnel steamer out of Shanghai was standing in toward the Fujian coast for a cargo of Foochow tea.[1] On its passenger list was Elizabeth Fisher, London, Ohio, USA, and Miss Carrie Jewel, another young missionary who had joined Elizabeth at St. Louis. The girls stood on deck watching the ragged skyline lift into range upon range of mountains, so different, (they told each other happily), from the yellow mud flats before Shanghai.

The journey from San Francisco had been one long delight to Elizabeth who had reveled in all twenty-eight excitingly stormy days to Yokohama on the old steamer *City of New York*. There had been ten days of sightseeing in the mist-shrouded cities of Japan, and then across the Yellow Sea to Shanghai. The most spine-thrilling moment of the whole journey had come about two days out of Shanghai. The girls had been watching the waves topple over in foam, like blue-green horses tossing white manes, when suddenly horses and pastures turned a dirty yellow. An officer standing beside them said, "Mud from the Yangtze. This is the Yellow Sea." Elizabeth felt as if China had come out to meet her. There was no welcoming committee

1 The beginning of this chapter is an enlargement of meager notes found in Elizabeth's diary.

waiting for them in Shanghai, however. The girls, not knowing what to do or where to go, stood on the dock surrounded by shouting, gesticulating rickshaw coolies. Finally an American man, seeing them just standing there, came up and introduced himself as a member of the Methodist Church South, and asked if he could assist them. Elizabeth still remembers his Southern courtesy with gratitude. He put the girls in rickshaws and sent them to the Shanghai home for missionaries, where they waited for passage south to Foochow.

Now somewhere behind those blue Fujian mountains just ahead lay home, and for a moment Elizabeth saw a white cottage on a tree lined street in London, Ohio, but just for a moment.

The steamer slowed down to take on a pilot who had been waiting near a rocky islet, called Matsu. Elizabeth gazed with eagerness at this outpost of Fujian, but saw nothing that looked important—just so many craggy peaks of drowned mountains with no life visible except a few fishing boats. If anyone had told her that the future of the world would one day teeter on this barren dot in the ocean, she would have laughed.

High on a bluff guarding the mouth of the Min, she saw some white buildings. "That's the new Methodist Rest Home. You girls will probably spend your summers there. They call this island Sharp Peak; it is just two tides from Foochow."

To anyone born in the heart of a continent, this was a novel way of measuring distance. But from now on, Elizabeth was to make no journey away from that shore without consulting the tides.

Just now, she was more interested in the hills that held the river in bounds. They looked like so many russet potatoes lying on their sides. The hills of Ohio on this seventeenth day of November would be hidden in scarlet foliage, but these were completely bare of trees.

The man who was pointing out the sights wanted them to look halfway up the mountains. "See those low, dark spots? Those are the forts with the guns that can shoot only downstream, and when the French gunboats came in here early this year, they just snorted and scooted past and that war was over."

Elizabeth laughed a little uneasily. She had read about that brief encounter in a newspaper in Ohio. But now that she was on the spot, and the spot was home, she wasn't sure it was funny.

They had been steaming along with the tide for some two hours when suddenly the mountains fell back and the river spread out into a sunlit harbor. On a little tongue of land, a white pagoda stood like a wedding cake against the sky. Behind it a village backed up the hillside. Hundreds of sampans bobbed on the wind-tossed water, under the watchful eyes of lumbering cargo junks which hovered around them like so many mother hens. This was Pagoda Anchorage.

The passengers hung over the rail watching the scramble below as the sampans converged upon the ship. One pushed its way through and quickly made its way to the gangplank. In it stood a Chinese man holding a letter out for inspection; he was allowed on board and was finally directed to the girls. His letter said the bearer was a houseboat owner who had orders to bring them to Foochow. Shanghai had taught them not to expect welcoming hordes, but where was their southern gentleman? They couldn't even talk to the houseboat owner.

With the help of other passengers he made the girls understand that if they hurried they might get to Foochow that night. The tide was still in and the wind was with them.

So, for the first time, Elizabeth put her trust in one of the black-haired people. She and Carrie found themselves and their luggage in one of the sampans without quite understanding how they got there. From there they were taken swiftly to the waiting houseboat.

From its sheltering cabin they watched the hill behind Pagoda Anchorage rise to a perfect cone. "Now that," thought Elizabeth, "looks like the mountains my first graders draw." She was giving her approval to Kusang, one of the three holy mountains of China.

It was eerily dark on the river when they eased up against something solid. Peering out of the dimly lit cabin, they saw glistening steps leading up to a little jetty. There were two sedan chairs and some coolies there, and a young Chinese man holding a flare aloft who jumped onto the houseboat. Once again they were handed a letter which said that because of the uncertainty as to whether they would make the tide, no one from the mission would meet them, but the bearer of the note would escort them to the hospital residence where they were to have dinner and spend the night.

With spirits slightly dampened by their continuing casual reception, the girls accepted hands stretched out to help them up the dark, slippery stairs. There, for the first time, they climbed over the carrying poles of sedan chairs lowered to receive them.

Elizabeth says she will never forget that ride into the night. In silence, except for the rhythmically squeaking chair, she was bounced through narrow streets that were tunnels of darkness. The dark walls hemming her in were striped with perpendicular cracks of light out of which voices leapt. The stench was sickening—a combination of rancid grease and cesspools, cut through with strange spices and whiffs of fragrance.

And then the chair-bearers were climbing, the chair tipping backwards. Elizabeth noticed that the street was almost covered by overhanging eaves. Then these disappeared, and she could see trees against the sky in which distant stars were shining. Here there were no narrow streets, only open country. Now and then, they passed along stretches of white walls behind which she could see lighted windows in what seemed to be very large houses. From one of these she heard piano music and a woman singing an English song.

On the girls swung through the darkness. They went through several more tunnel-like streets when the chair-bearers began to shout. From somewhere ahead, a voice answered and a gate creaked and closed behind them. They were in a great walled garden passing between two rows of some kind of flowering plants. Ahead of them they saw many lit-up windows. Without warning their chairs were lowered to the ground, and to their amusement their knees rose up almost hitting their chins. A door opened and a woman stood silhouetted in the doorway, calling a welcome to them. It was the voice of a young American.

Inside the girls tried not to show their amazement. The rooms were so large, so graciously furnished. The table standing near the glowing Franklin stove was laid with linen and set with silver. Everywhere there were flowers. This was lovely, but was it right, they wondered. They had expected hardship, not comfort. The sense of unreality continued as a pleasant woman served them dinner. Oddly enough, Elizabeth does not remember what she ate that night, but is willing to guess it was chicken.

Leaving dessert plates on the table, they gathered around the living room grate and were briefed on what to expect and what would be expected of them by this young American—a lady doctor who had arrived just a few months ahead of them.

Lying awake under her tent-like mosquito net that night, Elizabeth considered what it would be like never to cook and serve a meal, never again to wash dishes or clothes, never again to clean the house. She felt positively sybaritic. There was an uneasy question in her mind whether she could carve a chicken without scattering it on the white linen cloth, and how long it would take her to learn the language. With her prayer of thanks that her feet had been set in so pleasant a place, she renewed the promise to use every ounce of strength and every hour of time, thus released, to minister to these people as God should guide. And it was a promise kept.

The next morning the girls chose to walk to their school. The Bible School for Women, which Carrie was to head, and the School for Girls, of which Elizabeth was principal, were under one roof. They were eager to see it now and also to retrace their journey of the night before. The hospital cook was going to market and would guide them. Out in the sunny spacious garden, they trailed admiring fingers along the crisp heads of garnet-red and butter-yellow chrysanthemums which bordered the path to the gate. They wondered if the man sitting on his haunches cutting grass with giant scissors really did the whole lawn that way. He did.

Beyond the gate lay a small village. There, no grass was to be seen. A crooked road, edged by a dozen attached shanties of unpainted wood and stucco, had no space for trees. But a flower peddler was selling a bright, yellow marigold to a woman who tucked it into a shining black bun of hair. At the far end of the street a knot of blue clad figures stood around something that looked like a barrel. Steam was rising from its top. The people were drinking out of little bowls cupped in their hands. As the girls reached the deep shade of the overhanging eaves of the village they saw that the houses had no front walls. Each one seemed to be a shop with dark rooms behind it. One displayed stools of bamboo; in another lengths of heavy satin were being cut and stitched by hand; across the street children bent over embroidery frames; in another shop, live chickens squawked in a bamboo basket. Infants sat on their heels in the dirty street eating twists of fried dough, scolding the mangy, starved dogs that skulked near them.

Last night voices had leaped out through the cracks in what seemed a continuous wall. Now the planks that fit into slots at the floor and roof of each dwelling had been removed, and with them all privacy. A woman with a child at her breast combed her hair, shouting cheerfully at a woman nursing a baby across the street. A man rose from washing his feet and threw the water with a splash into the street. The knot of people drinking from bowls scattered as the owner picked up his travelling restaurant on the end of a bamboo stick and carried it away.

Behind the girls came the heavy thud of bare heels on stone, the cook stepped to one side and a woman with silver daggers in her hair swept past. From the two big buckets on her carrying stick came a frightful odor. Elizabeth had been warned about this last night. "Don't walk behind the women with silver daggers in their hair. They are carrying toilet slops in those big buckets."

But now someone had noticed the strange American women and the whole village rose up to look at them. The most curious came out and followed them to the edge of the village, shouting questions at the cook who flung back answers without turning his head. He was on his way to market and had to hurry.

The girls hurried after him as he turned left and followed a white garden wall up a steep hill. Through the tops of young trees and blossoming poinsettias, the red tiled roofs and great arches of a Spanish style house were visible. But in the grassy bank between the wall and the hard, white riding path on which they walked, were gaping holes in which decayed coffins could be seen. This, too, the girls had heard about. They had been told there were graves everywhere—inside the walled gardens and on every hillside where they could see buffalo cows and scrawny brown cattle grazing. The whole island was a burial ground.

At the close of the Opium War in 1842, Great Britain had demanded the opening of treaty ports along the coast in which she could sell the hated opium from India. She also demanded land in each treaty port for residences for her businessmen and missionaries. Naturally, the Chinese cities gave their least desirable land. Canton gave a rocky islet, Shanghai gave salt marshes, and Foochow gave an island in the Min River that for centuries had been used as a burial ground for the city.

As she panted up the hill, Elizabeth reflected on how strange it was that this long-ago, unhappy war now involved her. In the forty years since then, the energetic western powers had turned a rocky islet outside of Canton into the incomparable Hong Kong. They had turned the salt marshes of Shanghai into the Bund, famous to commerce around the world. Even the cemetery of Foochow was laced with white tree-shaded roads, and the merchant princes of the tea trade had built themselves palaces surrounded by fabulous gardens and hidden them from the eyes of the Chinese behind high walls with broken glass at the top. So that now the Chinese people, embittered by the injustice of the wars and resentful of the miracles the western outlanders had accomplished out of what they had thought worthless concessions, were beginning to ask themselves how they might learn the secrets of these blue-eyed people. Should they perhaps learn to read their books and speak their language so as to protect themselves in the future?

In the mission community and among some of the Christian Chinese, pressure was being brought to introduce English in the school curriculums. An English-speaking high school for boys had been endowed by a wealthy Chinese merchant. In the school for little girls, this pressure had resulted in a crisis. Two American women had worked for twenty years to build it up to an enrollment of thirty. Most of these were the daughters of Christians, but a few were from non-Christian homes who were paid a few pennies a day for coming—the same amount they might have earned for herding cows or cutting grass for fuel. The women principals contended, so long as the school taught only Chinese reading and writing and Bible, only good could come from educating these girls. But if they were to be taught English, the whole picture changed.

Was it necessary to call to anyone's attention the five o'clock parade of green sedan chairs carrying girls with painted faces decked out in brocaded satins to the great walled houses where the American, British and European bachelor merchants lived? Was it not obvious that girls who could speak English would be in much greater demand as night companions than those who could speak only Chinese?

The indignant women declared they would go back to America rather than agree to contribute to the corruption of the girls by their own countrymen. It was useless to argue with them, or to point out that teaching the girls to read and write Chinese colloquial made them more desirable to their Chinese patrons.

True to their convictions, the women had retired from missionary work, and Elizabeth and Carrie had come to the mission to take charge of their school. Peering in through the iron grill gate at the great house they were passing, Elizabeth wondered if this was a stop for a green sedan chair.

Gratefully the girls reached the top of the hill, and followed the cook around the corner of the wall into the bright sunlight. It was not only for breath that they stopped, wordless. Below, the upturned eaves of thousands of houses crowded each other to the river. To the right, the stone arches of the Bridge of Ten Thousand Ages stepped from island to island across the swirling waters to the city of Foochow spread out on the flat plain beyond. To the east, just four miles away, Kusang and Kuliang mountains rose in a towering wall against the sea, joining a chain of other peaks to throw a mighty ring around the valley of Foochow.

And for the first time, Elizabeth heard the vast hum which rose like a cloud from the city, the voices of multitudes of people living outdoors. But it was the river that fascinated her as she walked the road along the crest of the hill. She saw it emerge, a streak of light from the western mountains; she watched it swing, swift and strong, around the city plain; and on under the Bridge of Ten Thousand Ages, she followed it past the fleet of bold-eyed junks, to where it disappeared in a mighty curve against the foot of Kusang Mountain.

The cook was used to the view. He stood pulling a bell in a green door set in an adobe wall. Hearing the clang, the girls hurried to join him.

When the gate swung open, Elizabeth saw more flamboyant chrysanthemums, and behind them a row of little girls dressed in short blue jackets and wide-leg trousers, their thick, black braids wound around their heads. But their eyes were big with the imminence of tears. Seeing their fright, Elizabeth smiled and spoke softly. Then at a word from the pleasant woman in charge, the children chanted a greeting and fled like frightened birds into the building.

Both girls planned to inspect their schools that first day, but for Elizabeth other plans had been made. In a shadowy bedroom in one of the great houses she had passed the night before, a man lay dying. Thirty years before he had come as a medical missionary to Foochow but had been forced to leave because of ill-health. Now as an old man, he had come back as Bishop to China. Once again ill-health had overtaken him in Foochow. As he lay dying, he longed for his family and the friends in the brick churches of Ohio.

Hearing that a young missionary from Ohio had just arrived, he sent word asking if she would come to see him. So Elizabeth left her new school and hurried to Bishop Wiley's bedside. He could see that she was unafraid, both of the Presence in the room, and of the new land to which she had come. She could tell him much about Ohio—what men were preaching in different churches, who had conducted the summer camps and what was new in Cincinnati. He gave her messages for his wife and laid his hands on her in blessing and gratitude. He died on November 22. She spent her first Sunday in Foochow pleating rolls of white satin into lining for Bishop Wiley's coffin.

***

On a summer day under the trees at the farm, as Elizabeth folded laundry, I picked up the story again.

"It seems to me that lining a coffin was a depressing way to start your life in China," I said to Elizabeth. She considered that as she smoothed out a towel.

"Depressing?" she repeated. "Not to us."

"There was nothing depressing about Bishop Wiley's death—only sorrow for his family in Ohio. As for preparing his coffin, we were accustomed to caring for our dead in those days."

With a laughing grimace, she added, "Unless you call a rash depressing. We did get an awful case of skin poisoning, Carrie and I, from the fresh Ningpo varnish on his coffin."

Almost wistfully then, she continued, "No, that first year in China was wonderful—wonderful. I was literally born again—a new country—a new home—a new language—new work. I had become an entirely new creature. Joy had been mine ever since my conversion, but now I was gay, always ready for fun and adventure. My Ohio family would not have recognized me. I hardly knew myself."

She shook her head slowly as if in wondering disbelief at the beauty of the memory. Her hands lay quiet as she sat gazing out across the fields lost in inner contemplation. I could not tell whether she was looking back to that happy year so long ago or to the promise implicit in each such rebirth.

Eye hath not seen
Ear hath not heard
Neither hath it entered into the heart of man
The wonders that God hath prepared
For them that love Him.

This is Elizabeth's favorite quotation and her confident hope.

Picking up the towel in her lap, she went on with her work and her story:

"It was this new personality that gave me my Chinese name. You know Chinese names have meaning, so our language teachers tried to find suitable ones. For Carrie they had only to translate her own name, Jewell. For me they chose the surname, 'Sing,' meaning 'star.' 'Fisher' would have been unsuitable for me, they explained. Years afterward when we were all decently old, they told me they named me 'Star' because I was so little, so gay and twinkled like a star.

"What fun we had learning the language that year," she continued. "I had never studied a foreign language before and was amazed to find it was so easy. I guess speaking Chinese is easy for everyone because there's so little grammar. You do need a good ear to catch the tones, though, and that I got from Uncle Wyatt's musical training. I can still hear myself singing those seven tones, Remember?" As she raised her hand to indicate the positions, I laughed and joined her. "Sing, sing, sing, sing, sing, sing, sing."

For a moment the hot windy, Wisconsin day faded. Once again, we were sitting opposite a young man in a blue gown and black skull cap learning the intricacies of Chinese. How earnestly we exaggerated those sounds, remembering each one meant an entirely different word. The first one was Elizabeth's name, "Star," one meant soul, one meant new, etc.[2]

"The written language fascinated me," continued Elizabeth, "although it was by no means easy. So much of the philosophy and culture of the country was contained in those strange hieroglyphics, that I almost decided to become a scholar. I think the idea intrigued me because I had no degree from an American university. It would have pleased my pride to be known as a scholar of Chinese characters. That would have done the Chinese people no good, though, so I contented myself by studying classical characters and Mencius my second and third years in Foochow.

"How thrilled I was to be able to read the characters on the gravestones to the little children raking leaves for fuel. They helped

2 Meanings for all seven tones: 1. Heart, star, new; 2. To investigate, adding the sign for woman it becomes "aunt;" 3. Faithfulness, letter; 4. Ancient, chamber; 5. spirit, deity; 6. duplicating second tone; 7. Abundant, very; 8. Ten, the ordinals or cardinal numbers.

me with conversation and I helped them read.

"I learned enough of the language for conversation, and enough of the written language to pass my examinations."

As her grasp of the language increased so did her understanding of the people and their problems.[3] Her school was beginning to absorb her. From the beginning, the solemn-eyed little girls had won her love. The Chinese woman in charge while Elizabeth learned the language was doing a splendid job of administration, but Elizabeth felt the need of reaching out to increase the attendance. She conceived of her school as a training center for teachers who would open day schools in the villages where there was no Christian teaching and little of any other kind, either. She asked that visiting country day-schools be added to her language study and Foochow Girls' School assignment.

So in her first year, Elizabeth prepared for country travel. She bought a three-tiered travelling basket, as big as an old fashioned clothes hamper. In it she carried cooking utensils, food and dishes. She bought a heavy cotton quilt big enough to keep her warm in the unheated village churches and provide some comfort on the board beds used by the Chinese people. She hired a Christian Chinese woman to travel with her. She stocked up on Chinese coins—a thousand to a string, each hundred being separated by a knot. The cash on such a string was equivalent to a dollar.

"If I planned a long trip, I had to hire a man to carry my money," she laughed, remembering.

So equipped, she set out in the biting chill of winter or in the steaming heat of summer to visit the country villages. Usually she travelled by sampan up or down the river to the point nearest the village to be visited. From there she and her Bible woman and load-bearer walked the narrow mud paths between rice fields to the low-roofed cluster of houses which was their destination. If there were already Christians in the village, there was probably a bare room somewhere which served as a meeting place. If there was a tiny Christian day school, that was her destination. There Elizabeth would

3 The interview under the trees is augmented by notes from her records and other sources.

set up housekeeping surrounded by the villagers, who oftener than not, had never seen an American woman. The Bible woman would obtain boiling water for tea while the load-bearer hung her mosquito net and brushed the bed boards clean. Then, if the weather was fair, a table covered with a pretty cloth was set out in the open, and Elizabeth drank her tea and ate her lunch. Through all her years of travel, she carried her own food, knowing that, otherwise, the hospitable villagers would feast her and starve themselves.

After a long trip, it would have been pleasanter for her to retire into the chapel and rest and eat behind closed doors, as most missionaries did. On one of her earliest trips, however, she overheard a remark that guided her through a lifetime of country travelling. She was eating outdoors in the sunshine because it was so bitterly cold in the chapel. One of the interested onlookers said to another, "What a strange people these Americans are. Their strong men come to visit us and hide inside while they eat. But this young little woman eats out in the open and talks to us. She isn't afraid at all. Their men behave like women and their women like men."

Always after that, Elizabeth spread her table in the open. Men, women and children crowded around her, laughing as she cut her food with a knife, exclaiming in horror as she placed it in her mouth with a sharp tined fork. "I had never before thought of a fork as a dangerous weapon," commented Elizabeth, "but now seeing it through their eyes, I wondered about it myself."

They were very curious about the food she ate, so she always carried extra cookies and oranges to share with the children. Like all children they wanted to touch everything. This Elizabeth forbade, but gave to each one of them a section of an orange or a taste of a cookie to satisfy their curiosity and take the hurt out of her firm, "Don't touch." Although the time would come when she would be the protector of many, she never forgot that she was always a guest in China.

To the children crowding around her lunch table, she also gave small colored pictures and told Bible stories.

If the village had a Christian school she visited it, heard the children recite chapters from the Bible and paid a few dimes to those who knew the prescribed lessons. It was for these examinations that she had to be able to read the colloquial written language. To do so in her first year was no small achievement. She visited the homes of the girls who showed promise, seeking to win them as pupils in her Foochow school. She always fought the custom of foot-binding. No foot-bound girls were accepted in her school, so often she had a double barrier to break down. "Unbind the feet of your daughter and send her to us to be educated," was the challenge this blue-eyed foreigner carried into many a village home.

At the beginning of the winter term there had been an increase of ten in school enrollment and Elizabeth rejoiced. Among them were several older girls who were betrothed to boys enrolled in the Theological School. This presented a special problem. A son of any family, no matter how poor, could aspire to be a scholar and eventually a government official. In that case, his wife might support him by working in the fields or carrying loads while he studied with no damage to his prestige. But a minister was different. His wife was necessary in his work and had to be educated. Often Elizabeth's trips to remote villages were for the purpose of finding such girls.

In one of her diaries there is an account of a series of revival meetings held in the Foochow school that first year. There were girls from both Christian and non-religious homes in attendance, and as usual, Elizabeth sought to lead every one of them into a personal relationship with God. Inherited religion was never enough for her.

She made special note in one of her diaries of an older girl, a non-Christian, who was the wife of a theological student and who had been brought to school by her husband. She was sullen and uncooperative, Elizabeth reports. She would not unbind her feet or change her habits of speech and untidiness. That meant she could not remain in school—and Elizabeth grieved thinking how her husband's church would be affected by such a wife. So Elizabeth and the Christian pupils surrounded her by loving prayer. They were rewarded by a complete character change in the girl. She became an outstanding Christian, helping her husband establish a model church community. After her husband's death she continued Christian service as a Bible woman.

In every child gathered around her table, Elizabeth saw the possibility of another such Christian.

These trips into the country were no small adventure. The older, more experienced missionaries were anxious about excursions up and down the river and into the hinterlands. The Manchu dynasty was dying, and, as always in dislocated times, thieves and murderers rose to the surface and harried their brothers. There were various societies throughout the land with marked anti-foreign tendencies, such as the society of the Harmonious Fist, which the Europeans dubbed the Boxers.

Only thirty years before Elizabeth's arrival, one of the most devastating of China's wars had swept up this rich Min Valley which she frequently travelled. Its leader, an unbalanced man, had worked in the home of a Canton missionary and absorbed some half-baked ideas of Christianity. Using the theme of the Kingdom of Heaven, he brilliantly succeeded in drawing to him thousands of men and boys discontented with the decadent Peking government. Using Christian slogans and terminology he and his rabble army swept up the river valleys northward, pillaging and burning villages and cities, and killing twenty million people before he was stopped. So great was the loss of life that often there was no one left to rebuild.

Elizabeth saw the results of this devastation along the lonely river valley. Forests of feathery bamboo veiled tumbled ruins and wild animals made their lairs where men used to live. For centuries, farmers in mountainous Fujian have lived in villages for protection from bandits, but now the distances between inhabited villages was greater than ever. Sometimes during planting and harvest time when blue clad figures dotted the lonely fields, Elizabeth heard the clanging of cymbals and knew that tigers were in the vicinity.

She was moved by the desolation and stirred with the smoldering excitement of the times, but was never afraid. Even though she came using the same Christian terminology and preaching the Kingdom of Heaven, the people were always kind.

"Only once in all my travels in China was I rudely treated," she records.

"That was my first year in Foochow. I was shopping in Foochow and a child picked up some dirt and threw it at me. It was just after the French took Indo-China and invaded Foochow waters with a fleet of gunboats. For a while all foreigners were very unpopular."

In the Spring of her first year, a journey she made outside her territory became one of her most vivid memories. Two elderly missionary men were planning to make the trip to the island of Haitan, two tides off the Mainland, and were willing to take Elizabeth along if the mission was approved. Accompanied by her tireless Bible woman, she made the trip.

An American woman was a novelty anywhere in China in those days, but Haitan had never seen one before. A Chinese soldier who had become a Christian was holding evangelistic services on the island at the time. When he saw Elizabeth, he decided to use her as an object lesson. He asked her to go for a walk over the low hills to let the people see her. She was almost mobbed by the astonished people, who ran after her. They pressed so eagerly for a look at this strange creature that Mr. Ding himself had to go to her rescue. They all followed him back to the church. There she was asked to stand on a table so that everyone could see her and her size-three shoes, while Mr. Ding preached a sermon about her big heavenly feet. So far as Elizabeth knows, this was the beginning of the "heavenly feet" or "anti-foot-binding" movement in south China. With deep satisfaction, she remembers that she helped stop the practice which had tortured baby girls for centuries.

That night the women refused to go home. They filled the room, watching her curiously and discussing her among themselves. One of the wonders that engrossed them was a hammock which Elizabeth brought. This swinging bed enchanted them and they all had to try it. With the help of her Bible woman, she answered their questions and made them welcome. At last, worn out, she suggested that everyone go home and sleep so that they could come back the next day. She herself had to go to bed, she said.

"Oh," cried the women, "that is what we are waiting for."

To this Elizabeth answered with true Chinese courtesy. "I couldn't think of being so impolite as to undress before guests."

Reluctantly the women withdrew. While Elizabeth prepared for bed, holes for eager eyes were punched through the paper covered windows. With a little bow and a smile she snuffed the wick burning in the saucer of oil, and undressed in the dark. So Elizabeth added firmness to her growing reputation for courtesy and kindness, a combination which served her well through the years.

For at least one of these curious women, Elizabeth had made a permanent impression. During her last years in China, when health and political conditions prevented her from travelling in the country, the young ministers of the conference used to come to her for counseling. One of these brought her an echo of that long-ago visit to Haitan.

His grandmother, he said, had recently died. As is the custom in China, the whole family was gathered around her in loving farewell. Like Elizabeth's own father, the old lady had apparently died, when suddenly she opened her eyes.

"Please remove the bandages from my feet," she commanded.

"But grandmother, you have worn them since childhood. Why trouble your body unnecessarily in the moment of death?" they remonstrated. The old lady insisted, saying, "When I was a little girl on Haitan, I saw a foreign lady, called Miss Star, standing on a table so that we could see the kind of feet the Heaven Father gives his daughters. Just now at Heaven's Gate, I saw her again. She reproached me, asking, "How can you hope to walk God's golden streets with bound feet?"

"But, grandmother, removing the bandages will not correct your feet. It is too late for that now," her children protested.

"Nevertheless, unbind them. My Heavenly Father will accept my good intention and heal them."

Unwillingly, they removed the bandages, and straightened out her misshapen feet. As they watched in awed silence, she eagerly hurried away to her streets of gold.

Elizabeth, commenting on this story said:

"So often, a seemingly unimportant word or act of kindness

would sink into a heart with the most surprising result."

"Sometimes the word fell on my own heart," she laughed. "Take the time I quarreled with my language teacher. That was really strange, for we usually got along so well together. He not only taught me Chinese, but the history and customs of his people, for which I was very grateful. Once in a while he irritated me though, especially when he talked in a superior way about Chinese girls.

"One day he boasted about how well the boys at Anglo-Chinese College could sing."

"We can read music and sing foreign songs. No girls can do that."

"Oh, can't they," I snapped back at him. "We'll see about that."

"I shouldn't have lost my temper, but he did annoy me, as the children say. At least I put the energy released to good use.

"Hurrying back to school, I drew a staff and scale on the board. When my girls came in I explained what had happened. They accepted the challenge, beginning that very day to learn their do, re, mi's. At the Easter Church service they sang an anthem in English. Never since has there been any doubt that the girls of Foochow can sing. That year music became a part of our curriculum. In fact, the youngest girl in the school later went to America to be trained as a music director. She came back to Hua Nan College, where she taught music for years.

"Oh, there was no limit to what I wanted for my girls. I believe it was my second spring in Foochow that we organized the women's Annual Conference. We were assigned Saturday night for the presentation of women's work. The topic assigned to me was, "How Much Education Shall We Give Our Girls?" Carrie was to discuss the "Training of Bible Women" and a missionary wife had as her topic, "Woman's Place in the Church." Since I was the youngest, I was given the poorest spot on the program, the last hour before adjournment. My teacher and I toiled over that address until we both felt it was perfect in every detail, although, of course, he had his doubts about the subject matter.

"I sat on the platform clutching my manuscript while the other two women spoke. One by one the weary ministers dropped off to sleep—after all the conference had lasted for days. When I saw that

I was going to have no one to listen to my important message, I was ready to cry—I believed so strongly in my answer to the question assigned and I had worked so hard to present a good address. When my turn came, I stepped out to the edge of the platform and said,

"Please all wake up as I have something important to say," and waited while the men sat up and looked around, virtuously, to see who had been sleeping.

I have prepared a long speech in reply to your question, "How much education shall we give our girls," I told them.

"I shall not give it now. In answer to your question, 'How much education for your girls,' I shall only say: Exactly as much as you plan for your boys. The time for talking is past. It is time for you to act." Then I sat down.

"These were the men who had already been dissatisfied with the educational program for girls. They wanted them to have music and English, but to give them education equal to that of their brothers was revolutionary. Not only music and English for girls, but mathematics, science, history, architecture, theology and medicine were implied in my bombshell speech. From then on, the road was always upward: from primary school through high school, to college, theological or medical schools—for girls as well as boys. Even I wasn't audacious enough then to foresee co-education.

"Forty years later, when Hua Nan College for women was chartered,[4] I sat on the platform and heard the Acting President, beautiful Lucy Wong, say, "This is the college of your dreams, Mrs. Brewster." That, I think, was the high point of my life in China.

"I wonder what has happened to them all, she sighed, thinking of the hundreds of bright-faced young people who had gone out from her schools to become teachers, preachers, nurses and doctors, from whom no letters ever come now. The uncertain fate of these is the

4 In 1933, Hwa Nan secured registration as a college for women from the Chinese government, and the following year it was granted the "Absolute Charter of College for Women" by the Regents of the state of New York. In 2005 a new campus was built in the locality of University City in Fuzhou. With about 200 faculty and staff and 3000 students, Hwa Nan Women's College is the only private institution in University City and is proud to be writing a new chapter in history.

sorrow that shadows the end of Elizabeth's life.

"Knowing what has happened in China, would you go again if you could?" I questioned.

"You mean if it were 1884 again and I could look down the years and see the flowering of our work blighted by the Communist Revolution?

"Yes, I would do it all over, gladly, only I should work even harder. We plant beside all waters. This is not China's first revolution, and probably not her last. If we waited for a hundred years of peace, when should we find it? No, I have seen my own joy multiplied too many times in the lives of those people to have any regrets. Besides, I didn't 'go' to China, as you say. I was sent."

"That is something else I have wondered, Mother. Weren't you ever disheartened when you got there and found that the people didn't come flocking to hear what you had to offer? Didn't you lose any of your bubbling joy?"

"If I had, I should have left China. One of the older missionaries said to me one day, "My child, you have had a wonderful, religious experience, but don't expect to keep it here."

"If I can't keep it, I won't stay," I told him.

"No, that inner voice still guided me, giving me a joyous confidence always."

She laid the corners of a sheet neatly together, then smiled at me.

"Do you remember your first spring in Foochow, my dear?"

Sentimentally, I replied.

"I remember the moonlight, white as milk, and the shadows of the palm fronds like black daggers on the ground. I remember the wisteria that curtained our veranda and the pink drift of roses on Miner's wall."

"Of course, those are the things you would remember," chortled Elizabeth, "you and my Francis were in love. Even down in Hinghwa, I heard of the somewhat devious arrangement he made with the Miner's gardener to send you roses every day. Strange that you should live in the same house and same room as I had forty years earlier."

"My own first spring was very different. I was very tired and I saw more of the earthy side of the season—the mold an inch thick on my shoes, the mildew on every tiny spot on my clothes, and the flies that clung to the food in the shops. It was terribly hot. Cholera came early, and by autumn it was raging.

"One day, coming up from school, I met Dr. Cory. She was the young doctor who had made us welcome at her hospital residence our first night in Foochow. She had been taking sick calls around the clock and looked ill herself.

"Suddenly that inner guidance came with great urgency. 'Go home with her.'

"Kathryn," I said, "you look so tired. You live alone and if you should become ill in the night, you would have no one to help you. You probably would wait until the servants got up in the morning to ask for help, and that would be too late. I'll go along and sleep with you just to play safe."

"She was too worn out to protest, so we went off together. We had dinner and went to bed early. Oddly, no calls came for her and we slept soundly. About midnight I awakened feeling queer. I just reached the bathroom when I became violently ill. Dr. Cory heard me and came running. It was I who had the cholera. Dr. Cory wakened the servants and hurried them off for help. Carrie and others came at the risk of their lives. Caring for a cholera patient was neither safe nor pleasant. There was no medicine for the disease in those days, just a fight to keep the heart going while the body turned itself inside out. At four in the morning, I was cold to my knees, but the women kept on working and pulled me through.

"Whenever I read the verse, 'He that saveth his life shall lose it, and he that loseth it for my sake, shall find it', I recall that night. You see I, too, lived alone. Alone, so far as human companions were concerned," she amended, "but always within the shadow of His wings."

The sun had dropped behind the ridge of the barn now, and my husband, Elizabeth's son, Francis, was bringing the sheep in across the meadow. The golden collie puppy was behaving badly, leaping and barking in excitement.

The clothes were folded neatly and I had a book full of notes. It had been a good afternoon.

Come, darling," I said, helping Elizabeth to her feet, "That's enough for today."

"So much talking," sighed Elizabeth, "and we haven't even got to Hinghwa."

CHAPTER FOUR

All Things Work Together for Good

For a month after her nearly fatal attack of cholera, Elizabeth was hospitalized in Foochow. Since there were no nurses, the friends who had saved her from death now nursed her back to health. When she was able to work again, gratitude for life restored spurred her on to more than usual activity. She took up her full schedule of teaching, plunged into advanced language study, assisted in revival meetings in Chinese churches and exposed herself to the chill rains of a Foochow winter visiting country day schools.

"Why, Elizabeth, you ought to have known better, "I chided, looking up from her diary. Turning eagerly from her game of counting the cars that passed our farm, she listened, as I read the notes, then laughed.

"Yes, I should have known better, but it has taken ninety years to learn to slow down, and I don't see that I am any better for it. Anyway, God knew what He was about even if I didn't. He fitted my foolishness into a plan for my good, as you will see."

By the end of the school year of 1886, she was in a physical collapse. As the steaming heat rose from the flooded rice paddies, she lay listlessly in the long chair on her wisteria-curtained veranda. Forty years of experience had taught the Mission community that there was little hope for recovery in a Foochow summer. Accordingly, they sent her to Japan, where the cool air of a mountain resort revived her strength. By September, she was back at her desk in Foochow confident that she could finish the remaining three years of her term of service. Again her enthusiasm for her work overdrew her strength, and by midwinter Carrie and Dr. Corey were watching her anxiously.

One day in January, hearing that some of the school girls were sick, Carrie walked over to their dormitory. She found Elizabeth already there with the sick children, comforting them until the doctor's arrival.

Carrie Jewel was only five-years-older than Elizabeth, but for some reason she assumed a protective attitude over her. She must have been a very remarkable woman, for even at ninety, Elizabeth will allow none of us to make decisions for her. That, insists Elizabeth, is God's job. Sizing up the situation, Carrie ordered her home. A little later, she went to Elizabeth's study to report the doctor's findings—it was a combination of scarlet fever and measles among the girls of the school. Brusque with concern, she ordered Elizabeth to avoid the sick children.

"You run the school and go on with your teaching. I've had scarlet fever; I'll stay with the sick girls."

The next morning Carrie was ill with scarletina, so it was Elizabeth, after all, who nursed the sick. In spite of her round-the-clock care and Dr. Corey's skill, one of the girls died. She was the beloved daughter of a Christian family and the darling of the school. About the same time word came from America that Elizabeth's own adored younger sister, Carrie, had died. The double loss tested even Elizabeth's stalwart faith.

In an attempt to make up for lost time, the school continued classes until the end of June. In those last weeks of heat and strain, amoebic dysentery found an easy victim in the exhausted Elizabeth. Once again her friends began a battle for her life. When medicines failed to help, she was taken to the rest house at Sharp Peak.

A time of great trouble had come for her—illness aggravated by sorrow and indecision. Quite apart from her physical ailment, she was torn between wanting to stay in China and going home to comfort her mother. No answer came to her prayer for guidance. Instead, she was sent to a place of unimagined beauty and given time to regain her spiritual balance.

In her chair, high on the bluff above the ocean, she watched the cloud shadows race across the bright water, much as they had done in her father's hay meadow long ago. She saw the far-away waves blossom silently and scatter like white roses in a windy garden; she laughed with the Psalmist at the plight of the little fishing junks staggering through the stormy seas. The Psalmist's isles of the sea were there, too, strung in a purple chain along the eastern horizon. On clear days, she could see the outline of Matsu, where ships from Shanghai picked up their pilots before navigating the treacherous waters of the River Min. That was where she and Carrie had first seen the misty hills of Fukien three happy years ago. It had never occurred to her then that illness would rob her of months of activity.

Now when her friends walked down the steep path to bathe in the cove, she was content to watch the gulls tilt the wind that blew cool from the ocean, and meditate on their plaintive tale of lost destiny. They were the restless souls of those who had died without sons, her teacher told her, condemned forever to ride the wind and water with no resting place anywhere. So, she watched and dreamed, but could not sleep. The medicine that should have acted as a sedative stimulated her. The sea wind brought coolness, but not rest.

At night, covered with steamer rugs, she lay face up to the star-strewn heavens, tracing the constellations learned in her high school astronomy classes. At Sharp Peak, no spreading elms of friendly rooftops shut out the awesome sweep of the universe. This was the sky of the Bible, too, she mused—a vast tent pegged to the rims of the earth. Here, as at home, Scorpio dominated the summer night—his head rearing boldly into the zenith, his glittering body slipping down through fathomless space, his tail curling up just in time to foil the reaching sea.

The Dipper was there, and the Milky Way, brighter than she remembered it at home—River of Heaven, her Chinese friends called it. Low on the southern horizon, three blazing stars marked the

Southern Cross. It seemed to her that the story of life was written in the sky—the symbol of evil, the promise of life-giving water, the sign of forgiving love. All those shining worlds were rooms in her Father's house, and she was at home in it. She wondered if one of them might be the new home of her father, Ada and Carrie, too. Sometimes a bit of melting stardust streaked across the sky, and like the flashing nailhead that fell from Will Fisher's coffin, it spoke to her of love. People died, and worlds died, but God loved on. This was the certainty underneath her illness and grief, the floor that would not let her sink into despair. It was what she had come to share with the Chinese people who saw themselves in the homeless seagulls.

Again, she was overwhelmed by the wonder that she, Elizabeth Fisher, had been entrusted with this message for China. God, who poured worlds in a river across the sky, had held out His hand and drawn her close to Him. He had sent her here to witness for Him. This was as incredible as the jeweled night and more real. God, in all the world, had sent her to the millions of people who lived in constant fear of demons of earth and sky and sea. These people were her life responsibility, she was certain.

It was the persistent illness that worried her. She should be up and at work, but now after weeks of rest and care she was still chair-bound. More than that, a picture tormented her night and day—a small white cottage in Ohio with shades drawn against the summer heat and a hot wind moaning drearily around the corners. Her mother, who had begrudged her going to China when Carrie was alive, what must she be suffering now? As she stirred restlessly, someone would suggest that it was time for her to be in bed.

In Foochow and Sharp Peak her friends were praying. The mission needed Elizabeth's joyous presence of God, and feared they might lose her. When she did not improve, Nathan Sites asked her to go home. He and his wife had befriended Elizabeth upon her arrival and had become as father and mother to her. Missionaries in the area since 1861, they knew too well the toll the climate had taken in lives of young Americans. Their word carried authority with Elizabeth for they lived so close to heaven that she still remembers them as saints, beloved and trusted by the whole community. When Father Sites' message arrived, she heard again the assurance, "This is the way, walk in it," and accepted the assignment to go home.

In August of that year, a steamer that was to inaugurate the new Canadian Pacific Line made a courtesy call at Pagoda Anchorage enroute from Hong Kong to Vancouver. To Elizabeth's friends, this was a gift from heaven. She could be placed aboard in the care of Carrie Jewell, and not have to disembark until she reached Vancouver. Another missionary going on home from Japan would relieve Carrie, allowing her to return to her school in Foochow. So Elizabeth in her long rattan chair was carried aboard. The friends who had failed to meet them upon arrival assembled to bid the girls goodbye, and if anyone in that silent group doubted that she would return, it was not Elizabeth.

The loving welcome that waited her in London was tempered by concern for her health. Pitzer wondered if he had been right! It certainly looked as if his sister had thrown her life away in China. Right now a good breeze would blow her away. In an attempt to coax her to eat, he brought her a pint of ice-cream every noon, an unheard of luxury in those days, but not too good for his sister. Her mother, gentle Mary Jane Fisher, sat with her back turned as she sewed so that Elizabeth would not see her tears. What had she done that God could take everyone from her? Will and Ada first, then Pitzer's wife and two little girls, then Carrie just nine months ago, and now Elizabeth so ill! She vowed she would try to handle this problem without Him. If Elizabeth recovered, she was going to keep her at home.

Slowly Elizabeth regained her strength. When she was able to receive callers, the cottage took on the aspects of a celebrity's home. Mary Jane bloomed as a stream of friends and relatives came bearing gifts of esteem rather than pity. Their interest in her work was the tonic Elizabeth needed. Letters arrived from distant cities asking her for speaking engagements. The young people of the town came in groups to listen to her talk about China. "Say something in Chinese," was their constant request. When she obliged with a stream of musical language, or translated passages from books she was studying, they shook their heads in amazement. Was this the Lizzie Fisher they used to know?

In their imaginations, they went with her across the hills to the Stone Seat to watch the moon come up through the pink clouds behind Kusang Mountain. She invited them to a picnic at the top of Lone Pine Hill on a spring night when the flooded rice fields mirrored the white moonlight. They went to a formal dinner with her at the home of the American consul, a scene of elegance quite outside their own experience. They had never even heard of the foods she mentioned—sweet persimmons, tangy pumelos, crisp water chestnuts, dried mushrooms and tender bamboo shoots. They heard her say, "Even if life holds nothing but sorrow from now on, I have had more than my share of wonder and delight."

In the bitter cold, they huddled with her under the arch of a river sampan on a long winter trip; they sat with her among her school girls when cholera and bubonic plague were raging, and no one knew who the next victim would be. They tried to understand how it felt to get bad news from home and not be able to do anything to help. They felt with her the pain of living in a city of half-a-million people who knew cruelty and suffering and despair, but nothing at all of hope or of God. So this was what it meant to be a missionary! But there were some who remembered only the picnics, the lovely scenery, the good things to eat, who murmured among themselves, "Where's the sacrifice in that?"

Elizabeth laughed when she heard of these comments. So far as she was concerned, there was no sacrifice; there were plenty of hardships, but she was young and adventurous and took pleasure in dealing with them. The question of sacrifice, however, kept recurring during her wonderful year at home. There were, for instance, two young women who came to her in distress. They had hoped to go to India as evangelists, and hearing that a missionary from that country was speaking nearby, they had gone to hear her. They had been horrified to hear her tell of the amenities of life to be enjoyed in that country. Could they find sacrifice in China, they demanded of Elizabeth.

Looking at them, she understood their dismay. She herself had stepped off the edge of the earth without a question as to what would bear her up, eager only to do something wonderful for God. When she found herself set down in safety and comfort among friends, she, too, had been dismayed. Is this right, she had asked with misgiving? Where is the sacrifice in this? It had been given to her to understand that the sacrifice was the surrender of her own will in obedience to God, and that it was up to Him to set the conditions for the use of her gift. Joy, laughter and gladness were obviously acceptable to Him—perhaps good times were more useful than tears and sadness. Elizabeth told the girls her own experience, adding that she could not promise them sacrifice in China. She suggested that they wait until God made it clear where He wanted them to serve, and then obey gladly.

Elizabeth remembered the incident perfectly when I read it to her from her notes. "Do you know what happened to them?" I asked.

"I think they went to Korea; whether they found sacrifice, I do not know." Elizabeth, who loves parties, movies, games and laughter, shook her head. "So many Christians used to have the idea that to be happy was wrong and felt guilty when they were having fun. Because of those two girls, I never spoke in public of social life in Foochow.

Even when I was young the consulates and the homes of the business people were very beautiful. Some of the British tea merchants used to give magnificent parties. There were several where I was a frequent guest. I had never seen anything to compare with them except some of the old homes in Baltimore, where I was entertained just before going to China. I remember being very much impressed then by the size of the houses, the beautiful furniture, the solicitous servants and the gracious manners of the people who owned the houses. I couldn't help thinking, a little enviously, that this manner of living was mine by inheritance, if only the Minshalls could claim their fortune from the chancery. Then, in Foochow, I was a part of it myself, whenever I was invited to one of those beautiful merchant houses. It all seemed like a bit of heavenly humor, and I enjoyed every moment of it.

"I was invited back to Baltimore as soon as I could travel. This time the pier glass mirrors, the polished mahogany furniture, the thick Oriental rugs and the solicitous servants didn't make me envious at all. I was used to it. But the graciousness of the people of Baltimore! That was still something very special.

"That question of sacrifice came up again in the spring of my year at home. There was a very lovely woman teacher in London who had just experienced the blessing of complete consecration, as we used to call it. She was waiting to be shown where God wanted her to serve. She had a particular gift for teaching boys, and since I knew the president of Anglo-Chinese College was in the States looking for such a teacher, I wrote him at once. After considering the position for several months, she decided that she would return with me in the fall.

"Everyone seemed very happy about it. Later on in the summer Dr. Thoburn, who later became Bishop Thoburn, met her at Lancaster Camping Grounds. He was very much impressed with her wonderful Christian spirit, and asked her to go to India to start the deaconess work there. Among other things that meant a salary of $8.00 a month, and the wearing of the somber uniform and cap. All of us young people were shocked at the thought—she was so gifted a teacher, so beautiful to look at and always so handsomely dressed. But she accepted the invitation, turning down the chance to do what would have been pure joy for her in Foochow. It was the sacrificial aspect of the deaconess work that had won her. Of course, no one can know what the will of God is for another person, but I have always wondered about that decision.

"Then there was my mother. My sailing date had been set for November twelfth. Invitations kept coming from churches to come and tell them about my work. I couldn't bear to leave her at home alone, so insisted that she accompany me. That too turned out to be very hard for her, because she constantly had to listen to me openly rejoice in the fact that I would soon be on my way back to China. Everywhere, people made much of both of us, invariably bidding us goodbye by singing what was then the very new and popular, 'God Be With You Till We Meet Again.' All of us knew how very possible it was that we might never meet again on earth, and the farewells became increasingly difficult for my mother to endure. She was truly making a sacrifice, though not gladly. Joy lay ahead of me; sorrow and loneliness for her.

"One day, we both went into an empty church to lay our burdens at the foot of the Cross. We were kneeling at the altar when something very wonderful happened. I am not given to visions, but as I knelt there, I saw Jesus upon His cross, and oh, the glory that streamed from His blessed face! Not pain, not sorrow, but glory! I was caught up in the vision, forgetting everything else until my mother touched me, exclaiming joyfully, 'Elizabeth, I can let you go now. I'll not rebel any longer. I have seen Jesus, and I give you gladly to Him for China.'

"Mother lived until 1927," Elizabeth's diary records, "she saw me come home many times, and usually came to keep house for us so that I could be free to go out speaking. She was living with Will in Kansas the last time I saw her. She had only one wish—that she would not die alone. So far as we know that wish was denied her. The family was out on a brief shopping trip one day, leaving her in good health. When they came back she was dead."

Toward the end of October, Elizabeth and her mother went to Cincinnati where Elizabeth was to be one of the featured speakers at a conference. After the address she was surrounded, as usual, by an admiring group of people who wanted to shake her hand and make flattering remarks. A friend, closely followed by a handsome stranger, broke through the circle.

"Lizzie, may I present Mr. Will Brewster, a leading member of the Cincinnati Conference.

Elizabeth looked up at him. So this was Will Brewster! She knew his father, Samuel Brewster, a leading member of the Cincinnati Conference. She had heard that the son was to become a preacher, too. He was tall, his blonde hair waved back from a high forehead; his eyes, a bright sea blue, were looking at her severely. Here was something new—no smiling flattery, no trifling conversation—just a word of courtesy, followed by a blunt question.

"I have been hoping to meet you, Miss Fisher. How many days a week do you work in China?"

Nettled, Elizabeth relied flippantly, "Six and twice as hard on

Sundays."

He nodded. "Exactly. No wonder you broke down in three years. Don't you know the commandment 'Six days shalt thou labor and do all thy work?' Those are words of divine wisdom. To be sure those of us in church work are busier on Sunday than on any other, but we can choose a week day instead. Wednesday is my day of rest. Are you going back to China?"

"Yes. November 12th."

"Promise me, then, that from now on you will rest one day a week."

Elizabeth heard herself meekly promising. He asked her if she could possibly squeeze in a talk for his Sunday school children on October 28th in the afternoon. This she also promised. During the next few days she had little time to think about the young man with the extraordinary approach, but when Sunday came, she remembered her promise. The streetcar conductor was so occupied with a load of jolly German picnickers that he forgot to let Elizabeth off at the right corner with the result that she arrived at Will Brewster's church an hour late. He had almost concluded that the pert young woman from China had decided that Sunday was her day of rest, when she hurried in laughing and apologetic. It was for both of them a day to be remembered.

Before she left for China, she heard that the astounding Dr. Thoburn, now Bishop, had secured Will Brewster as a missionary for India. Later she heard that he was to preach in Singapore for a year while the pastor of the English-speaking church was on furlough. Elizabeth was not greatly interested in the report, or in the man. The last time she had talked with him, he had told her that he liked the people of India better than those of China. Indignantly, she had accused him of judging a whole people by his laundry man, and flounced off, leaving him puzzled and amused.

****

She reached Foochow in January. Several new young women had arrived during her absence. One of them had been assigned to her position in the school for girls. Another had taken her place in the close friendship with Miss Jewell and Dr. Corey, which had prompted the Mission to call them Faith, Hope and Charity. Perhaps, it was the cold rain that enveloped the city; perhaps, the year of adulation in America had spoiled her, she thought to herself—whatever it was, she felt that she had bitten into a beautiful red apple and found it bitter. She waited for guidance, but none came. Finally she asked to be assigned to country work visiting and organizing day schools.

Accompanied by her faithful Bible woman companion, she travelled up river by sampan for sixty miles, and then was carried in a light rattan chair swung on long bamboo poles thirty miles through the mountains to the city of Kucheng. Other men carried her three-tiered baskets of bedding, dishes and food, and her little organ. She planned to stay for two months, but when she saw the lovely scenery she wished she could stay forever. No missionary had set up residence there, but land had been bought for that purpose on a beautiful hill outside the city of Kucheng. The site overlooked the city, the river which bordered it and on to the mountains on all sides.

Elizabeth herself looked like a small black bear. Since there was snow on the mountain tops, and no heat in any of the houses, she wore quilted outer garments. She had known the discomfort of chilblains in Ohio, when she had toasted her cold feet on the polished steel bars of her mother's parlor stove. Now, unhappily, that misery visited her hands too. When they became stiff and blue with cold, she held them over a little basket of glowing coals as the Chinese people did. The result was swollen itching hands.

In spite of the weather, the two women worked purposefully. They visited existing day schools. They heard the children recite passages of scripture, not to claim them as converts for a church, but to give them something to draw on for comfort in times of great need. They helped the teachers with their problems, and visited preachers' wives and widows in hopes of finding new teachers, these being the only women in the village who might be able to read. They sought out older women willing to become Bible women, and started teaching them to read. The schools they organized taught only reading, writing, numbers and Bible. Even so, they were the only schools in the country areas.

Every night her load-bearer set up the little organ in the village street so that Elizabeth could play and sing the story of Jesus, attracting a crowd of amazed and curious village folk. How often she blessed Uncle Wyatt for teaching her to sing and insisting that she learn to play a three-fingered accompaniment. (Whenever I pass a Salvation Army unit singing and preaching on a street corner, I think of her singing and telling stories on a narrow, dirty street in China long ago.) The crowd that gathered around her was made up of the children of the neighborhood, the load-bearers and the beggars. They stopped to watch this amazing blue-eyed being and the strange box that made music.

To those who could stop long enough to listen, the story she told must have been even more amazing. God, if they had ever heard the name, was the Being that only the Emperor could approach at the altar of Heaven in Peking. Love was something fathers felt for their little children. What was this she was saying, that the King of Heaven was not far away, but right close at hand, and that He loved each man, woman and child as a father loved his little children? He had sent His Son, Jesus, to tell men on earth of His love for them, but they wouldn't listen and killed the boy by nailing Him on a Cross. And instead of destroying the earth in anger, the Heaven Father forgave those who did the evil thing, asking only that men be sorry, stop being cruel to each other and believe in Him instead of evil spirits. If they would do this, they would be safe even when they died. The Heaven Father would take them to live with Him, and care for them and love them always.

Who could imagine a stranger and more wonderful story? The men who heard it told it over and over again with variations whenever they stopped for tea or soup in remote mountain villages. Many people listened and some believed. Once a frightened family from a village many days journey away appeared on the streets of Kucheng asking the way to the blue-eyed outlander who could speak to the Heaven Father on behalf of their baby who was about to die. So Elizabeth knew that the lovely message was spreading.

The cold winter rains were over when she and her companions started back to Foochow. The pines where putting out fresh green shoots and flowers were everywhere. Elizabeth laughed with the chair-bearers as they pointed out one peak called "Flower Mountain." Why should one mountain bear that name when all of them were gay with azaleas, they wondered. Not until the River Min lay before her did Elizabeth realize how much she would miss the lovely Kucheng hill country. "I should like to come back and spend the rest of my life doing country work among these hills and these people," she said to her companions.

Back in Foochow, she was dismayed to learn that one of the promising new missionaries, Miss Mabel Hartford, was about to be sent home because of ill-health. The Mission had delayed only because the girl was so unwilling to go. She had no relatives in the States, and asked to be allowed to work out the rest of her life among the Chinese people. No one knew better than Elizabeth how she felt. Only a year ago she had been in the same position. Turning over in her mind how much devoted missionaries were needed, how much it cost to send one to the field only to withdraw her permanently after a year of two, Elizabeth had an inspiration. She proposed to the Mission that she be allowed to take Miss Hartford to the Foochow mountains for a few weeks. The Plumbs had built a stone cottage on the top of Kuliang Mountain just a few hours' journey from the city. If they and the doctors were willing, would it not be worth experimenting to see if the air there could restore Miss Hartford to health? To the delight of both girls, permission was granted, and they went to Kuliang.

Elizabeth took a teacher along, so that she could continue advanced language study. From the founding of the Mission, proficiency in native languages had been considered of utmost importance. Elizabeth studied not only because the Mission required her to, but because she loved the language of the people among whom she worked, and the written language which opened up to her the history and classics which only the scholars could read.

That spring, she was also commissioned to superintend the building of a stone house for the Women's Foreign Mission Society.

This was the first of many building projects that were to occupy her for the next sixty years.

Elizabeth had recorded that a Church of England missionary, a Miss Apperson, decorated the walls of the house with illuminated texts. I was intrigued by the name and the artistic talents of the girl and spoke to Elizabeth about her.

"This Miss Apperson, Mother dear, I never heard of her in China."

"She was married years before your time to a Mr. Phillips. You may have known her daughter, Kathleen."

I certainly did! She had helped me through the most terrifying night of my life. So now I stopped to tell the story to Elizabeth, realizing as I talked, that with her as an audience, the whole episode sounded overly dramatic and not very unusual.

"The summer our son Bill was born, I was living with friends, the Cannons, on Kuliang Mountain. When Bill was eleven days old, we knew a typhoon was near because of the typical pattern of strong gusts of wind followed by dead calm. I thought it very kind of Kathleen to venture up our hill in that wind, and told her so.

"She laughed, saying she was eager to see the house as well as me and the baby. When she herself was an infant, her mother had had quite an experience with a typhoon there. Maybe I should tell you about it; the club was flying typhoon flags as I came up," she laughed.

"Mother was up here alone with me, when the storm came up the coast, but she felt quite safe because the house is solid stone and the stone typhoon wall out back is sixteen feet thick. But the storm swerved inland and the winds hit the unprotected front of the house. When the glass began to fly, she put me in the top drawer of one of these chests for safety. When the partitions began to go, she knew she had to leave. She pinned an English bath blanket across her chest, like a sling, and put me in it, then she crawled on her hands and knees down the mountain to a safer house."

"I thought it a very interesting story, but almost too close for comfort. While we drank our tea the wind gusts increased in violence and frequency so that Kathleen had to hurry downhill.

"At dinner my friend, Harriet, and I were nervous. Her husband was on a tiny coastal steamer coming down from Shanghai, my husband was in Foochow. The amahs put the children to bed early and happily they all went to sleep.

"Never having been through a typhoon, I kept asking Harriet with each blast of wind, 'Is it a typhoon yet?' She always answered, 'Well, the tiles are still on.' Looking up, I realized that the tiles were laid right on the rafters. If they blew off, we should have no protection from flying debris. I went to my room, cleared a chest drawer and put my baby in it and pushed it nearly shut. Almost immediately, there was a fearful clatter overhead as the wind swept a section of the roof clean of tiles. Harriet shouted in my ear, 'This is a typhoon.'

"Then the front storm shutters began to rattle. It was Kathleen's typhoon all over again. The wind was hitting the unprotected front of the house. Harriet and I stood guard over the children for more than an hour as windows blew in and tiles blew off, and the wind tore around the inside of our house. Harriet's children were awakened by the clamor. She wrapped their heads in Turkish towels and yelled in my ear that she was taking them down the mountain to a more sheltered house. Her amah (a nurse maid) offered to go along. My amah, expecting to die, went to her own room and combed her long black hair. Harriet's bathroom had a ceiling in it and a lantern still burned there. She carried the baby still sleeping in the chest drawer in for me and told me to stay there—she would come back for me if she could make it. I watched the five white blurs crawl along the floor and out the open door.

"It might have been half an hour later when our dog set up a dismal howling. I looked up and saw that the walls were bulging. I could hear partitions and furniture crashing in the other rooms. Through the paralysis of terror that gripped me, I remembered how Kathleen's mother saved her baby. In the cupboard I found a great bath towel, pinned it around me, put the baby in it, and crawled out into the shrieking night. Somewhere along the way I bumped into Harriet who had come back for me. Sitting there exposed to the wind, she took the baby from me, wrapped him in the towel and crawled away. Automatically, I stood up and was promptly blown away. I landed in a rice paddy ten feet below, unhurt, but I almost frightened Harriet to death when she came crawling down the steps and found me waiting for her."

"You and your storms," chuckled Elizabeth. "I remember hearing about your experience, but I didn't know it was Kathleen Phillips who had prepared you for it. That house was never occupied again, did you know that, my dear? Too bad you didn't have a cellar to hide in!" (Somehow it didn't seem necessary at the moment to tell her that though the house where we sought refuge was destroyed inside, the bathroom was intact!)

This was a wicked gibe at me, and we both laughed. At the farm this summer we have had exceedingly villainous weather. One evening the sky looked so sinister that I led Elizabeth into the cellar, where my son had arranged a tornado shelter consisting of an old cellar door laid across two cupboards. The unwilling Elizabeth sat on a chair underneath and tapped her fingers, while I ran up to look at the weather and back again to see how she was.

"I'm perfectly comfortable here, but I'd be much happier upstairs where I belong," she announced wryly. "The good Lord has always cared for me in danger and he would never think of looking for me down here under a cellar door!"

Her faith is as uncomplicated as that. God expects her to act like His child. She trusts Him with her life.

Her son Edward recently told me a story about Elizabeth in a storm which illustrates this faith. It was told him in laughing wonder by one of the men who shared the experience. Accompanied by a Bishop of the Methodist Church and a well-known missionary, she sailed one day across many miles of open ocean to an island off the coast. They were overtaken by a violent storm which threatened to swamp the open boat. The crew bailed valiantly, but could not keep up with the water. Seeing their peril, the two men passengers grabbed buckets and worked furiously. Elizabeth had been wedged into the bow of the boat to keep from being swept overboard. From time to time the exhausted men had to stop to rest, grimly hanging on while they recovered their breath. Finally, the boat reached the island. Everyone climbed out, and stood wringing the water out of their clothes, too tired to talk. Finally, one of the men said to Elizabeth, "That was a close call, Mrs. Brewster. If it hadn't been for you, we would never have made it."

"For me? What did I do?" asked Elizabeth in surprise.

"Why, several times we stopped bailing because it seemed utterly useless to continue. Then, when we looked at you sitting there, soaking wet but calm and smiling, we took courage. It was evident that you expected to get across safely, so we went back to bailing, and here we are!"

"Well," laughed Elizabeth, "you are wrong. I didn't expect to get across safely. I thought our time had certainly come, and I was just sitting there waiting to meet my God. That's why I was smiling!"

***

To everyone's delight the mountain air cured Miss Hartford. Elizabeth notes in her diary that this might well be her greatest contribution to the missionary cause, for Mabel Hartford was a valiant woman, and a radiant missionary. Like Elizabeth, she was completely surrendered to God and, therefore, completely unafraid. She reveled in country work, and for most of her life lived alone far up the Min River perfectly happy and secure among her Chinese neighbors.

That fall the Plumb family was going home on furlough. Because Mrs. Plumb was ill, the doctors recommended a long sea trip via Singapore and the Suez Canal. Elizabeth had loved the Plumb children, Horace and Florence, from the time she first saw them, tearfully, dropping flowers into the grave of their beloved Bishop Wiley. The children were also members of her music class and Florence was a frequent and always welcome guest in Elizabeth's study. It now occurred to her that she might do them all a favor. That abrupt young man, Will Brewster, was living in Singapore. Perhaps he would meet them and take them around the city. She wrote him, recalling their Ohio encounter, and the promise he had extracted from her not to work seven days a week. She had kept her promise, she said, and now would he be kind enough to see that her friends had a good time in Singapore?

About a month later a pile of mail from Singapore and Hong Kong was dumped on the floor of one of the mission houses. As was the custom in Foochow at that time, everyone came and sorted eagerly through the pile for their own letters. It did not pass unnoticed that Lizzie Fisher had a letter from Singapore. For three years, every mail delivery from the States had brought at least one letter addressed to her in a strutting masculine hand. Since her return, there had been no such letters. Now there was one from Singapore, obviously from a man. Elizabeth was pleasantly aware of the interest, which unaccountably, she shared. The letter announced his delight to meet her friends and show them the city. Of course, that necessitated a thank-you note, and soon there was a flourishing correspondence between Will Brewster and Elizabeth. She felt satisfaction in what he had written. He was discovering for himself that the Chinese were the most superior people in Singapore; that he was not satisfied to be pastor to an English speaking congregation; and that he intended to study their language and work among the Chinese people.

During the following winter, she noted with gratitude that the old zest for her work had returned. Advanced language study was progressing satisfactorily, and in her heart Elizabeth was beginning to wonder if God would allow her to do for the girls and women of China what Isabella Thoburn had done for the women of India. Miss Thoburn had started teaching the children playing around her door and now had founded a college for women—the Isabella Thoburn College! How wonderful to found a college! "Elizabeth Fisher College!" Wouldn't that be wonderful?

Meanwhile down in Singapore, Bishop Thoburn was worried about Will Brewster. It was obvious that the climate did not agree with him, and, in the early summer, the Bishop called him in for conference, suggesting that he go north to China for rest and a change of climate. Will Brewster agreed to go. As they visited, the Bishop had another idea.

"Will, you ought to have a wife."

"Yes, I have been thinking of it," agreed Mr. Brewster.

The Bishop, an astute man, sat looking at the young minister, speculatively. He had certainly been very cooperative about going to China for a vacation. The conference at Cincinnati the year before passed in review before him. Will Brewster was there; so was that lively young woman, Lizzie Fisher, now back in Foochow, China.

"Ah, yes, Will. To be sure. Lizzie Fisher! Fine, that will be just fine. She knows the Chinese people and I hear she is doing splendidly with the language. She can work there with them. That will be wonderful, Will, just wonderful."

So with the Bishop's blessing on a proposal not yet made, Will Brewster started north.

In Hong Kong, while waiting for a coastal steamer, he became acquainted with a young couple who were waiting transportation to America. They had been out only a year, but the husband had applied himself so enthusiastically and exclusively to language study that his health had broken down and now his place in the mission was vacant. He had been preparing to serve in a place called Hinghwa, south of Foochow, and spent hours pouring out to Will Brewster his love for that city and his disappointment that his missionary career was over.

Mr. Brewster arrived in Foochow with a lively desire to see Hinghwa as well as enjoying the wisdom of older missionaries and doctors there who believed that tennis, walks, golf and social good times were health preservers. Apparently in the Orient, resting one day a week was not enough. He would speak to Lizzie Fisher about taking exercise too. He was a guest of the Nathan Sites family, Elizabeth's most loved friends.

Everything about Foochow agreed with him; he liked the people, who accepted him as one of themselves. He wrote Bishop Thoburn asking for a transfer to China; the mission wrote their Bishop requesting his appointment to Hinghwa. Everything was progressing satisfactorily, except his proposal to Lizzie Fisher. Together they walked the narrow roads out into the hills and sat on the stone tables in the horseshoe-shaped graves while Lizzie tried to make up her mind.

Finally, in exasperation, Will said to her, "Do you know what I think? It's your pride that stands in your way. You want to do for the Chinese women what Isabella Thoburn did for India, and are afraid marriage might upset those plans. Am I right?"

Lizzie could only interpret this astonishing baring of her heart's secret as an indication that God was helping Will Brewster, and accepted him at once.

As soon as the transfer from Singapore was granted, Mr. Sites took Will to visit Hinghwa. He, too, fell in love with the city set on a coastal plain, laced with canals and circled by mountains. He preached through an interpreter to the Chinese ministers gathered to meet him, and when they reacted favorably, he and Mr. Sites negotiated for land on which to build a residence. They purchased a hill outside the city just inside the city wall, much like the mission site Elizabeth had admired up in Kucheng.

Will and Elizabeth chose the 28th of October for their wedding day because that was the anniversary of her visit to his church in Cincinnati, when Will first realized what it meant to get along without her.

They were married in the big bare church of Heavenly Peace in Foochow. The little English Episcopal Church would have been more suited to the traditional bridal outfit of white, brocaded satin with a train and long veil which Elizabeth wore, but she wanted to be married in the Chinese Church of which she was a member. It was her wish to have Father Sites read the service. He was accustomed to marrying Chinese brides in vivid pink, using the Chinese wedding service. The English ceremony was strange to him and he was emotionally moved by the marriage of this girl who had been like a daughter to him.

All went well until he came to the lines, "I pronounce thee, Will and Elizabeth, man and wife." The service used the initials M and N, and Father Sties read as it was written, "I pronounce thee, M and N, man and wife," much to the delight of the audience and the amusement of the bride and groom. The American Consul who gave the bride away made everything legal, with a properly worded marriage certificate, so for Elizabeth and Will, it was just an added fillip to their most wonderful day.

Elizabeth of the silver curls leaned forward eagerly as I closed the little blue notebook and laid down my pencil.

"Did you get to the wedding?"

"Yes, I got to the wedding, darling. What a lovely bride you must have been! And I see what you meant by saying God knew what He was doing when He sent you home on sick leave."

"Ah, yes. He always does, dear." She sat smiling at the memories. "All the years since were decided by that sick leave. The twenty-six years Will and I had together were pure joy. Even after he was gone, there was still our work to do in Hinghwa, our home—our beloved home."

Sensing a note of melancholy, I turned on the radio. The six o'clock news was on, and immediately Elizabeth leaned into the blast of words—a soldier of the Lord eager to hear from the battlefront.

CHAPTER 5

Elizabeth and Will

Some weeks before the wedding, Father Sites[1] took Will Brewster on an introductory visit to Hinghwa and the surrounding district. When they arrived at the river that formed its boundary, Mr. Sites pointed across saying,

"There lies your territory."

Halting his chair, Will Brewster got out and stood looking at the mellow landscape. Then picking up his Bible, he opened it to Paul's first letter to the people at Corinth. At the beginning of the second chapter he read the words that were to be his guide through all the years to come.

When Elizabeth told me this incident, I picked up my Bible to read the passage.

"Read it aloud," she said.

"And I brethren, when I came to you, I came not with excellence of speech, or of wisdom, declaring unto you the testimony of God. For I determined not to know anything among you, save Jesus Christ, and Him crucified."

Holding up her hand, Elizabeth stopped me.

"That was his vow. 'For I determined to know nothing among

1 The term "Father" is merely one of endearment. Elizabeth uses it frequently when referring to Mr. Nathan Sites.

you save Jesus Christ,' making 'and Him crucified' secondary, as Paul did. It seemed to us there was too much emphasis on the last part of the statement in those days. We missionaries spent too much time preaching 'and Him crucified' to a people who needed a living Lord. So Will determined in so far as he was able to demonstrate to the people of Hinghwa the Jesus who taught and healed and lived the love of God.

"He used to say, certainly, he wanted to get people into Heaven, but he also wanted to make their Earthly life as worthy as possible, as sons of God. He was always trying to improve their physical as well as their spiritual condition. There certainly was need for both.

"One of the purposes of that first trip," she continued, "was to buy land on which to build our home. The men bought a hill just inside the wall southwest of the city. It was like the site I had admired so much in Kucheng, high up and overlooking the city. It would be cool and clean and far enough from the crowded city to be quiet. I was delighted when they described it to me.

"On the night we returned from our wedding trip up the Ing Hok River, there was a reception for us. Our two best friends, Mr. Gracie, the American Consul, and 'Father' Sites avoided us all evening. When we finally cornered them, they told us there was unpleasant news from Hinghwa which they had hoped to keep from us until morning. It seemed the people of Hinghwa had not been pleased with the sale of the land for our home. In the first place they were afraid to have us live among them. We looked strange and acted even more strangely, they said, and no one knew what ills might befall the city because of us. Moreover, if we were allowed to live on a hill above them, the good luck of everyone would be endangered. The hill was higher than the city's 'heaven touching' pagoda, and a house built there would absorb the good luck which the pagoda had been erected to insure for the people. Besides, being the nearest point to heaven in the whole area, the hill was sacred to the dead whose graves dotted its surface. So indignant and fearful were the people, that Hinghwa officials had felt it necessary to warn the American Consul that riots were threatened. Mr. Gracie told us of all these developments, and strongly advised that we postpone our contemplated trip to Hinghwa on Tuesday.

"Will and I would not agree. We asked him to notify Hinghwa officials that the land purchase was cancelled; that we understood perfectly the feeling of the people, and hoped they would help us find a dwelling that would be satisfactory to everyone. Aside from that, we saw no reason to postpone our journey. I could speak Foochow fluently and was sure there must be people in Hinghwa who understood that dialect. Mr. Gracie reluctantly consented to our departure on condition that we spend two nights enroute. This would allow ample time for his official message to arrive in Hinghwa ahead of us.

"All was quiet in Hokchiang where we spent the first night. It was evening of the next day when we approached the port city of Antau, (Hinghwa is about six miles inland), and quite dark as we rode through its streets."

That was Elizabeth's matter-of-fact description of what seemed to me an exciting, if not perilous, journey. I could see the little procession of chairs advancing into the night, escorted by a coolie carrying a flaming torch as protection against tigers and thieves. Doubtless there were also other travelers, merchants, farmers and load-bearers keeping as close as possible for safety's sake, speculating loudly as to the destination and purpose of the foreigners.

Certainly, both Elizabeth and Will must have wondered what awaited them. Was Hinghwa rioting in protest against their coming? What would it be like to be mauled by a mob? Would they be required to die before they had a chance to tell the people why they had come? Didn't Will worry at all for the safety of his bride of a week? Thus, I questioned Elizabeth.

She thought for a while. "I can't remember worrying about anything. I was just eager to get to Hinghwa and start working. I have told you before I didn't expect harm. I never wasted energy in fear! Sixty-six years would have been a long time to be afraid! As for Will, why should he worry? I knew China and its risks far better than he; he wasn't taking me anywhere against my wishes. We were two intelligent people with one purpose—to do the work of God according to His will, and we left our safety to Him."

How truly she spoke for her husband, I discovered later in his book, *Evolution of New China*, written in 1907. He, too, must have been asked such questions. The following quotation is his reply:

"The saintly Bishop Ninde visited the Eastern Asia Missions of the Methodist Episcopal Church in 1894-95. It was wartime and winter. He was advised by many not to undertake the journey into Korea. His reply might well be graven upon the medals of highest award for deed of bravery. 'It is my duty to go; and I am too much of a coward to step out of the path of duty.'"

Will Brewster continues; "The Father's care is the essential thing, not the external conditions. In doing the Master's will, any place is safe. It is this that makes the life of the foreign missionary, even in the interior of China, one of joy and peace. He hears the assurance from the lips that never deceived, 'Let not your heart be troubled, neither let it be afraid.'"

In spite of their indifference to danger, it must have been with real thanksgiving that the travelers found the little city of Antau, dark and silent except for the loud voices of their own chair coolies. Replying to the pounding on his gate, the sleepy but cordial minister of the little Methodist church came out to receive them. He understood Foochow dialect, and in reply to Elizabeth's eager question, assured her all was quiet in Hinghwa. Then with the wonderful hospitality of China, he invited them in, asking just time enough to move his sleeping family from their beds. This Elizabeth refused to allow. Instead she and Will spread their thick cotton comforter on the four-by-six-foot platform in the little chapel hall, hung their mosquito net over it, and crawled in. Elizabeth laughed remembering the countless nights in diverse places they were to sleep like that.

On November 7, 1890, they entered Hinghwa as unobtrusively as possible. Children ran in fright and the people were unsmiling, but no voice was lifted against them. When they reached the chapel, the minister made them warmly welcome to the three-room apartment which had been prepared for them. They were at home.

Since there was no one to tell them what to do, their work was real pioneering. Throughout the district there was a Christian community of about a thousand people; there were also some small day-schools established by a presiding elder, one of a family of brothers of such outstanding Christianity that they were known as the Six Golden Candlesticks. Otherwise their field was as unlimited as their faith.

For both of them, the first job was language study. Their teacher was one of the scholars of the city, a man who was to be their friend and counselor for many years. With his help, Will was able to write out and read a sermon after six months study and in a year's time could preach from notes. Elizabeth spoke of this accomplishment with pride, undiminished by the passage of almost sixty years. "Will was able to do this," she said, "because as he learned to speak the language he reduced it to phonetic sounds. The Chinese written language or classical, as foreigners called it, was extremely difficult—a language more foreign to Chinese adults than Chaucer would be to a six-year-old in present-day America.

Nevertheless, Will acquired such mastery in the language that the proud literati of Hinghwa invited him to become one of them, a scholar of the classics of China. To this invitation Will replied that he would let them decide whether becoming a scholar would be more useful to China than the work he was doing. They did not urge the invitation.

All this came years later, however, not during that first difficult year, when the two men, wrapped in quilted coats, sat in the unheated apartment, pouring over Bible and dictionary. It was not difficult to learn the names for material things, but to express in Chinese religious concepts was not so easy. Will marveled at the magnitude of the task undertaken by Robert Morrison, himself ignorant of the language, who had spent eleven years compiling the English-Chinese dictionary with the help of one man who knew Latin.[2]

Of even more immediate concern, was the purchase of a home. In a little alley off a busy street they found a deserted house which they were able to buy. Since it had the reputation of being haunted, no Chinese family would live in it. After making sure the neighbors

2 English missionary, Robert Morrison, took up precarious residence in Canton in 1807, thus re-opening China to Christian missions after a lapse of a hundred years.

would not object, the Brewsters bought it for two hundred and fifty American dollars. Carpenters were brought from Foochow to do the necessary remodeling, both because they were accustomed to foreign building innovations and because Elizabeth could speak their language. Although better Chinese homes had long windows covered with lattice and painted paper, this one was a humble windowless home. Elizabeth ordered glass windows for every room, even the bedrooms. This brought protests from neighbors who feared evil spirits would take advantage of the occupants in their sleep. Folding glass doors formed the partitions between rooms, and board floors were laid over the existing ones of pounded earth and stone. Every inch of wall and ceiling was scrubbed clean, and painted white. There was not a dark or dirty spot to be found when the job was finished, and all in good time for the New Year's celebration. According to local custom, Will and Elizabeth planned to hold open house for the whole community during that holiday.

Entrance from the alley gate was into a courtyard, much like our flagged terraces. A narrow strip running around the courtyard was covered by a tile roof which sloped steeply toward the middle of the court. Rain drained off this roof into a basin in the center of the yard which formed a pool to reflect the sky. Such a pool was always appropriately referred to as the "Heaven's Well." In the windowless Chinese houses, the only light that reached the living quarters came through doors which opened to this courtyard. In wealthy homes, rock gardens, fish and flowers ornamented the pool, and in all seasons of the year, plants blossomed on the terrace around it.

Like any bride, Elizabeth wanted her furniture in place before guests arrived. There had been considerable discussion over the transportation of their household goods, which were in storage in Foochow. Will was too new in China to accept with equanimity the use of men as beasts of burden. His own shoulders could feel the weight of that heavy furniture. To carry it sixty miles was unthinkable. Elizabeth on the other hand worried about the winter rains which were due to begin. Water would ruin all her furniture. Finally, she and Will decided to ask Father Sites to ship it by junk to Antau; from there it could be carried by canal boats to Hinghwa.

This plan was frowned on by their Foochow friends. The season was stormy for one thing. The junk might sink or take on water enough to ruin everything. There were also pirates operating along the coast who might steal it! Besides, if people refused to hire load-bearers, how would they earn a living? When, in spite of all opposition, Will and Elizabeth stood firm, Father Sites made the necessary arrangements. He had all the furniture placed on two freight boats and he accompanied them to Pagoda Anchorage himself, where a junk had contracted to meet him. Its captain had already accepted bargain-money for moving the furniture to Antau. Upon arrival at Pagoda, Mr. Sites inquired for the junk only to learn that it had sailed away at dawn on other business. There was nothing to do but return with the furniture to Foochow.

When the discouraged Mr. Sites stepped from his houseboat, a man he recognized as a member of the Hokchiang Church, hailed him.

"Do you know where Miss Star's furniture is?" he wanted to know.

Upon being questioned, he explained that he had heard her speak at his church, and that many weeks ago she and her husband had spent the night at the church enroute to Hinghwa. He said,

"Some nights past, while I was sleeping, an angel told me to take a junk to Pagoda to get Miss Star's furniture and take it to Antau. That was very strange, but here I am. I have been very anxious, though I have several junks, they were all at sea. After five days, one returned and I brought it up myself as fast as I could. My crew is all ready to load the furniture, if I can find it." With some misgiving, the puzzled Mr. Sites saw the precious cargo transferred to the junk. He learned the following week that it was safely delivered.

"Even the rain held off until the last article was in the house," Elizabeth told me. "The captain would take no pay, explaining that he was under orders from Heaven. We didn't know what he was talking about until Father Site's letter came, telling his side of the story. We tried, in vain, to find some natural explanation for the episode, but never could. We finally accepted the captain's simple statement, 'An angel commanded it.'" It wasn't the only time they were so mysteriously blessed.

I offered various explanations which Elizabeth, smilingly, brushed aside. "We weren't so naive, my dear, we were as unwilling as you to accept a supernatural explanation—we finally had to."

Moving to more prosaic matters, I asked, "What kind, of furniture did you have in those days, mother dear?"

"In those days!" laughed Elizabeth, mimicking me. "Why, in those days we had chairs, tables, beds and dressers made according to our specifications in Foochow, just as you did when you and Francis were married. We did have American springs for our beds, though. I never could sleep on the hard, stretched-rattan platforms the Chinese people used. Our living room furniture was the tapestry-covered Queen Ann sofa and chairs that Faith Baldwin's grandparents, the Stephen Baldwins, brought around the Horn to China back in 1858. It was still in perfect condition and my choicest possession.

"Our dishes were purchased from a tea merchant who was going back to England. The everyday set was blue and white. I gave the last of it to Dorothy Fisher years ago. Our Sunday dish set was patterned green on white. I don't remember what became of those."

Because I have an interest in old dishes, I wrote Cousin Dorothy Fisher in London, Ohio, asking about the remnants of the blue-and-white set. She wrote me that it was a Wedgewood, William II pattern.

"By the New Year's holiday, everything was in place. Our newly remodeled house and pretty furniture made a lovely home for us. We sent out invitations by word of mouth through church members, food shops and school children, and waited eagerly for company. Men came first, and, when no harm came to them, women and children followed. The question was whether we or the house were the greater curiosity. Our blue eyes, brown hair and strange clothing were wonders to them, subject to much comment and touching. Our house they recognized as one of their own, but they shook their heads over all the windows and the white walls.

"We learned to expect certain questions from everyone. Weren't we afraid? Didn't we know that the devils could see everything that went on in such a house? We were glad that so many came to see for themselves that there were no dark corners in which to hide the evil deeds foreigners were supposed to do, such as making medicine out of the eyes of Chinese babies. This rumor got started because some missions in big cities used to pick up abandoned babies and try to nurse them back to health. Naturally many of the waifs died, and when the town's people saw them being carried away for burial, trouble-makers started the rumors that they had been maltreated. The Chinese people, unaccustomed to foreigners and ignorant of their intentions in China, had been aroused to mob-attack more than once by such falsehoods.

"Through all the years in Hinghwa, we were grateful for the threatened riot that made us give up the hill site. If we had lived out there, surrounded by a high wall, the people would always have been fearful and suspicious of us. In our house, on the busy city street, they saw us every day. Our gate was always open, the doors unlocked. Anyone could walk in to visit with us or the servants. There was always a pot of tea on the table so that guests could help themselves if no one was around. They could see there was nothing to fear, although there were new things to wonder and laugh about."

I was amazed at this picture, so different from the China I knew. Our home was surrounded by a high wall with a gate that was guarded night and day. No one was allowed in the lovely grounds unless he had business there; no one entered the house unannounced.

"What about diseases," I questioned, "and thieves?"

"Well," Elizabeth chuckled, "we weren't so germ-conscious then as we became later. Even in America, people were still sharing an unwashed dipper in a bucket of water for drinking. There weren't many houses screened against flies and mosquitos, either. I can remember only one theft. We were all at church one Sunday morning, except A-Siang, who was preparing dinner. He thought he heard a clock striking outdoors. Looking out, he saw a man holding our parlor clock in outstretched hands, watching in terror as it struck eleven. When A-Siang shouted at him, the man, already frightened out of his wits by a clock that talked, set it down and ran. A-Siang was still laughing when we came home to dinner.

"As for flies and rats, I can't remember either during our first years in China. They tell me flies came when bean curd began to be imported from Manchuria. Where rats came from, I don't know; probably on some ship from Europe.

"We had one bad scare from illness in those early days. It might have been brought by Chinese visitors, but since Will and I were out every day among the people; we probably brought it home ourselves."

[The following story is excerpted from Elizabeth's husband's book, *Evolution of New China.*][3]

"When we went to Hinghwa in November 1890, there was no other family living nearer than Foochow. To secure a physician, in case of urgent necessity, a messenger must go to Foochow overland, a journey of two days and nights, and an equal time would be consumed by the physician in coming. Living in Chicago with the nearest physician in San Francisco, one would be closer in time than we were. Good friends remonstrated with us for being so rash. Our second child was born there, attended only by a Chinese woman who had taken a course at the Woman's Hospital in Foochow. We lived there for nearly five years before we had any resident physician, and in all that time only once did we imperatively need a doctor, and then one was on hand more promptly than if he had resided half a mile away.

"One day in January 1894, a servant rushed in with the news, 'There are two foreign men out in the front yard.' I hastened out to welcome the strangers, and, as the door of the court opened, a tall, slender young man almost fell into my arms, saying, 'I am sick'. I recognized his companion as Doctor Kipp, a veteran evangelistic missionary of the Dutch Reformed Mission of Amoy. The sick man was Doctor J. A. Otte, a medical missionary of the same society. They were on their way to Foochow from their station of Chang-chau, a five days journey south of Hinghwa. Doctor Otte seemed to have an acute attack of what was then called the 'Grippe'. We took the best care of

3 Brewster, William Nesbitt, *Evolution of New China, pp. 229-31.*

him we could, and he improved rapidly. The second day he thought himself able to proceed on his journey, and they were about to start when my wife asked our faithful Chinese nurse to bring our baby boy, Francis, ten-months-old, saying that he had been restless during part of the night and seemed to have a fever. The doctor carefully examined the child, and noticing suspicious symptoms, turned to Dr. Kipp, saying:

'I think I would better stay here for a day or two and see what this is. You can go on to Foochow, and I will follow as soon as I can.'

"Before that day closed, the doctor's suspicions were confirmed—our baby had the small-pox! Doctor Otte told us that he himself was taken ill only a few hours after leaving home, and prudence directed an immediate return, but he could not make up his mind to order the 'chairmen' to about-face. He reached the large station of Tsuen-chau on the third day and here was a hospital with an eminent physician, Dr. David Grant, and his junior colleague, Dr. Paton. It seemed folly not to stay there for treatment, but in spite of the protests of friends, he pushed on two days farther, until he reached the place where, unknown to himself or any of us, he was soon to be needed so imperatively. Had he arrived in health, he would have gone the next morning before the dread disease had shown itself."

Remembering the episode, Elizabeth ruefully shook her head. "That Francis! Everything happened to him. He was only a few hours old, when a leaking, hot-water bottle scalded his arm. You can still see the scar, I imagine. He was the only one of our seven children to catch small-pox. He almost drowned learning to swim in the canal. Once in the middle of the Pacific Ocean, a ball bounced out his cabin porthole, and he went after it. I heard children screaming and ran in just in time to grab his feet and drag him back to safety. We never could have brought him up without God's help."

Thinking, though mistakenly, that I could always get these stories from my husband, I steered Elizabeth back to information only she could give me.

"What was the reaction of the Chinese people to your house,

mother? Can you remember what they admired and what they laughed at?"

"Oh, they loved the spring beds. They had never seen the like before. The mothers used to bounce their babies on them, and how everyone laughed. The mirrors on the bureaus, too, were a marvel. Almost no one had seen one. Their mirrors were pieces of polished brass and the image they saw was far from clear. The women and girls would cry out in astonishment when they saw themselves in a glass mirror. It must be a shock to see yourself as you really are for the first time. They used to come back, again and again, for another look. I felt sorry for some of them."

"I suppose they felt as I do when I see myself in a three-way mirror in a dress shop", I laughed. Elizabeth, who is also weight-conscious, nodded in agreement.

"Of course, everything was strange to them; they had never seen a rocking chair, for instance. They liked the motion, but disliked stumbling over the rockers and bruising their ankles. The idea of soft chairs was new to them. They loved to try out the upholstered Baldwin furniture. All Chinese chairs were hard and straight-backed. I suppose the white walls and board floors astonished them as much as anything. White was their color for mourning, and they couldn't understand why we wanted a house full of it. They thought the shining painted floors very beautiful, but thought it was a great pity to walk on them.

"It was a happy place for all of us. Mary and Francis were born in that house. A-Siang, who was Will's travelling companion and later mine, came to help us there. He took care of us for something like fifty years."

In the little silence which followed, I looked up to see Elizabeth staring with unseeing eyes at the orchard beyond the window. Her fingers began to trace the rough-textured chair covering. For the moment, she was lost in lonely memories.

"Can you tell me, Elizabeth, how you started your work? When I went to China, all I had to do was to teach English in an already established high school. How did you know what to do?" Instantly, she rose to the challenge.

"Well, the first thing we did was to find teachers to help us learn the language. I thought I was good at learning Chinese, but Will was wonderful. As I told you before, he could compose and read a sermon in six months, and in a year preached from notes only. He accomplished this by reducing every word he learned to phonetic symbols. He used the German system, which reproduced the Chinese sounds so accurately that his Chinese teacher learned the symbols, too, in order to use them in correspondence with Will.

"I already was well along in the writing of characters, so, while Will worked at that, I began calling in the homes, accompanied by the pastor's wife as interpreter. Sometimes for a change from so much studying, Will and I took trips into the country to get acquainted with the Christian community and the pastors who served them. I had known some of these men as students in the Foochow Theological School, and it was a great joy for me to introduce them to Will. They were like brothers to him for the rest of his life.

"The country itself was so beautiful that every trip was like a visit to paradise. Oh, that fairy valley of Sien Yu!"

Her allusion to paradise recalled to my mind that someone once said that paradise originally meant a garden of trees, with flowers and running water, shut away from the heat and dirt of the Orient by high walls. That is a perfect description of Fukien Province where Hinghwa and Foochow are located. Towering mountains shut the rest of China out, and divide the province itself into magnificent valleys, through which rivers wind past a mosaic of green rice fields, ancient red-roofed villages, hoary banyans and orchards laden with fruit.

"I have never been up the valley to Sien Yu, Mother, but I am willing to take your word that it is a fairyland."

Elizabeth smiled, "I don't know why everyone says 'up' to Sien Yu. It is really southeast of Hinghwa toward the sea. It's like the New Yorkers referring to Boston as 'down east.' The pastor at Sien Yu was one of Will's best friends, so we went there often. His father and mother had that wonderful poise and dignity that seems so remarkable in people who have had no advantages of education or travel.

"These trips often furnished opportunities for our work. I remember visitng in a wealthy home in another village. The grandmother was binding the feet of a tiny girl. Since such feet were the accepted mark of a lady, I had to choose my words so as not to offend. 'I hear the son of the magistrate has chosen as his bride a school girl with natural feet,' I said in a gossipy tone of voice. 'Apparently he prefers education to lily feet.'[4] Later, I was delighted to hear that the child's feet had been unbound, and inquiries were being made about school for her.

"On one of these trips we heard news that horrified us. In a village down on the seashore, two of our finest Christians, an elderly brother and sister, had contracted leprosy. As was the custom, they quietly left their home, voluntarily immuring themselves in the leper houses outside the village."

"Leper houses?" I questioned. "what kind of houses are they?"

"Just a cluster of ancient windowless mud houses set by themselves in a field—a desolate, dreadful place, I assure you. Not long after the exile of those two fine people, we received an invitation from them to attend the funeral of a member of their community."

"You didn't go, did you Mother?" I protested, remembering the repulsive beggars on the streets of Foochow.

"Certainly, we went. It was a humbling and moving experience. The old man had a request to make. 'So long as I live, I will comfort these people, but when I die, what then? Will you build us a chapel and help us start a church and school?'

"Will promised. The very first new building he undertook in the district was that chapel for the lepers. The old man lived to see it completed. He spoke at the dedication, using the words of Simeon, (Luke chap 2, v. 29) 'Lord, now let Thou Thy servant depart in peace, according to Thy word: For mine eyes have seen Thy salvation.' He died shortly afterward, happy that community would have the gospel preached to them. We organized a regular church there, with officers, records, and weekly services. Sometimes I preached; sometimes other Christians helped out.

4 One legend is that centuries ago an emperor had a favorite concubine whose feet were deformed. To save her embarrassment, he decreed that all beautiful ladies must have feet on which they, too, could sway like lilies as they walked.

"That was the first of three churches for lepers that I supervised. We established another one just outside of Hinghwa on the way to our mountain house; the third one was in Yellowstone. I visited them every week during all my years in China. Such happy, appreciative congregations they were; always so glad to see me come; always contriving gifts of oranges, eggs and firecrackers for me on Christmas and their own holidays."

"How did they live, Elizabeth? How could they afford to give you gifts? I thought they were all beggars."

"Some were street beggars, but most of them received subsistence from home. Their own people brought them as much food and clothing as they could afford. It was wonderful that the Chinese people did not cast out members of their families afflicted with leprosy, as was the custom in Biblical lands. There was no organized charity to help them, but, by tradition, those able to walk could go to a home where a wedding was in progress to receive a gift of rice. At harvest time, it was customary for farmers to give generously to lepers who came to the fields. We wrote to churches at home for aid and to the Leper Society in Shanghai for medicines. At Christmas we gave the lepers cloth, clothing, stockings, and food for a feast in the chapel which they decorated for the occasion.[5]

"The front of each chapel had a private entrance and a wall-to-wall railing to segregate the sick from those of us who were well. It wasn't necessary, though. Those dear people used every precaution to protect us. The Chinese understand the disease, and seldom transmit it from one member of the family to another. In those early years when our children were small, I took extra precautions, such as, always wearing gloves during my visits, and always changing clothes and bathing before going into our home."

"Were there any children in the leper houses, Elizabeth?"

5 Dr. Harold Brewster, Elizabeth's youngest son, is very unhappy over my use of the word "leper." He wishes I would use the term "people afflicted with leprosy" or "Hanson's Disease." He feels that the use of the word "leper" makes these people sound subhuman, when actually they are no different from anyone else; just unfortunate to contract a disease. I use the word only because Elizabeth does and. as she does, always with love.

"Yes, a few. Children are born to lepers, but never many. The parents always tried to keep them 'clean' as the Bible says. In the case of the elderly brother and sister I spoke of, the sister had two adopted children who accompanied her to the leper houses. She had some education, and after her brother's death she conducted a school in the chapel for all the children in the group. Later, when we had developed a phonetic reading and writing system, I taught it to the adults so that they, too, could read their Bibles and hymn books. What a joy that was to them! It was always a great sorrow to us that we could not teach them handcrafts, to give them some interest in life and a little money; their poor hands were so deformed by the disease that this was impossible. They were a happy sociable lot, though, gathering in the chapel for recreation, visiting and holiday feasts.

"When the elderly teacher died, I took her children home to Hinghwa. We rented a room for them, and kept them there until it was certain they were not infected with the disease. We already had several other orphans for whom we were caring. One was a charming boy who won our hearts during our first year in Hinghwa. Will had seen him in one of our country schools and had talked so much about him that I, too, had to go see the child. He had the most beautiful laughing eyes I have ever seen and an irresistible charm.

"A year later, Will came back from a visit to that village to report that the boy's father had died leaving his family in great need. The beautiful boy was to be sold to a theatrical troupe. This we couldn't endure. We gave the family the price offered by the theatrical troupe and brought the child to Hinghwa, undertaking his support and education ourselves. There were several other children, too, those we found on the street or who had been left on our doorstep wrapped in rags. If I remember correctly, we already had a few children of deceased preachers whose mothers were in training for teaching jobs.

"It so happened, that an elderly couple came out from the States looking for work in the mission field. Since they loved children, it wasn't long before they had gathered around them a handful of blind and other unwanted youngsters. The mission suggested that they organize an orphanage, whose support they were to solicit from

American churches. When enough money was in hand, they built a missionary residence and four cottages outside the city, which became the home of all our orphaned protégés. These Americans were wonderfully kind people, but not suited to pioneering in China. The wife, a particularly lovely woman, was so exquisite a housekeeper that she used to dust the floor after the departure of each guest.

"Unwittingly, we caused her trouble, and a great fright. For eight years, our house had been open to everyone—fishermen, farmers, mountain woodcutters and city folk of every description. When the New Year's holiday arrived, all these people flocked to the new orphanage, of whose function many were still a little suspicious. They found the gate locked and the gateman under orders not to open it to them. A few early arrivals had walked past the gateman into the garden where some of the children were playing. When the new missionary saw the strangers, she hustled the children toward the house. The little boys, reacting to her fright, picked up dirt and stones and pelted the visitors. When they protested noisily and angrily, other people gathered in sympathy, and the missionary fled out the back door to Hinghwa, where luckily she found me at home.

"I got out to the orphanage as fast as I could. An angry crowd was milling around the wall. I walked among them, explaining the situation, and soon had them laughing. The whole affair ended harmlessly, proving once more that the ability to speak Chinese and to understand the customs of the people could avert unpleasant incidents.

"Several years later when the supervision of the orphanage was added to my duties, we moved it back to Hingwa, right next door to our own home. Our children and the orphans all grew up together, like one huge family. I was mother to all of them."

"Were you still living in the Chinese house then, Elizabeth?"

"Oh, no, we had outgrown that house some years earlier. It was torn down to make room for the girl's school. We had built a large red brick house to take care of our family of seven children. The orphan asylum and the cottage for the blind boys adjoined it."

She paused smiling, and then began to laugh.

"I was thinking of all the noise and joyous living of those days. Such squeaking and scraping and tootling that went on! The Chinese children loved music, and I helped them as much as I could to play and sing. We started with my little organ, soon adding native flutes and stringed instruments. Then I sent to America for accordions for the blind children. Drums, violins and horns of all descriptions followed, until I think we must have had every known instrument for them to play. I played tunes on the organ, gave the pitch and time, translated the directions which came with the instruments, and the orphans did the rest. It was amazing the way they taught themselves and each other, but no more amazing than the noise they made!

"One day, a very solemn preacher came to call. He was hardly seated, when a homesick donkey which had just arrived that day from Peking, set up a most raucous braying in the back garden. It was the first braying ever heard in Hinghwa, so it was no wonder that the poor preacher almost fell off his chair with fright. Recovering himself, he asked politely, 'And what kind of a musical instrument do you call that?'"

"It sounds as if it were a happy place, Elizabeth," I said with some surprise.

"Of course, it was. It was a very happy place for all of us, although sometimes our own boys complained that the orphan kids shared all the fun, but never got the whippings! That wasn't quite true. We tried to be impartial, but I suppose parents are always harder on their own kids. Anyway, the orphans knew we loved them, which was the important thing. They had clean rooms, good food, and decent clothes. They had regular hours for school, work, church and play. The blind children had excellent instruction in Braille, and all the children, including the blind, were taught skills so that they were self-supporting. They went to school half-time, and worked half-time; all of them becoming very proficient in weaving bed mats out of the grass that grows so abundantly in Hinghwa's salt marshes. Those smoothly woven mats were very popular with the Chinese who used them like a sheet over their rough rattan beds.

"Cloth weaving too was taught to all our children. Because

Chinese looms were so narrow, we imported others from Japan. Some of our older orphan boys were sent there to learn to operate and repair the newer, wider looms before we installed them at the orphanage. The children paid for their food and part of their clothing with the money they earned weaving. They made their own shoes, did the gardening and washing. We hired a woman to do the cooking. Each child had spending money and plenty of play time. We were really a busy, happy family.

"I suppose Francis has told you of his escapades with the orphanage boys. He was the leader, but then they were always most willing confederates. More than once, they sneaked out in the middle of the night and ate themselves sick in neighboring lengeng orchards. Several times they nearly drowned in the canals learning to swim. Once they had a yearning to taste puppy meat, because someone had told them it was delicious. Francis bought a puppy for a quarter and asked our cook to prepare it for them. He was promptly chased out of the kitchen. The orphanage cook was persuaded to roast it at a price—the biggest share of the meat went to the cook! Although the boys got only a taste, they insisted that all dogs ran from them for six months afterwards. How importantly they strutted around!

"Then there was the time Mary went with them on a hike. Like all boys, they objected to having a sister trail after them, especially, Mary, who they said had turned into a lady in America. She got whooping cough while we were on furlough and had to be left with my mother for two years. According to the boys, she was never the same again!

"On the way home from the hike everyone was hot and tired. The boys decided to go swimming in the river, which had been forbidden. Mary did her best to stop them, but they just laughed at her. She must have been about nine then, and Francis eight. The boys stripped and went in, while Mary stood on the bank crying and begging them to come out.

"When they finally did, they were terrified. Each of them was covered with hair which stuck to them like glue. They ran home, howling, thinking that the hairy covering was punishment for their disobedience. We almost had to skin them to get that hair off. No other punishment was necessary. The spot they had chosen for swimming was just below a tannery and they were covered with cow hair and pig bristle. Fortunately, no one got anthrax, so that turned out all right, too.

"You, of course, remember that horrid white scab that covered the heads of so many Chinese children. Whenever I think of the orphanage, I shudder to remember how I struggled with those heads! We used ointments of every kind. We kept the children very clean, sponge baths every day, and a hot tub bath once a week. Nothing helped. At last we tried a really heroic treatment. We wrapped the afflicted child in a sheet in such a way that his eyes, nose and mouth only were left uncovered. Then we put him on a chair, setting a pan of burning sulphur under him, draping the sheet like a tent over the chair. The idea was that the sulphur smoke would penetrate the skin and remove the scab, but it didn't. The hours I spent on that treatment! It wasn't until Mary took charge of the orphanage that she discovered the scab was a nutrition deficiency disease, and cured it with diet!"

"What became of the orphans, Elizabeth? Did they really become self-supporting men and women?"

"Oh my, yes! Many of them became teachers; others attended Bible school and became preachers. The blind girls were much sought after as wives, because they were such skilled housekeepers and had such sunny dispositions. They could knit, sew, weave, and cook and keep house better than most seeing people. Some of the brightest boys and girls went to universities in America, and are now working in China, or were when I left. The best loved of them all, the boy with the laughing eyes was educated in America, became a government official and later a foreign diplomat. If I judged by gifts, I would have to say he loved me more than my own sons. Through all the years, until his recent death, he remembered my birthday and my work. He sent thousands of dollars to support it, and hundreds in personal gifts for me. Even after his death, his second wife, whom I have never seen, sent me four hundred Chinese dollars as a birthday gift."

The resonant voice stopped. Elizabeth's lips moved, speaking words I could not hear. She was back among her beloved, black-haired children. The interview was over. I had asked her how she started her work and she had told me. When the sick had asked for help, she had given it to them. After they died, they left children to her care; these children she had fed, clothed and sent to school. When the schools proved inadequate, she contrived something better. From several of her slim notebooks, I have gleaned that story.

When she first visited Hinghwa, a year before her marriage, she found several schools for boys and one for women already in existence. This was the work of the Christian brothers known as the Golden Candlesticks. What was more surprising, a few girls, who had been admitted, were already teaching in day-schools.

"Since I was still identified with the women's work, my first task was to start a school for girls. In the winter of 1892, the first class met in a house across the alley from us. At that time, only one woman in 10,000 could read, so it was not easy to find teachers for our twelve girls. We found two, one suffering from elephantiasis and the other the only child of a Christian family. The first woman had been rejected by her fiancé because of her disfiguring illness. Instead of committing suicide, she turned to study, and had become a famous scholar. Both were wonderful women and excellent teachers of Chinese classics and Bible. I taught the new subjects of arithmetic, English and geography.

"One day seven years later, I was visited by a committee of boys. 'Unless you teach us these new subjects, too, Mrs. Brewster,' they moaned, 'we shall find ourselves married to women better educated than we are, and shall have to be walking five steps behind our wives for the rest of our lives!'

"Realizing the seriousness of their position, I turned the girls' school over to several new missionaries, and concentrated on teaching the boys. In 1897, I was given charge of the boys' school, and began teaching English, science and mathematics. We also added geography, history, Mandarin and astronomy, all taught through the medium of Chinese classical characters.

"Because of all my other work, I never taught a subject twice. I tutored the brightest boys so that they could teach and keep ahead of their classes. That released me for more advanced teaching in algebra, geometry, and beginners' trigonometry. In time these also were handed over to my students."

Through all the years, Elizabeth kept up a voluminous correspondence with churches and individuals in America. Since all her work depended for support on these letters, it had to be faithfully done.

"We never finished a year in debt," she records. "The money always came in time and in sufficient amounts to balance our books. One year it looked as if we would have a deficit. We needed $500, and the only known contributor whose check had not arrived always sent us $100. When her check came, it was for $500. The accompanying letter said, 'I took up my pen to write $100. The Spirit said, "Write $500." Here is my check for that amount.'"

Among my treasures are two testimonials which Elizabeth left with me years ago. They were given her by Chinese friends on the 50th anniversary of her arrival in Hinghwa. One of them follows:

We call her mother, this little lady,
Who came to us from far shores, long ago.
We are her people now, and she is one of us
For she has been with us in weal and woe
To outcaste, leper, orphan, she is Mother;
The friendless and the poor her kindness know.
Herself has ministered to our misfortunes
Herself was tireless when our hopes ebbed low,
Her heart is wide; all need and care embracing,
Her daily acts of grace, her spirit show.
She is our mother; our faith and hope and wisdom
To her unwearied, loving heart we owe.

A father's smile to remember, his faith to emulate, a coffin nail to treasure! Not much of an inheritance for Elizabeth, but invested with God, enough to bear such great fruit!

CHAPTER SIX

As the Apple Tree Among the Trees of the World

Like most of his colleagues on the mission field in 1890, William Nesbitt Brewster was young, college educated, and devoutly Christian. He was graduated from Ohio Wesleyan University in 1883 and from Boston University School of Theology in 1886. Unlike many young missionaries, he had the added advantage of two years in the ministry before going to Singapore. So far as Elizabeth is concerned, no man in the mission field or elsewhere was his equal. It is like listening to one of the Songs of Songs when she speaks of him.

> As the apple tree among the trees of the wood
> So is my beloved among the sons.
> I sat down under his shade with great delight
> And his fruit was sweet to my taste.

There is no doubt that he had much to do with the transformation of a small-town girl into the world-aware Elizabeth I know. His children, too, give him legendary stature. His oldest son, my husband, remembers him as a kind of King Arthur, clad in immaculate white linen, white topi, and spotless shoes, forever striding in the China countryside doing good. His youngest child knew him only as a man of prayer, who rose daily before dawn without the aid of an alarm clock, to find time for study and prayer.

It must have been those quiet hours with God that gave him the vision of China, which he set down in 1907 as the thesis for a series of lectures given at Boston University. Knowing the moral and political weaknesses which rendered China helpless, he had the love and courage to write:

"The qualities inherent in the land and its inhabitants will probably place China among the greatest of the world's empires before this new century has reached is meridian."

Perhaps his dream could best be stated in the words of Lord Elgin, Great Britain's Christian statesman, speaking fifty years earlier, in April, 1858. "But the great task of construction, of bringing China with its extensive territory, its fertile soil, and its industrious population, as an active and useful member into the community of nations, and making it a fellow laborer with ourselves in diffusing over the world happiness and well-being, is one that yet remains to be accomplished." In Will's day, the task was still undone, and he gave his life to it.

So in the predawn darkness, as he opened his Bible, he laid China and her needs before God. As the city around him wakened, the sounds of hunger filled the air. From everywhere rose a nerve-jangling scraping of metal. He winced as he listened to the women of the city scraping the soot of yesterday's fires from the bottoms of their shallow rice kettles. Even in the dark, every good housewife must make that soot fall in a perfect unbroken circle, inside which she must never step for fear of contracting elephantiasis.

From farther away came the piteous squeal of pigs and squawking of chickens under the knives of their butchers; and everywhere an all-pervasive rhythmic thumping told him that men and women were already treading the rice-hullers. Hunger, endless work, ignorance and superstition were the problems which he battled constantly. For him the day was always too short; life itself was over before he had even come to grips with the tasks his vision had set for him.

As a missionary, his first interest was, of course, religion. He had grown up in the brick churches of Ohio where Sunday school and worship services had been the very heart of his life. Even in Singapore, he served a congregation which met regularly for worship in an adequate building. In Hinghwa, not a single steeple pointed Heavenward; no church bells announced the Sabbath. Time was measured by the waxing and waning of moons, a cumbersome method to anyone accustomed to seven-day weeks beginning with a day of rest and worship. The few people who attended Christian services in the bare little rooms called "chapels" made no impression on the life of the city. In Cincinnati he had been challenged by occasional unbelievers, a tiny minority in a community of believers. In Hinghwa, he and other Christians formed an even smaller minority in a vast body of men and women who had hardly heard the name of God, much less his earthly incarnation, Jesus. In Ohio, the cause of Christian missions had been challenged.

Why interfere with the religions of other peoples? Why don't you leave China alone? Those people are probably happier with their own beliefs. Why try to force yours on them?

With one such objector, a prominent lawyer, Will had entered into a spiritual combat from which he did not withdraw until the man was won for Christ.

His first contact with the composite religion of Hinghwa's population was in their terrified reaction to his purchase of the hill outside the city for a home. The Taoist priests had told the people a building there would rob the whole city of the good luck their pagoda had been built to insure. Unhappily, not only that, but every hill, tree, stone and stream hid spirits waiting to do someone harm. Only by consulting Taoist priests could the people protect themselves from the malevolence of nature. The very ground on which they walked, the air they breathed, were body and breath of an all-pervading dragon, which could be angered by stubbing its toes on a building a shade too high, or wounded to savage retaliation by the digging of a well, except as sanctioned by a Taoist priest for a price. The ornate temples of the city had become headquarters for charlatans and soothsayers, who set the lucky days for weddings or kept the dead waiting in mat-sheds outside the city walls until the prescribed propitious time for burial.

It did not take Will long to come to the conclusion that two-thirds of the damaging superstition and idolatry in Hinghwa was Taoist in origin. He marveled that a religion, originally almost Christian in teaching, could have become so degraded. Often when cholera or drought plagued the people, he watched as grotesque "scare-devils" from the temples were carried through the narrow streets to drive out the evil spirits responsible for the calamity. At such times, he dreamed of the day when ordinary elementary scientific education would bring an end to Taoist terror. At other times, he wondered, whimsically, how such education would explain the strange orderliness of nature in China, which made it possible to set the day for the "stirring of insects" in spring. Invariably, insects appeared on that day. Again, at the end of summer, a day was set for the fall of white dew, on which day the terrible heat always broke.

The Buddhist facet of the prevailing religion was also present in the teeming streets. Mangy dogs dodged underfoot, too sacred to be killed outright, but starved and kicked and mutilated by boiling water thrown at them as they scrounged for food. Sometimes Will saw live fish being dumped into the river, or a cage of birds set free, as a prosperous-looking man waited with money in hand. He would be purchasing merit in the existence to come by saving animal life, a Buddhist tenet of faith. Although the same religion offered merit for providing coffins for the poor, or the burial of unclaimed bones on the hillsides, it did little to encourage the care of the sick, homeless starving people.

Will read with his teacher how Buddhism came to China. In the year which Christians reckon as 65 A.D., the Emperor Ming-Ti had a vision of a great new God born in the West and he sent envoys to find Him. Even to that emperor of antiquity, the combination of Confucian philosophy and Taoism had seemed inadequate. The envoys traveled until, in faraway India, they discovered Buddhism and brought some of its priests back to China. Will liked to speculate on what might have happened had the envoys travelled until they met St. Paul. Would China have become Christian and sent missionaries to Europe and America, or would it have impaled St. Paul's message on the rock of ancestor worship, making it a mere palliative to existing philosophies?

In Will's opinion, Taoism was an attempt to provide for the invisible present; Buddhism, for the invisible future. There remained the third facet, the great Confucian philosophy, to provide for the visible present. Will had great respect for truth wherever he found it, whether in Plato or in Confucius. For millenniums, his teachings had formed the cornerstone of all Chinese life. In a country divided by government, language and lack of communication, it was the one great unifier. Everyone, from the "foreign" Emperor on the throne in Peking to the lowliest coolie, observed its cardinal doctrines of filial piety and ancestor worship. All Chinese believed that the ancestral spirits actually entered into the little tablets of wood bearing their names when as children they began to worship, and left when the ceremony was over. Even the last emperor, tormented as he was by his aunt, the Empress Dowager, was restrained by filial piety from disobedience, which might have saved him his throne.

In most cases, Will could see great good resulting from the respect and obedience of children to those in authority and the responsibility families assumed for their members near and far, in accordance with Confucian teaching. That many of his other hundreds of rules of behavior, scrupulously observed by the Chinese, were both stultifying and ridiculous, was obvious. Will attributed the weakness of China as a nation, to the great doctrine of ancestor worship, because it turned the loyalties of men exclusively to family.

Japan accepted the five relationshps laid down by Confucius, that of father and son, ruler and ruled, husband and wife, elder and younger brother, friend and friend. Japan gave priority to the ruler and ruled relationship, resulting in a strong national state. China, giving priority to the father and son relationship, built indestructible families, but a very weak state. Perhaps this may explain why the present Chinese Communist regime has been merciless in its attack on families, removing them from their ancestral homes, separating children from parents, refusing aged parents the presence of a son to comfort their last years—a beautiful custom observed for millenniums.

Will had no desire to destroy what was obviously a good system in the family, only to subordinate it to God for the benefit of both the individual and the nation. Men became pirates, robbing and killing their fellowmen to enrich their own families. Public officials engaged in huge-scale corruption for the same reason. Elizabeth tells of a Hinghwa official, a Christian who refused to engage in the common practice of diverting public funds to enrich his family, suffering the wrath of his own mother, who denounced him as an unfilial son. Ancestor worship had other adverse effects upon people. People could be enslaved by it throughout their lives. Men believed that the spirits of their ancestors had the power to help or harm, and so lived in fear of them. In moments of crises, families appealed to their ancestors, offering incense and begging their blessing.

Added to all the spirits of Taoist origin, there were others even more powerful to be placated. The ever-present desire for sons which caused so much unhappiness to the women of a family, was the other side of the picture. A man must have sons to worship him and offer sacrifices to him after death, otherwise he would have no peace or happiness in the life to come. Sometimes several wives were required to insure this happy state. The great Christian doctrine that our happiness on earth and in the next life is wrapped up in God and is safe with Him, released thousands of converts of enslaving fears, although they retained always their reverence for the dead and their obedience and respect for their living parents.

It was a matter of profound regret to Will that the beauty and purity of the prayers offered by the Emperor at the Temple of Heaven could not be shared by all the Chinese people. Since only the Emperor was a son of Heaven, any of his subjects who dared to offer prayers at the Temple erected to Him in Peking, would have been guilty of treason. So the masses of the people lived and died without any awareness of God whatsoever. Will's conception of his first great responsibility in Hinghwa, was to introduce Jesus, the Redeemer, to men who had lost all knowledge of their stature as sons of God, to cast out fear with love, and to provide hope both for the present life and the one to come.

To do this, he first of all, had the sure knowledge of the presence of God, then the rudiments of a church organization consisting of eighteen preachers, most of whom had little or no theological training, along with one thousand scattered church members, and Elizabeth. In those early years, the most visible Christian witness was their shared work among the lepers, the orphans and the school children.

In his second year in Hingawa, he organized a small theological school to replenish the Chinese preachers which his growing church required. Students were bright boys he found in Christian homes in the country villages. Classes were conducted in a Chinese house across the alley from his own first home.

One Saturday when he had gone, as it was his custom to spend the weekend preaching in the country churches, Elizabeth, alone with the infant daughter and the cook, was startled to hear an angry uproar in the courtyard. Carrying her baby, she went out to investigate. A group of boys from the theological school were the center of attention.

When shouts of "Kill the foreigner! Burn down his houses!" reached her, she went down among the people, pushing her way to the man who seemed to be leading the disturbance. She recognized him as a neighbor and begged to know what the trouble was. He told her he had been giving a theatrical party in his garden when the boys from the theological school, passing by, had made unsuitable remarks. He and his guests were now demanding satisfaction, as they did not choose to be insulted by foreign rudeness. Elizabeth told him that her husband was away, but that on Wednesday, when he returned, he would most certainly look into the matter and make proper amends. "You know he is a man and a true friend," she added.

The man listened to her, courteously. After a moment's consideration, he announced to his followers that it would indeed be improper to destroy a man's family and property in his absence; that this would be entirely contrary to the Confucian rules of behavior between friends. So saying, he departed, followed by the now amiable crowd. When Will returned, he found that his boys had indeed been at fault. Proper apologies, accompanied by the prescribed firecrackers, were offered and peace was restored according to both Christian and

Confucian principles.

One of the Chinese proverbs they both tried to obey urged, "When entering a village, learn what is customary; when entering a country learn what is forbidden." In their first ten years, both Elizabeth and Will were constantly breaking a custom which attained the force of law, when the Empress Dowager proclaimed that foreign teachers and preachers were disregarding the proprieties of the land in their work. Not only did unmarried foreign women travel in the company of foreign men, but they taught Chinese men, both married and unmarried. Foreign men also preached to audiences in which Chinese women were present, with Heaven knows what improper results. Suspicion of the good intentions of missionaries thus aroused, caused many unfortunate incidents throughout China. Although Elizabeth and Will were never endangered, they had one unpleasant experience.

At one of the country churches where Will frequently preached, a fine, young couple became Christians. Within the year, the birth of their first son caused great rejoicing. The jubilant mother-in-law went around saying, "See what happens when you join the new foreign religion. You get a son!" Malicious village gossip soon had a rumor started that Will was the father of the child. Fortunately, both Elizabeth and Will had become so well known among the people, that the gossip died out without harming the church or themselves. Elizabeth says, however, they shuddered to think what might have happened if the child had been one of the rare albinos sometimes born in that vicinity.

More often than not, Will came home from his country trips to tell Elizabeth of beautiful experiences. One day, he went down the coast to attend a quarterly meeting at an ancient seaport. Among the men who were baptized, he noticed one of such purity of countenance that he engaged him in conversation. His amazement deepened as he realized the spiritual qualities of the man. Prayer to him was as natural as it was to Will. Upon being questioned, the man explained himself as follows.

For twenty years he had been seeking a balm for his troubled spirit. Other religious zealots in his community had gathered around him and together they had discarded idols, but continued to burn incense to spirits and to the Emperor's "Lord of Heaven and Earth." He had visited holy men and Buddhist shrines. For a short time, he had attended services in a Christian church, but he was not convinced it was the one true religion. Nothing seemed to assuage the hunger within him. Finally, he decided to seek guidance about organizing a "Three Religions Society," following the teachings of a holy man who had lived three hundred years earlier in Hinghwa. For three-days-and-nights he fasted, most earnestly praying to the Lord of Heaven and Earth to reveal to him if doing this would bring him peace. A voice did, indeed, answer him, saying, "I have already established the Christian church. Christ is the only savior. Believe Him, and bring your followers into His church."

He and all his family were baptized and became most earnest Christians. Twenty years later, another missionary asked him if he had really found satisfaction for his soul's hunger in Jesus, the Christ. "I have, indeed," he answered, "and now that I am old, I greet each day with joy in the hope of seeing my Savior." One can only guess how much satisfaction such an experience brought to Will and Elizabeth.

The most amazing part of the story to me is the comment with which Will closes it. "But during those twenty years while he was seeking the light—praying to God, keeping himself pure from all defilement of the flesh, gentle and forbearing in all his dealings with his fellowmen—who could doubt that he would be accepted by God as a soul redeemed by the Blood of the Lamb?"

It's no wonder that a man with such spiritual insight and understanding as Will had was able to fulfill Nathan Site's prophecy, and almost single-handedly carve out a conference consisting of 5,628 members in six-years' time.[1]

The travels that accompanied such an accomplishment brought new problems to Will. Not only did he struggle with the burden of a "religion without God," but of a society using tremendous "brawn without brain." It bothered him to see men used like animals. Most

1 Walter Lacy, *A Hundred Years of China Methodism*, 1948.

people from the West are shocked the first time they are carried by men, but they soon get pleasantly inured to it. With Will, being carried by men was always distasteful. Whenever time permitted, he walked to nearby churches, but when his destination was at either extreme of his seventy-five-by-forty mile territory, he had to be carried.

Not even the time this gave him for necessary study and reading, could make up for backs shining with sweat and muscles bulging under his weight. The roads were too narrow for carriages, which would also have allowed study during transportation. He noted that the steep mountain trails were set with thousands of smoothly worn stone steps, indicating that for millennium barefooted people, not animals, had carried loads over them. The only horses in the province were those belonging to the military personnel; spindly ponies hardly able to bear a man.

The time came when he found a partial solution to this problem. On a trip to Peking, he bought two animals; one, the jackass which so startled the gentle clergyman visiting the orphanage, the other, a handsome stallion. With Elizabeth's help, Will designed a double basket to be hung across the back of the jack. After tea on pleasant afternoons, their two oldest children were seated in the baskets and taken for a ride out into the country, accompanied by their parents on foot. Everywhere people stopped to gaze at this new thing; they laughed and asked questions.

Both Will and Elizabeth had long since learned the dignity and pride inherent in the people around them. Whenever possible, they allowed their Chinese neighbors to do their own thinking. One day the hoped-for question came. "If the beast can carry children, why couldn't it carry a load?" Within his lifetime, Will saw long lines of donkeys plodding over the mountains carrying the loads that formerly burdened men. The beautiful stallion became his riding horse, and before long, the military encampment in the city was equipped with horses shipped in from the north. No blessing is free, it seems, for it was then, according to Elizabeth, that flies began to plague the city. My husband thinks it more likely that they accompanied the bean curd which was being imported for the first time from Manchuria.

Another problem of transportation that bothered Will was the slowness of water travel. There were canals and rivers all through the Hinghwa plain which were in constant use by hand-poled sampans. For the ever-hurrying American the slowness of man-propelled boats was a constant irritation. It wasn't long before Will purchased an engine from the States and brought in a man from Foochow, where motor launches were in use, to install it.

The first motor-driven boat drew only jeers from the crowds along the bank. The native boat in which it was installed lay too deep in the water, causing the propeller to churn up mud from the bottom of the irrigation canal. Will had a boat with shallow draught built, and acquired one of the new outboard motors, which drove it smoothly and swiftly through the water, cutting travel-time in half. In all, there were ten passenger launches that became widely used. Unfortunately, the owners of the land through which the canals passed were angry with boat owners, because the motor-churned water washed away the banks of their precious fields.

In their first Hinghwa home, Elizabeth noted that they only had candles and wicks floating in saucers of oil to give them light. Within a few years, Will was able to import cans of kerosene for lamps, which were greatly admired. When he sent home for several kerosene lanterns to carry on night trips into the country, the people were frightened, expecting that the entire population of evil spirits, reveling in the dark, would target so visible a light. When nothing frightening happened, oil lanterns, too, became very popular, replacing the inefficient torches and paper lanterns. Such was the demand for kerosene, that the pleased oil companies offered Will a sales opportunity in the prefecture of Hinghwa. Although the offer was tempting, financially, he refused it, wanting no business entanglements to blur his mission of love and service. Upon his recommendation, the job was given to two Christian families, whose integrity and enterprise accounted for many years of mutual profit.

Providing milk for their growing family was not easy for Elizabeth and Will. Cows were almost nonexistent. From the sandy sweet-potato country of Binghai peninsula, across the lush green plains, to the tops of the hills, there was hardly a cow to be found. Scraggly chickens and scrawny pigs were everywhere, because eggs and pork were important in the Chinese diet. A few little brown cows furnished beef to those of the population who, for religious scruples, could not eat pork. Milk was not used except to raise calves. When Will had one of the refractory little animals brought to his door, its legs had to be tied before it could be milked.

With the advent of a whole community of "outside people," the demand for fresh milk was greater than the local cows could supply. Their milk, though exceedingly rich, was very scanty. On one of his infrequent trips to the United States, Will brought back a huge Holstein bull and two cows. When the amazed Chinese dairymen saw the buckets of milk that the black and white foreign cows produced, there was both joy and consternation. Probably from fear of losing his new source of income, someone managed to poison the cows, which Will had brought across the ocean with so much trouble and expense. This was a blow to him; he had envisioned a profitable dairy business for many Chinese farmers, as well as a good supply of milk for Chinese and American children.

The big bull, unfortunately, had a white star on his forehead, which the superstitious farmers considered a spirit mark and refused to allow their brown cows to be bred by him. Finally, the Christian widow of a former family cook was set up in the dairy business, and did very well. Forty years later, her cows were still superior in size and production, thanks to that one Holstein sire. It wasn't easy, Will learned to change the ways of people who had been in business for thousands of years, but he was not willing to concede defeat.

As he rode through the rice fields at harvest time watching the laborious work of hand-cutting of grain with a six-inch blade, he resolved to send home for a "cradle" scythe. Local Chinese blacksmiths could forge the blades and carpenters could copy the long curved handles. What a blessing it would be! When it arrived he took it to a village where he was known and loved, and offered to cut a little field of rice for them. Cries of admiration and gratitude accompanied each swish of the swinging blade.

Sweating and triumphant, he offered the scythe to one of the laughing men following him. Then the village elder spoke, "Think what it would mean to have knives like that around. A thief could cut and carry away a whole field of rice in a couple of hours of darkness." The hands outstretched to try the new knife dropped, the laughter stopped, the interested group melted away. Ruefully, Will carried the scythe back to Hinghwa and hung it up on a nail.

The purchase of motors, cows and small tools were all hard on the family budget, but the flour mill, which Will introduced hoping to replace hand-grinding, was very costly. One of the children remembers asking her mother, "Why do we have dessert only once a day?" Elizabeth's answer to this question and many like it was, "Because we have to pay for the flour mill." The $1200, which that mill cost, ate up desserts, new clothes, and savings alike; but to Elizabeth, as well as Will, it was money well spent.

For untold centuries, rice had been ground into flour between soapstones, which added a bit of themselves each grinding. Even so tiny an increase in the weight of flour as this represented, made the rice millers unwilling to change to a mechanical mill. For a time, the mission tried to operate the mill, but the lazy and unscrupulous in the community thought the mission should grind their grain for nothing. Since pauperizing the people through charity was the one thing Will wanted to avoid, the mill project, too, had to be abandoned.

Even the industrial weaving project in the school, although it supported the children successfully and happily, caused Will and Elizabeth trouble. There were friends in China and America who felt that the work of missionaries was evangelistic only, and they should never be involved in the material aspects of life. Elizabeth recalls that in 1905, criticism of their work was so severe that both she and Will considered resigning. But the original conviction still burned in their hearts, "Woe is to me if I preach not the gospel." They were willing to say with Jesus as he faced death in Jerusalem, "To this end was I born, and for this cause came I into the world, that I should bear witness unto the truth," even if it cost their lives.

Nevertheless, if their presence was a stumbling block to the

Christian community in Hinghwa, they wondered if they had misinterpreted their call. After days of prayer, they wrote to a Bishop who was to be in Hong Kong for a few weeks on church business, offering their resignation. Two weeks later, their letter was returned unopened. The Bishop had left before their letter arrived. Feeling that their prayers had been answered, Elizabeth and Will went on with their work.

It would have been so much easier had Will been content to limit his work. Apparently, no one ever told him that "to save one is, to save a whole world." To be sure, he was forever seeking individuals to save, but he could never shut out the vision of what might be for the whole country. Her greatness in land, in resources, in population and in the, as yet, untouched reserves of ability in her people, haunted him. He foresaw the China of 1950 and planned for her a place of honor in the family of nations.

He did not doubt that somehow she would have electricity, railroads, heavy industry and modern education. What concerned him was who would provide them. He knew the sodden people working endlessly to earn the cent-and-a-half-a-day necessary for life, would not always be content with such living. The question was not will a change come, but who will bring it about. So in 1907 he wrote, "Has Christianity nothing to do with all this? This material expansion may be for the Chinese people spiritually a savor of life unto life or of death unto death. If materialistic philosophy, or no philosophy at all except minding of the things of the flesh, takes the place of the old superstitions, then will the last state of China be even worse than the first. But if the spiritual forces of Christendom will recognize that these material things too are holy, then the very forces that tend to be a savor of spiritual death may be made a mighty savor of life unto life."

Because he saw all nations against a background of the Eternal purpose, whose Builder and Maker is God, he was bound to meet rebuffs and disappointments. It was not in him or Elizabeth to be discouraged permanently. To meet the needs of the people, in spite of ignorant opposition, he repeatedly urged the building of a huge industrial school where the best artisans of Europe and America could "incarnate themselves" into the brains and hands of young Chinese men and women, who in turn would go home to their villages and demonstrate a better way of doing work, where brains would direct the huge reservoir of brawn.

In the meantime, he contrived new approaches. When building was going on, he encouraged his young sons to hire themselves out to the Chinese mason. With the help of their donkey, they carted sand and brick, and did odd jobs for pennies a day. This was to undermine the paralyzing tradition that people who could read and write did not work, and set a good example for the bright orphanage boys, who were sent to the States to work their way through college.

Another work-project he suggested to his sons, was the growing of sweet potatoes. Although he never stopped work during the hot season, he sent Elizabeth and the children for a few weeks every summer to the top of a mountain just outside the city. For the first years, he made arrangements with a friendly Buddhist priest to rent a couple of bare rooms in a little temple. Later, he had a stone cottage built to accommodate his family. He also rented some of the abandoned terraces for his sons' project of growing sweet potatoes. It was not nice clean work for small boys. The only fertilizer known in China then, was human waste collected from houses and stored in cisterns. The boys took turns carrying buckets of the stuff to their potato patch.

My husband, Francis, came padding down the stone steps one bright summer morning with two loaded buckets on a bamboo pole over his shoulder. He stubbed his bare toe on a stone and with a howl of pain and dismay, fell headlong down the steps, covered in the fertilizer. His amah, the beloved Chinese woman who cared for all the children while their parents worked, came running to his aid. Ordering him to get up and strip himself of his clothes, she hurried away to get charcoal and wood and a bucket of water. She built a fire nearby and threw the water over the boy to rinse him off. While the fascinated family and neighbors watched, she made her small charge hop across the leaping flames until the stench was smoked off. Meanwhile, the amah told the world, in loud and angry tones, what she thought of people who encouraged their children to do work fit only for coolies. It was a day to remember.

One late September Saturday, the three older boys, aged 12, 10 and 8 were allowed to take the donkey up the mountain alone to dig sweet potatoes. The plan was for them to finish their work and be home before dark. But there was so much visiting to do along the way! Everyone knew them and wanted to chat. The boys were enchanted with this opportunity to show off their donkey and to strut importantly before these friendly folk. It was noon before they reached the mountain top. Then, of course, they had to eat their picnic lunch and see what had changed on the hill since the last time. By the time the potatoes were dug and sacked, the sun had dropped behind the mountain. Darkness comes very quickly in South China, and man-eating tigers prowl the mountain at night. Frightened, the children looked around. Hinghwa lay far down in the valley. Out in the dark ocean, a beacon of the lighthouse flashed silver across the purpling sky. Night was almost upon them. There wasn't a person on the mountain except themselves and the old priest in the little temple.

The boys slowly filed down toward the temple leading their laden donkey. They weren't exactly eager to face the old priest. They had scampered away from his displeasure when their vacation was finished a few weeks earlier. One of the idols in the temple hall had a beard of long black human hair and more than once the priest had caught them pulling out hairs, as he had that last afternoon. It was with some inner-quaking that they knocked on the plank wall which had been set up against the night.

The old man asked who was there. With becoming humility, they announced themselves. More kindly than they had reason to expect, the old man took out a plank and stood looking at them and the bulging donkey. "So you played too long and don't dare go home in the dark. What will your father say now? Well, come in, come in. You don't deserve to be received as guests, but he is my friend."

He gave the boys tea and boiled some of their own sweet potatoes for supper, grumbling as he worked. It was most improper and irreverent, but there was no place large enough for them and the animal except the temple hall. The donkey couldn't be left outside because of wild animals. He would give them one of their father's lanterns to keep them company, he said. Since the temple was separate from his apartment, there was no use in calling to him in the night. He wasn't going out in the dark for disobedient boys. Then addressing them directly, "Mind you, if the Buddha comes down to snatch you away, it will be your own fault. Who is it that is always so handy about pulling hairs from his beard?"

He left them in the shadowy temple where the boys watched as he walled them in by sliding long boards side-by-side into top and bottom grooves. Then he hurried away to his own quarters. The boys tested the sheltering wall, their perpendicular cracks large enough to insert their hands. The boards rattled, but didn't fall out. When they turned back to the small sanctuary, there, in the dim light, the glass eyes of the enormous Buddha glared at them. Suddenly, the boys felt cold. Pulling their thin cotton garments close, they huddled at the foot of the Buddha, their faces turned toward the flimsy outside wall.

Sometime in the night they were roused from their uneasy sleep by the snorting donkey. They sat up and watched in terror as the beast, ears laid back and rump turned toward the outer wall, twisted its head to follow a snuffling outside the upright planks. The children hid behind the sacks of potatoes until the noise stopped and the donkey relaxed. They were awake and waiting in the chilly dawn when the priest came to let them out. Peering through the cracks, they saw him stop, look at the dust in front of the temple and exclaim, "Are you in there?" pulling at a plank. When the tired boys stumbled out, he looked at them in relief, and then pointed at the tracks in the dust. "Tiger!" he said.

There were those in the community who felt that the Brewsters went too far in preferring their work to the welfare of their children. They said Elizabeth treated the children, the boys in particular, just like her orphans, except for the month she took off from work to give them birth. They had to admit though that the work accomplished was prodigious. "She is one, and he is one, but together they are more than three," was a frequent comment.

Except for meal times, the children rarely saw their father, but then they saw him at his best. In addition to a magnificent presence and rare conversational abilities, he managed to read enough to keep abreast of the thinking of the times. This he would discuss with Elizabeth at meals. The result was that his sons, to this day, cannot participate in small talk. They sit in glum silence waiting for some allusion to a world problem, and then there is no stopping them.

Their parents must have realized that there might be too much adult conversation. Sometimes a dinner hour was given over to the children. On one such occasion, special family friends were to be guests. It was planned that each child should prepare in advance something elevating and interesting to talk about at dinner. With the greatest skill, Will brought each one into the conversation and, with delightful courtesy, heard him through. To one little son, he turned with some anxiety. The boy almost never spoke, and Will and Elizabeth both wondered what he would have to offer. With the air of one about to die, he began somberly,

"There was a man who worked on the third floor of a rubber factory. One day a fire broke out on the lower floors. He put on three pairs of rubber boots and jumped out the window. When he hit the ground he bounced back up again. He bounced and bounced. Finally they had to shoot him to bring him down."

Upon telling me this incident, Elizabeth rocked with laughter, remembering the amazed incredulity on Will's face at this unorthodox contribution.

He was not without humor himself, as the following incident indicates. His own growing family and that of other missionaries was a source of worry to the Board of Missions in New York. To the small original salary of a husband and wife, an increase was granted at the birth of each child. Someone in the treasurer's office proposed that Protestant missions might profit by the experience of the Catholic Church, whose personnel were all celibate. Not only did this save in salaries, but it also did away with the need for furlough, so expensive in time and money. Upon hearing this, Will wrote the home office that he found this to be an excellent idea, adding that he thought celibacy should begin with the men who proposed it. Apparently, the suggestion was indefinitely tabled.

In his capacity as superintendent of the mission, Will received unfavorable comments of another kind. He was advised, for instance, that an official of the church had been designated to make a field inspection of reported luxurious living among missionaries. Will received this news with indignation. Knowing how many early missionaries had died as the direct result of housing inadequate for the stifling summer and wet, cold winters, he offered no apologies for the big adobe houses being built in South China. After one of his weekly trips into the country, he always returned to his own home with real gratitude.

At some time or other he had spent the night at every inn his territory owned and although all of them were filthy, some were unspeakable. It fell to his lot to conduct the visiting dignitary from station to station. Telling Elizabeth about the tour afterwards, Will grinned, guiltily, as he named one inn.

"I suppose I should have spared him that, but you and I have stopped there more than once."

"What did he think of it?" inquired Elizabeth, laughing.

"Oh, after he looked around a bit, he looked so sick I asked him if we should step outside," recounted Will.

"And?" prodded Elizabeth.

"Oh, he said, 'Thank God, there is an outside,' and rushed for the door," chuckled Will.

Perhaps his most ambitious project was the Borneo colony. He recognized the all too obvious fact that over-population was the chief cause of poverty. Even this overwhelming problem he sought to bring to heel with a two-pronged attack. First, by teaching the people that their security in the life to come depended upon God and not upon the number of earthly sons they possessed, encouraging monogamy and fewer children.

More directly, he planned for migration. There was no accurate census of China's population, but he estimated it at certainly no less than Japan's 1,922 people per square mile of arable land. To Will's dismay, the United States with 61 people per square mile, had closed her doors to the Chinese. Japan was already overcrowded. Far to the south, there were the great fertile areas of Java, Sumatra, Borneo and the Malay Peninsula, which welcomed men from China to pull rickshaws, work the fruitful soil and do mining. Java at that time had a population of 200 people per square mile, but the land was so fertile that this figure could be greatly increased. Borneo was so sparsely populated that Will computed forty percent of China's 400,000,000 people could be moved there without overstraining the fertility of the island.

Tens of thousands of Chinese men had discovered the South Seas for themselves and were migrating annually. Many families in the Hinghwa area were supported by men working in those faraway lands. This, however, did not greatly reduce the population. Women and children of non-Christians were left behind to tend the ancestral halls and tablets, and the men returned home as soon as they had earned enough money to raise more children to their honor and future happiness.

It was Will's observation that Christian young men found it difficult to resist the sensual customs of the tropics, and so they were lost, as he said, to the Kingdom of God. For that reason he planned emigration of families. In 1901, such a colony of Christian families had left Foochow, and had formed a very successful colony on the west coast of the Malay Peninsula. A few Hinghwa families had joined the migration and never returned.

Will had so identified himself with the Chinese people, that he was unwilling to propose such a migration without some assurance that the plan would mean happiness for them. In the year 1910, he visited the Malay Peninsula colony. He found one of the Hinghwa families there, prospering on a small rubber plantation they owned. All its members continued their Christian way of life. He was overwhelmed, when they presented him with $180 American currency for his work in Hinghwa and urged him to encourage more Christian families to join them.

Upon consultation with Chinese leaders and Bishops of the

Methodist Church, it was decided to promote the new Hinghwa colony in Sarawak, a British Protectorate in Borneo. The government was willing to give as much free land to the colonists that they could keep cultivated, and was willing to support the immigrants until their first rice crop could be harvested. After that they must be self-supporting. Once again Will, accompanied by a Chinese pastor, made a trip of inspection. They found the soil incredibly fertile to the depth of the twenty-foot-deep water wells.

The government was willing to make almost any concession to induce the Chinese families to come. In all Asia, probably in the entire world, there were no workmen so capable of grueling work, cheerfully done under any climatic conditions, whether steaming heat or arctic cold, than the Chinese. The native population of the islands were cheerful, but, had neither the strength nor inclination to do the hard work necessary to clear the jungles or work the mines.

Twelve miles along the Rejang River was the first grant of land set aside for the Hinghwa colony. Will thought the delta of the Rejang and its beautiful valley could support as many as 10,000,000 Chinese. Already 3,000 from Foochow were settled there. He foresaw a thriving Christian Chinese state in that magnificent spot.

Back home in Hinghwa, Will rallied his people. He carefully chose them from the hungry, the poor and those who had lost their land through poverty brought on by exorbitant taxes or lack of rain. Because he himself had to provide boat passage, he chose those most likely to succeed. In the end, only 100 had the courage to go, among them, sixteen of the older boys from the orphanage went along under the care of a fine young preacher. The next year those boys owned their own land, were tithing their income for the church, and wrote back that each one would underwrite another boy, since the government was no longer offering subsistence money.

Here was the next problem that Will and Elizabeth prayed about. In order to send the people who wished to go but could not afford the original cost, they sought a Christian way which would neither burden the colonists with debt nor offend dignity by being forced to accept charity. In the country beyond Hinghwa, 230 acres of land, which had been salvaged from the sea in generations past by the building of a dike, was up for sale. Five villages had owned the land, but through the years, dissension had risen among them about taxes and who was to pay for the upkeep of the dike.

This rich piece of land was offered to Will Brewster. Immediately, a solution to problems in the Borneo colony came to him. The land was flat and rich like the Rejang River concession. Unlike the small terraced fields which Chinese farmers were accustomed to working, the new land could be worked by modern machinery. He decided to raise money from his friends in America, buy the land, secure an agricultural missionary to establish a school and teach Chinese boys and men the newest methods of farming. The student farmers would be paid the highest current wages, all of which, except the cost of their education, would be set aside to provide boat fare to Borneo, and the subsistence money necessary for living until their first crops were harvested.

The settlers already in Borneo were handicapped by not knowing how to farm the large flat fields available to them. They still used the old hand methods used for millenniums on the room-sized fields to which they were accustomed. The men who learned to farm on the new "plantation," as Elizabeth refers to it, would have learned the new style of farming before going to Borneo. Whatever profits accrued to the mission, would be used to support Christian schools in Hinghwa. Will bought the land, and so one more dream, perhaps the most ambitious of them all, occupied his heart and energies for the rest of his life.

Agricultural interests of lesser significance had interested them both through all the years of their residence in Hinghwa. Whenever they went on country trips, they carried with them vegetable seeds, particularly cabbage, carrots and cauliflower, which were new to the area. The people accepted them gladly and these foreign vegetables became an important part of the people's diet. Tomatoes, so dear to all Americans, grew in the Brewster garden, but were much more slowly accepted by the Chinese. They still are known as "serpent's eggs."

Love of flowers was a bond between Elizabeth and her neighbors from the first. Nowhere in America had she seen such chrysanthemums or lilies, but the roses she felt could be improved upon. It was her custom to send to the States for the newest roses, filling her garden with them, to her own delight and that of all her neighbors. When she left China, she had sixty different varieties growing in lovely profusion. These were always in great demand for weddings or celebrations of any kind.

For most Americans, strawberries are a favorite fruit. In China, they were not frequently eaten because human waste used for fertilizer on the fields and gardens made it unsafe to eat raw fruit or vegetables.

In his book, Will takes note of this American partiality to strawberries. He quotes Henry Ward Beecher, "The Lord doubtless could have made a better fruit than the strawberry, but He never did." To this statement, Will took exception. In Hinghwa there grows a fruit, the lychee, which everyone, including the Brewsters, prefer. It is about the size and color of a strawberry, but grows upon a large tree. The rough, red shell is brittle, like a peanut shell, and covers a delicious white flesh with a black pit inside.

Will decided to transplant this fruit, and a close competitor in deliciousness, the longan, to the United States. In the year 1903, when he was going home on furlough, he had his Chinese gardener pot several grafts of both the lychee and longan fruit trees. He cared for them himself throughout the long ocean journey, thinking with pleasure what a surprise he would have for his California relatives. At the customs shed in San Francisco they were not only passed as free of disease, but coveted by several agricultural agents of the Federal government, who wanted to experiment with growing them in California and Florida. In the hope that someday Americans might know these delicious Chinese fruits, Will gave away his little trees. Fifty years later, Elizabeth was to hear about them again.

CHAPTER SEVEN

So Was My Beloved

During the winter, with Elizabeth away, I have tried to understand the political background of China against which all of us worked. How was it possible that so great a country and so ancient a civilization, even lacking religious conviction, would leave the care of her sick and orphaned, the education of her children, and the establishment of colonies for her poor and dispossessed, to people from other countries? A sentence from one of Will's lectures gave me the clue. "A great country, and a still greater people, yet, politically, a cipher." This, I reflected, was true; I had experienced it myself. Why it was so, had never been explained to me at any stage of my American education, nor was it made clear to me during my years in China. In those days, there were no radio broadcasts or daily newspapers to inform and confuse us.

During my residence there in the 1921-1931 decade, I had been grateful more than once for the Shanghai International Settlement, with its turbaned Sikh police force to keeep order and insure the safety of Hong Kong, even for the U.S. gunboats that occasionally anchored off the Bridge of Ten Thousand Ages in Foochow. I often saw pitiful hordes of Chinese, their babies and bedrolls tied on their backs, streaming across the bridge to the comparative safety those gunboats gave us on our Island. During one such a time, when a friend came back from Formosa, reporting the quiet conditions there, I remember wondering if the Chinese people might not be better off if the Japanese took over our province, too, as rumor reported they were planning to do. But when long lines of students paraded past our residence shouting something about the Twenty-One Demands and the return of Dalny and Port Arthur, I was more concerned with giving aid to the girls who fainted from heat exhaustion than in the reason for their marching. It seemed to me, China had problems enough with what she had, without asking for more.

There was certainly cause for protest. I had been in Foochow less than a year, when, on a hot spring day, I decided that we should have ice cream for dinner. The cook shook his head. "As you know," he said, "the city is in the hands of soldiers belonging to another warlord. They are on their way home, looting as they go. If the gardener or any Chinese man goes over to the electric-light plant for ice, he will be kidnapped and forced to carry their loads until he drops dead from hunger and exhaustion. "But," he added with emphasis, "If you go with the gardener, he will be safe."

So the two of us walked across the old bridge, the gardener holding fast to my belt, to show that he was my man. We were challenged several times, but walked calmly on, secure in the knowledge that I was an American. We got our ice, and on the way back, since the gardener's hands were occupied, I held onto his shirt tail. On that return trip, we were threatened with bayonets, since it was quite obvious that the gardener could carry a load. Somewhat shaken, but otherwise unharmed, we reached our own gate. That day, I had occasion to wonder about the state of a country where an unarmed American girl could protect one of its own people from seizure by his own countrymen in his own home town.

In Elizabeth's absence, I asked my husband about it and received a typically Brewster reaction. Since the incident had taken place several years before our marriage, he had never heard of it before. Nevertheless, he was properly shocked at the foolhardiness of this small adventure of long ago.

"You were not in much danger," he said, but you had no business risking the gardener's life. All of China still remembers the reprisals they suffered from attacks made on Europeans and Americans in the Hua Sang Massacre and Boxer Uprising. That is what saved you. But why those soldiers didn't grab the gardener, I don't know. They wouldn't have had to answer to anyone for doing it."

Both of the events to which he referred had taken place during the early years of Will's and Elizabeth's service, some twenty-five years before my arrival in China, and had affected their lives deeply as their notes reveal.

The massacre took place on beautiful Flower Mountain near Kucheng, the mountain city which Elizabeth had loved so dearly before she discovered Hinghwa. Hua Sang, or Flower Mountain, was used as a refuge from summer heat by the Kucheng missionaries, just as Kuliang Mountain was by all the Foochow missionaries.

In that summer of 1895, Elizabeth was at her own cottage on still another mountain outside the city of Hinghwa, with two small children and several unmarried ladies for company. One night in early August, as Will was hiking across the plain to join them, he was overtaken by a breathless messenger who handed him a letter from the consul in Foochow. Will could hardly believe what he read. Eleven missionaries, some of them children, had been murdered by knife and spear at Hua Sang. The consul ordered Will to bring all Hinghwa missionaries to Foochow at once, because it was not known whether the massacre was only an isolated incident or part of a greater movement.

As Will ran up the mountain to see if his own little family was safe, he tried to make sensible plans. He and Elizabeth had always felt perfectly secure; they knew of no enemies anywhere. The work was going well; if he left, what would happen to it? He found Elizabeth and the others well and happy, until he told them his ghastly news. Sick with grief, Elizabeth remembered that her special friend, Mabel Hartford, was spending her vacation at Hua Sang. Knowing how greatly Mabel was loved by the Chinese people, Will and Elizabeth felt the massacre must be the work of ruffians sent in from some other place. In that case they too might be in danger. Their little group made hasty arrangements and were soon on their way to Foochow. Never had a two-night trip seemed so long.

Upon reaching Foochow, they learned more of the tragedy. The man who later married one of Elizabeth's friends, had been enjoying a leisurely climb up Hua Sang to join his friend on the afternoon of July 31, 1895. About halfway up, overcome with heat and weariness, he stepped off the path into the luxuriant ferns and flowers which gave the mountain its name, and went to sleep. He was awakened by excited voices, and raising his head, he saw a mob of rough-looking men armed with spears and knives. It was obvious they meant exactly what they said. They were going to kill his friends. Unable to warn the missionaries or protect them from the howling mob, he ran down to the city to notify authorities and get help, which, of course, arrived too late.

To Elizabeth's joy and rather rueful amusement, she learned how Mabel Hartford had escaped death, when one of the mob had thrust a pitchfork at her throat. The Chinese pitchfork is much smaller than one of ours, but is more deadly, because the tines are sharp on both edges and set closer together. Nevertheless, at the first fierce thrust the tines passed one on each side of Mabel's neck, instead of piercing it. As Elizabeth had told me in an earlier conversation, the mission had wanted to send Mabel home because of her frailty. Now her extremely thin neck had saved her life. As her enraged attacker pulled the fork away to try again, loyal Chinese friends watching in horror from a window in the house from which Mabel had run, threw a suitcase down on top of him. It opened as it hit the ground. While he scrambled around picking up its precious contents, Mabel escaped into the woods, where she hid until the madness subsided and the mob went away. Although both sides of her neck were cut and bleeding, she was not seriously hurt. Eleven of her British friends were brutally murdered, as reported.

The New York Times voiced the sentiment of the moment by calling sternly for "condign" punishment, meaning a penalty suited to the crime. To Will and Elizabeth as well as to other mature missionaries, one of whom is quoted in a New York paper, the tragic incident was explainable. The men responsible were members of a strict Buddhist sect known as "Vegetarians." They ate no meat because they believed the souls of their dead passed into animals. The sight of men eating meat filled them with horror, and to see uninvited men from other lands doing so was almost unbearable.

This was no mere intellectual belief. One of the sights of Foochow, that I vividly remember, is that of an elderly woman walking along its hard white paths, holding animated conversation with a grunting pig, as she gently switched it toward greener pastures. Her dead husband had moved into the pig, she told me, and was obviously receiving gentler treatment than many husbands still embodied as men. I could never, knowingly, have eaten that pig myself.

The tragic Hua Sang affair was finally settled in a most condign manner. Years later, I saw how it was done. An Englishman showed me a picture, which I thought must be a scene from a Gilbert and Sullivan opera. It portrayed a gaudily dressed Lord Executioner posing with a huge knife, a circle of men kneeling around a cloth, (red, he said) their necks stretched out over it, and a group of relatives waiting to receive the heads as they fell. My friend said it was a photograph of the execution of the men guilty of the Hua Sang massacre. I only hope the victims were the men who did the wrong, which was not often the case in China those days. This memory of justice was part of the reason for my safety on the streets of China a quarter of a century later, although I was ignorant of the whole affair.

There were other causes for bitterness and misunderstanding among the Chinese people those years. Their loyalty to Confucianism and Buddhism, religions so old that they had become inseparable from the cultural and political life of the people, was an ongoing source of friction. It seemed to them that converts to Christianity must be traitors to their race.

There was also the question of war. Countless generations had been taught that war was sin; that the soldier was the lowest grade of man. Yet the Manchu rulers, also foreigners, were calling for men and money to fight Japan, suddenly anxious to protect Korea. For at least a thousand years, there had been a parental relationship between big China and tiny Korea, which was often rebellious on the part of Korea, of course. Between Japan and Korea no such relationship existed. Japan, to China's dismay, had learned from Europeans how to fight with modern weapons. There was no question of the outcome in a contest between these weapons and China's antique spear-bearing armies. This, too, was the source of anger for the West.

With the war and Korea lost, every household in China felt the burden of new taxes, to pay indemnities and army expenses. It was little wonder that in many parts of the empire, angry men were throwing stones and insults, and occasionally murdering innocent men and women from other lands. The Hua Sang massacre was an isolated example of this empire-wide indignation over inroads on Chinese territory. It made the people feel they were a melon about to be sliced and handed over to greedy outside nations.

For months, Elizabeth and Will fretted, waiting permission to return to their work. They hated having their personal safety made a matter of concern by their own government. They had given themselves to God and were content in His hands. The fiery Civil War veteran, who was a U.S. Consul in Foochow, wasn't afraid either, but his trust for security was not in God. He went to investigate the Hua Sang disaster, shooting every barking dog along the way, creating a fearful respect among the harmless village people, so they say.

Finally, Will, desperately concerned for his work, wrote a letter to the Consul announcing his intention to return to Hinghwa. Since no comment was made either in writing or when they met socially, Will and Elizabeth returned. To their intense relief and joy, they found the work they had been so worried about flourishing. The Chinese pastors, finding themselves wholly responsible, had called a conference at which they had decided they had been depending too much on foreign missionaries and money. Then and there, they pledged themselves anew and tithed their tiny incomes of less than $100 a year. When Will returned, they had over $300 in hand. With this gift of faith, they endowed a Home Missionary Society.

Two weeks after their arrival in Hinghwa, a special messenger arrived with a letter to Will demanding his immediate return with his family, threatening them with arrest if they did not obey. Will, however, referred to his letter announcing his plan to return to Hinghwa to which no objection had been made, and refused to leave his work again, saying that, if it was necessary, he would take the case to the U.S. Courts. There was no more said about his return. Thus began the tradition which Elizabeth maintained throughout her stay in China, "Others may go, I stay. I absolve the U.S. from all responsibility for my safety. I cannot represent Jesus, if I am protected by soldiers or gunboats. Right or wrong, that is my stand."

This position became increasingly important in the next three years. While the U. S. was emerging as a world power through her war with Spain, other nations were following aggressive policies in China. Japan won Korea and Formosa, as well as a huge indemnity. Russia had acquired important concessions in Manchuria and the ports of Port Arthur and Dalny. Germany, using the murder of two priests as the excuse, had caused the governor of Shantung Province to be removed, with subsequent dire results; imposed a huge indemnity, and had taken the magnificent harbor of Kiaochow, plus mining and railway privileges.

Worried Great Britain felt her security needed a great harbor on the Chinese coast opposite the one acquired by Russia and, in addition, land on the mainland opposite Hong Kong. France acquired a harbor on the southern coast. The Empress Dowager, on the throne in Peking, had no defense except that of playing the cupidity and fear of one power against that of another, hoping desperately to save some of China for the Chinese.

This was what Will meant when he referred to China as, politically, a cipher, adding bitterly, "For the past half century, no country has been so feeble as the Chinese. Whatever European powers have demanded, China has been compelled to yield whether it be land concessions, punitive indemnities or the morally destructive opium trade."

During these years the secret societies, which for centuries have flourished in China, became active, directing their anger at the Manchu government for its corruption and weakness. The people of the Empire had been taxed mercilessly, not only to pay indemnities, but for equipping Chinese armies and navies, the money unhappily being squandered on pleasure palaces and profligate living by the Empress Dowager and her court.

In South China, Mr. Sun Yat-sen, a man of integrity, ability and personal charm, was preaching revolution. At great peril, he traveled throughout the empire in disguise, always pursued by the vengeful arm of the Empress Dowager, and always escaping. It began to look as though the Manchus, who had ruled the Empire since 1643 must fall. The early emperors of the dynasty were men great enough to win the respect of their black-haired captives. During their reign, however, came two of the most corrupting disasters ever to befall the Chinese people; the forceful imposition of the opium trade by the business interests of England, and the equally devastating custom of selling government offices to the highest bidder; a Manchu importation. It was tacitly understood that the price that was paid for the office and the subsequent salary of the official were to be squeezed out of the people.

The last emperor, worthy of the name, had died in 1854, broken-hearted because he had not been able to save China from the opium habit, to which three of his own sons were said to be slaves. During the early years of the service of Elizabeth and Will, a weakling was emperor, but the throne was occupied by a powerful old lady, the Empress Dowager, who had chosen him and then set him aside. So far as her personal selfishness and her ignorance of world affairs permitted, she was devoted to China, its culture, its learning and its religions. Because of the latter, she was responsible to her ancestors for the empire they had won and passed on to her. Slowly, she began to see what could be done to save it.

As early as 1887, a prince of her race had dared to address her on behalf of western education for China, no doubt with a coffin waiting outside the door, as was the custom, should she be displeased. With eloquence and passion, he pled for the introduction of astronomy and mathematics into the curriculum of a scholar's education. On these sciences, he said, the western nations based their knowledge of things mechanical and military, which had made them so powerful. Without such knowledge, the prince said, China could never defend herself. Because the statement is so quaintly apropos to the thinking of our own time, I quote it as follows:[1]

"Your Majesty's servant and other ministers of the Council for Foreign Affairs, on their knees, present this memorial in regard to teaching Astronomy and the selection of students. The sciences, being indispensable to the understanding of machinery and the manufacture of firearms, we have resolved on erecting for this purpose a special department in the Tungwen College to which scholars of a high grade may be admitted and in which men from the West shall be invited to give instructions.

"The scheme having met with your majesty's approval, we beg to state that it did not originate in a fondness for novelties or in admiration for the abstract subtleties of Western science, but solely from the consideration that the mechanical arts of the West all have their source in the science of mathematics. Now, if the Chinese government desires to introduce the building of steamers and construction of machinery, and yet declines to borrow instruction from the men of the West, there is danger lest, following our own ideas, we shall squander funds to no purpose.

"We have weighed the matter maturely before laying it before the Throne. But among persons who are unacquainted with the subject, there are some who will regard this matter as unimportant; some who will censure us as wrong in abandoning the methods of China for those of the West; and some who will even denounce the proposal that Chinese should submit to be instructed by people of the West as shameful in the extreme. Those who urge such objections are ignorant of the demands of the times.

"In the first place, it is high time that some plan should be devised for infusing new elements of strength into the government of China. Those, who understand the times, are of the opinion that the only way of effecting this is to introduce the learning and mechanical arts of Western nations. Provincial governors, such as Tso Tsung-tang

1 Mrs. Little, *Intimate China*, p. 13

and Li Hung-Chang, are firm in this conviction, and constantly presenting it in their addresses to the Throne. The last-mentioned officer, last year opened an arsenal for the manufacture of arms, and invited men and officers from the metropolitan garrison to go there for instruction; while the other established in Foochow a school for the study of foreign languages and arts, with a view to the instruction of young men in shipbuilding and the manufacture of engines. The urgency of such studies is, therefore, an opinion which is not confined to us, your servants.

"Should it be said that the purchase of steamers and firearms has been tried and found to be both cheap and convenient, so that we may spare ourselves the trouble and expense of home production, we reply that it is not merely the manufacture of arms and the construction of ships that China needs to learn. But in respect to these two objects, which is the wiser course in view of the future—to content ourselves with purchase, and leave the source of supply in the hands of others, or to render ourselves independent by making ourselves masters of their arts—it is hardly necessary to enquire.

"As to the imputation of abandoning the methods of China, is it not altogether a fictitious charge? For, on inquiry, it will be found that Western science had its root in the astronomy of China, which Western scholars confess themselves to have derived from Eastern lands. They have minds adapted to reasoning and abstruse study, so that they were able to deduce from it new arts which shed a luster on those nations; Europeans learned it from us. If, therefore, we apply ourselves to those studies, our future progress will be built on our own foundation. Having the root in our possession, we shall not need to look to others for assistance, an advantage which it is impossible to overestimate.

"As to the value to be set on the science of the West, your illustrious ancestor, Kang Hsi, gave it his hearty approbation, promoting its teachers to offices of conspicuous dignity, and employing them to prepare the Imperial calendar; thus setting an example of liberality equaled only by the vastness of his all comprehending wisdom. Our dynasty ought not to forget its own precedents, especially in relation to a matter which occupied the first place among the studies of the ancients.

"In olden times, yeomen and common soldiers were all acquainted with astronomy; but in later ages, an interdict was put upon it, and those who cultivated this branch of science became few. In the reign of Wang Hsi, the prohibition was removed, and astronomical science once more began to flourish. Mathematics was studied together with the classics, the evidence of which we find in the published works of several schools. A proverb says, "A thing unknown is a scholar's shame." Now, when a man of letters, on stepping from his door, raises his eyes to the stars and is unable to tell what they are, is not this enough to make him blush? Even if no schools were established, the educated ought to apply themselves to such studies. How much more so, when a goal is proposed for them to aim at?

"As to the allegation that it is a shame to learn from the people of the West, this is the most absurd charge of all. For, under the whole heaven, the deepest disgrace is that of being content to lag in the rear of others. For some tens of years the nations of the West have applied themselves to the study of steam navigation, each imitating the others, and daily producing some new improvement. Recently, too, the government of Japan has sent men to England for the purpose of acquiring the language and science of Great Britain. This was with the view of building steamers, and it will not be many years before they succeed.

"Of the jealous rivalry among the nations of the Western Ocean, it is unnecessary to speak; but when so small a country as Japan is putting forth all its energies, if China alone continues to tread indolently in the beaten track, without a single effort in the way of improvement, what can be more disgraceful than this? Now, not to be ashamed of our inferiority, but when even a measure is proposed by which we may equal or even surpass our neighbors, to object to the shame of learning from them, and for even refusing to learn, to be content with our inferiority—is not such meanness of spirit itself an indelible reproach?

"If it be said that machinery belongs to artisans, and that

scholars should not condescend to such employments, in answer to this we have a word to say. Why is it that the book in the Chao-li, on the structure of chariots, has for some thousands of years been a recognized textbook in all the schools? Is it not because, while mechanics do the work, scholars understand the principles? When principles are understood, their application can be extended. The object which we propose for study today is the principles of things. To invite educated men to enlarge the sphere of their knowledge by investigating the laws of nature is a very different thing from compelling them to take hold of the tools of the working man. What other point of doubt is left for us to clear up?

"In conclusion, we would say that the object of study is utility, and its value must be judged by its adaptation to the wants of the times. Outsiders may vent their doubts and criticisms, but this measure is one that calls for decisive action. Your servants have considered it maturely. As the enterprise is a new one, its principles ought to be carefully examined. To stimulate candidates to enter in earnest on the proposed curriculum, they ought to have a liberal allowance from the public treasury to defray their current expenses, and have the door of promotion set wide before them. We have accordingly agreed on six regulations, which we herewith submit to the eye of Your Majesty, and wait reverently for the Imperial sanction.

"We are of the opinion that the junior members of the Hanlin Institute, being men of superior attainments while their duties are not onerous, if they were appointed to study astronomy and mathematics, would find those sciences an easy acquisition. With regard to scholars of the second and third as also mandarins of the lower ranks, we request your Majesty to open on portals and admit them to be examined as candidates, that we may have a larger number from whom to select men of ability for the public service.

"Laying this memorial before the Throne, we beseech the Empress-Regent and the Emperor to cast on it their sacred glance, and to give us their instructions."

Some years later, the young emperor called for just such reforms in education and also for the modernization of the government. As a result the Empress Dowager had him imprisoned in the Peking Palace. One of the secret societies, the so-called Boxers, then began to whet their knives in earnest for an attack on the Manchu Dynasty. The Empress was an extremely clever woman, and with much reason on her side, persuaded the Boxers to direct their anger against the western nations, who, she said, were the real enemies of China. Having succeeded in winning their loyalty, she virtually declared war on the world. The U. S. had taken no part in the aggressions against China, but the bulk of the population had no way of distinguishing Europeans from Americans, so all were in danger.

That summer of 1900, Elizabeth was again at the beloved mountain-top home, this time with four small children. News came of the tense atmosphere around Peking, where both the Chinese and foreign populations were fearful of the struggle to come. Chinese Christians, especially, had almost more to fear than the missionaries, who could look for some help from their governments. The Chinese could expect no help from theirs. On June 24 of that year, an order was issued from the Palace to kill all foreigners, even those who had left their work and by slow car or on foot were trying desperately to reach some port of exit.

In and around Peking, the order was carried out with chilling results. The governor, who had been dismissed from his Shantung post at the insistence of Germany, satisfied his loss of face and anger at that injustice by having fifty-four men, women and children slaughtered at his official residence. Breathlessly, the rest of China waited for the Boxers to strike. When no word came to the Palace of vengeance against the Christians in the southern and other distant provinces the Empress Dowager began to investigate. She discovered that the two high officials who had been assigned to send her fateful telegram to the faraway provinces had been guilty of treason.

Conferring with each other, they had decided that the future of China lay in their hands. The Empress and her ministers might temporarily be satisfied with the spilling of much innocent blood, but the wrath of the whole world so aroused, could easily mean the death of China. Their own death by torture and perhaps that of their families, too, seemed a small price to pay to prevent such a calamity. They changed the word "KILL" to "PROTECT," and sent the message out.

The puzzling telegram, coupled with news that thousands were being massacred in the north, and that foreigners were barricaded and besieged in Peking, alarmed the governors of the southern and central provinces. Many of these men were more familiar with Western civilization than the Empress Dowager, who still entertained the conviction inherited from her ancestors that Americans and Europeans were merely savages from some unimportant faraway islands. Conferring by wire, the governors decided to control as far as possible the now inflamed tempers of their provinces. The two officials responsible for the telegram were brutally killed, as they expected, but because they died to save others, they are remembered as martyrs. Rumor says they were sawed apart.

As soon as the gravity of the situation became known, Will was besieged by anxious Chinese Christians. For ten years these people had looked to him in times of trouble. More than once he had saved them from injustice and persecution from government officials interested in them only as a source of the squeeze.

With pride, Elizabeth has told me that Will was never accused of unfairness, or of using his position as an American missionary to obtain undeserved or special privileges for his parishioners. Such was his reputation for impartial justice, that even some officials called on him for help, and many an innocent person had Will to thank for protection from the infamous police of that day.

When an order was received to locate the person guilty of a certain crime, it was the custom of policemen to threaten with arrest any number of innocent people, reprieve them for a price and continue this practice until some poor person was discovered who was unable to ransom himself. He then became the criminal, unless someone like Will would plead for him before the magistrate.

With terror mounting, as smoldering resentments against all Christians were fanned by news of violence in the north, Will used his reputation for justice and his friendship with the local Manchu magistrate to save the city and surrounding area from looting and violence. At his firm insistence, placards proclaiming protection for Christians and warnings against looting were posted throughout Hinghwa and the surrounding counties. In any civil disturbance, the merchants were the heavy losers, it being the custom to blackmail them for large donations or subject them to looting.

Throughout the summer, while murder and looting went on in many places, the Hinghwa missionaries lived in an uneasy quiet. Since the only means of escape was by water, Will had a friend anchor a junk in the harbor. This was for Elizabeth, who was expecting a fifth child, and for the children and other missionary women, in case killing began. When the people of the city became aware of the junk, they guessed its purpose. To avert a panic, Will had to send it away.

Day by day, he went on with his work, purposely walking the streets, clad in his customary immaculate white linens, calling on the magistrate and chatting calmly with the shop owners. One day, as he passed a barber plying his trade on the open street, he overheard the man say to the interested bystanders, "There goes that foreigner. They are killing them up north. When we get around to it, it won't take us long. We haven't so many around here." When he heard the excited laughter that greeted the remark, Will turned back.

"What do you mean by such a remark?"

"Oh, nothing, nothing. I was just talking," replied the barber.

"This is a poor time for talk of that kind. You know as well as I that such a remark could easily start a wave of killing and looting that would spare no one. I demand an apology as public as your remark." So saying, Will walked off leaving consternation behind.

"Goodness!" I protested when Elizabeth told me this story. "That sounds awfully autocratic!"

"It was a time for firmness," she explained. "If Will had reported him to the magistrate, the man and his family would have been destitute by the time all the police and petty officials got through with him. Will didn't want that to happen. Since so many people had heard the remark, something impressive had to be done. The safety of the whole city might depend on how the case was handled. As soon as Will got home, a mediator arrived to arrange for a private apology, which he refused. Pretty soon he heard firecrackers in the distance. As the sound approached the house, Will knew the apology was on its way, no doubt accompanied by a crowd of curious folks attracted by the noise. In his reception hall, Will received the written apology, resting on a tray covered with red cloth, the man was forgiven, and the temper of the city considerably cooled."

By the end of the summer, nerves were worn from constant news of atrocities. The Consul in Foochow, a man of long experience in China, notified Will he could remain in Hinghwa if he wished, but that many other Americans and Europeans were evacuating, and it might be well to get the women and children to some safer place. On the mountain with Elizabeth, were several women who refused to leave if Elizabeth stayed. This posed a problem. Elizabeth explained it to me this way:

"We felt perfectly safe. Neither of us had received any guidance to indicate we should leave. But guidance for us was always personal, and couldn't be applied to the rest of the mission. We were troubled by a sense of responsibility for the other women, who wouldn't leave unless I did. Finally, the solution came when the only remaining doctor, an Englishman, was ordered out by his government. Then I had to go, because I was expecting my baby in a month and needed help.

"We all came down to the city and prepared to leave. All of us needed money, so Will went to the street to cash the checks. The money-merchants were so upset when they heard he was leaving, that they refused to give him the cash we all needed. Will explained that I had to have a doctor and that was why I was leaving, but that he would come back as soon as he had us all safely settled at Sharp Peak. He promised that would be no later than Monday night and knowing he would keep his word, they cashed the checks.

"Will settled us all safely in the apartment at lovely Sharp Peak and then went to Foochow to confer with the Consul. He was disturbed because so many friends were going to Japan, Hong Kong or elsewhere. Yet, at the boat landing, we had met our Hinghwa messenger whom Will had sent to Foochow for supplies the previous week. He reported that the Hong Kong Bank was doing business as usual. This upset Will. He wanted to find out from the Consul why business was more important than missionary work. If businessmen were allowed to remain at their posts, he didn't want to be ordered away from his."

There is no use my arguing this point with Elizabeth now, but it seems quite clear to me, that men engaged in business in a large city accessible to their own navies, travelling only between home and office, were less exposed to the hysteria of the time than men and women in lonely country stations. But danger does not mean the same thing to Elizabeth as it does to me. To her danger is not until it happens!

There is, for instance, a delightful story Elizabeth's youngest son told me about her.

The country around Hinghwa was far from peaceful. Some of the villages were feuding over grievances hundreds of years old, others over water rights or recent insults. One quarrel began at the end of the Ming Dynasty, 250 years earlier. At that time, the so called Black Pirates were devastating the coast of South China so frequently, that the ordinarily peaceful people formed themselves into bands of vigilantes to fight the marauders. When finally the pirates were subdued, the vigilantes turned on each other, and their descendants were still at war when Will and Elizabeth travelled the Fukien roads.

Another feud, of even longer standing, was fought annually by the inhabitants of two villages. More than three hundred years earlier, a gang of boys from one village visited the other village. One of the visitors stole a few peanuts from a shop. The owner immediately gave chase, caught the boy and beat him severely. While this was taking place, the boy's companions ate the rest of the peanuts. Every year since, between the harvesting of the first rice crop and the planting of the second, the two villages have waged war.

When Will or Elizabeth travelled a road that lay within range of any of these local battles, it was only necessary for them to show themselves, hold up a hand, and pass in safety. All firing ceased until they were well out of reach.

During the warlord period, before Chiang Kai-shek's time, when soldiers from the north were in possession of the territory, Elizabeth was travelling alone one day. Entering an embattled area, she was challenged by a northern sentry. Either by intention or habit, she walked calmly on. The irate sentry ripped her dress from top to bottom with his bayonet. Indignant and ruffled, Elizabeth walked on. The astonished sentry let her go.

One day, when she was telling someone that she had never been insulted or harmed during all her years in China, her son reminded her of this incident. Elizabeth snorted.

"Well, that was only an ignorant northern soldier He didn't know me. Anyway, he didn't hurt me. He just ripped my clothes!"

To her the incident was not even exciting, merely disgraceful, and to be ignored.

It was with this same lack of personal concern, that Will visited the Consul requesting assurance he would not be ordered out of Hinghwa. The assurance was given with a request that he stop at one city and the villages enroute home, to call upon the Manchu officials to remind them of their duty to post placards announcing the protection of Christians and the severe penalties for looting. The Chinese Christians in those places were in terror of violence.

All of this took time. It was almost midnight the following Monday when he reached Hinghwa. The city gates were locked. Will borrowed a ladder from a friend outside the gates and climbed over the wall. "Did he wake up the money merchants to let them know he was back?"

Elizabeth considered my question. "I don't think so. Why should he? They knew he would keep his word."

The discussion group composed of literati and officials met with increasing interest throughout that summer. Current events became of primary importance. They no longer dared trust rumors or messages from Peking. Anxiously, they checked them in light of information Will had to give them.

For some years, he had published a weekly sheet called "The

Revivalist," which was printed in the Romanized form of the spoken language, the medium on which he counted on so heavily for the enlightening of the people. In addition to church news and devotional material, it contained a digest of current events. The literati had always scorned the Romanized medium, but now, Will records, it was a strange and moving sight to see them gather around a little child to hear news read from The Revivalist. Some of them secretly learned the printed language and subscribed to the paper themselves.

Seeing newcomers reading The Revivalist, he saw in capsule form, what could become his great vision of all China, where ignorant and learned, alike, could read Romanized print and almost overnight have access to the Bible. He once visited a remote village where a Chinese Bible teacher had formed a training class. Up to that moment, the people of the village literally rose no higher than the ground. From the fields came the vegetables and potatoes on which the villagers lived. To the fields returned the waste of their bodies and the burned ashes of the rags no longer fit to cover them. They settled their continual sullen arguments in bloody fights. If a dream existed, it was for food to satisfy hunger. The infinitely vaster dream that one of them might become a student and learn to read, was as remote as becoming President is to a child in America.

Within eight weeks after the coming of the Bible teacher, five young men stood up and read with understanding news from the current Revivalist which Will, there on his first visit, had brought along. A dozen girls read from the catechism at sight. They could read the gospels, hymnbooks and religious tracts. The rawest, darkest, most pagan community imaginable had in eight weeks turned its face toward God.

I can imagine with what joy Will printed the news that the Boxer trouble with its slaughter of thousands of Chinese and hundreds of foreign Christians was over. Of even greater importance to his readers, was the message that the United States was determined that the Chinese people should not be held responsible for the sins of the Empress Dowager and her ministers.

Our Secretary of State, Mr. Hay, took the stand that the real ruler was the young Emperor, whose power had been usurped and abused by the powerful Empress Dowager. So out of this most disastrous encounter of the West with China, came the "Open Door" policy, which sought safety for China from aggressive nations and the preservation of her territory and government for herself, but asked China to safeguard equal trade rights to friendly nations. The indemnity demanded was punitive. The United States returned millions of her share for education of Chinese students abroad. In gratitude, China designated this sum for the education of students in the United States.

Several years later, the Empress Dowager, chastened by the Boxer disaster, began in earnest the reforms, so long overdue. Commissions were appointed to modernize education, to reform and modernize the army, navy and judicial system. The most astounding concession on her part, was the commission sent abroad to study constitutional governments and to recommend one suitable for China.

All this was exciting and stimulating to Elizabeth and Will; it was part of their dream coming true. Sciences, mathematics and English were now routine in their schools. The problem was textbooks and teachers to do the job. The trained students coming back from abroad were needed in government, business and industry as well as in schools and hospitals.

Some of the returning students were ashamed of the corruption and personal selfishness they found in men in public life. They openly advocated the adoption of the Christian religion on a national scale in public affairs, so that China, too, might be strong. When others pointed out that Japan had become strong without adopting Christianity, one of the former group replied with a prophetic statement, which we have seen realized. A religion such as Japan's, he said, which substitutes a man for God as the object of a nation's worship, sets too low a standard, one that is likely to fall from Heaven, bringing ruin upon all his followers.

Will, too, believed that only the application of Christian principles could save China. He knew also that the strength of a nation depended upon the spirit of its people, which can never be legislated into being. Without a Christian spirit the people would still be minding only the things of the flesh, and the resulting materialistic society would be no better than the one founded on the old superstition. Will dreamed of something infinitely better. He wanted a new life related to God, in everyone; families God-centered instead of ancestor-centered; a whole nation claiming the privileges and responsibilities of being sons of God, instead of relegating that responsibility to the throne in Peking.

A nation of agnostics trained in the sciences was a prospect he dreaded. He knew the indifference to life around him. When a man was killed in one of the numerous village fights, the price of a good fat pig would satisfy his family. Scientific knowledge in the hands of a nation with so little regard for human life, was not a pleasing prospect. One of Will's great friends, Arthur H. Smith, writing some years earlier, had voiced the following opinion:

"No science lies nearer to our modern advancement than chemistry. Would the spread of a general knowledge in China, therefore, be a moral agency for regenerating the people? Would it not introduce new and unthought-of possibilities for fraud and violence throughout every department of life? Would it be quite safet...to diffuse through the empire, together with an unlimited supply of chemicals, an exact formula for the preparation of every variety of modern explosives?"[2]

Although Will foresaw so clearly the importance of China in the middle of this century, he did not share the view of those who referred to her as "The Yellow Peril." He knew the Chinese people had never made war on outside nations, although their conquerors, the Mongols, had devastated both Asia and Europe. The China he knew, hated war, despised soldiery and showed no desire for conquest. It was for the Chinese people that he feared the introduction of western knowledge, before their spiritual awakening had begun.

So he began in great earnest to count the cost of winning China to God. He was not alone in his concern, of course. In America those years, there was a keen sense of individual responsibility among

---

2 *Chinese Characteristics*, Arthur H. Smith, D.D, p. 327

Christians. Men were asking a wonderful new question. For too many years now, we have given huge sums of money through church budgets and taxes for the evangelization and relief of the world. Not often do we ask ourselves, "What is my individual responsibility to God for making His world aware of Him?" Will, and some of his colleagues set about answering this question. In a booklet called, "The Cost of Christian Conquest," he sets down his figures. He estimated that in the year 1908, the responsibility of each member of the Methodist Church was evangelizing 53 people, at a cost of about 5 per cent of his income. To Elizabeth and Will who always tithed, this seemed a small amount of money for so great a work. For churches with smaller membership, the individual cost and responsibility was naturally higher.

For Fukien Province where he worked, Will figured the responsibility of his church was 7,500,000 people; that in money cost it would be necessary to increase annual-giving by one-cent-per-capita of the population, until ten-cents-per-capita or $750,000 per annum were reached, and then continue that rate for a generation. This would also establish and equip schools, both secular and theological, for the training of Chinese leaders to carry on the work; establish hospitals and other works of mercy, such as, care of lepers and the otherwise handicapped people, that must accompany schools and evangelistic work. He stated that only the Chinese could win their country; that no alien could ever do more than set spiritual forces at work.

He differed from many, who thought that Christian responsibility consisted of announcing from door-to-door that Jesus had come to be the Way to God. He insisted people needed to see among them someone who was like Jesus, continually going about doing the will of God. Only a great army of Christian Chinese could do this for their people. So, he said, whereas America must give four times the existing number of missionary personnel, China must produce fifteen times as many local evangelists. Even if so great a treasure in men, women and money were poured out, he declared that it would all be in vain unless accompanied by an equal amount of loving prayer. That is always harder to raise than money or men.

He was under a stern conviction that he worked in a crisis of the ages; that all Asia was in a state of flux. Every country was questioning religions and customs which had commanded its loyalty for centuries. Should they harden with new cultural and religious patterns not Christian, he wondered if winning them could ever be accomplished, certainly not for generations. This was the anxiety which energized his campaign to make his churches Bible-reading communities.

Knowing the ease with which they memorized chapters and books, he planned for a contingency he hoped never would arise. Earlier attempts to Christianize the Chinese people had failed when missionaries had been driven out, or when the monarch supporting the movement died. The people were left with rituals and symbols, but not the Bible. The Bible had never been in their hands, nor had the ability to read it ever been given to the common people. If they acquired the habit of Bible-reading, no new book-burning era, with which China was already familiar, could deprive them of the words of Life. This was a part of the great burden which drove him to his knees every morning before dawn, sometimes keeping him there for days at a time.

Will and Elizabeth were aware of another danger in their work. We recognize it today with increasing anxiety. A friend voiced it to me recently in the poignant declaration, "I have an uneasy feeling that there is more to being a Christian church member than appearing on an increasing number of committees, and participating in a multiplicity of other organizations and duties." In China, laying aside superstitions and abandoning ancestor worship in order to join a church, was a much graver decision than most of us are ever required to make.

Will and Elizabeth knew from their own personal experience, however, that this was only the beginning of becoming a Christian. As a result of years of work and prayer, the church community in Hinghwa, missionary as well as Chinese, knew several periods of that spiritual warming and awakening that first came as Pentecost. In one of those great revivals, a little Chinese boy, nine years old, became a real Christian. I first heard of him one day last summer.

Elizabeth was waiting for me by the kitchen door as I came up the driveway with the mail. Among her letters, there was a questionnaire from a man in England. Since she cannot see, I read it to her.

"Someone wants you to answer a lot of questions for a biography about a man named John Sung," I said. Do you know anyone by that name?"

A stillness came over Elizabeth. "John Sung! Yes, I know John Sung. He became a Christian at one of our great revival meetings when he was only nine years old." She stood tapping the letter thoughtfully.

"What is the matter with him?" I questioned. "Didn't you like him?"

"Yes. He was one of our boys. He died some years ago. He was a great preacher, as his father was before him, but he went off on the tangent of faith-healing. I wish he hadn't done that!"

"Don't you believe in faith healing?" I asked.

She thought about this for a moment.

"I believe Jesus healed people. It was necessary then. But now we have doctors whose healing knowledge is also from God, and I believe we are expected to use new light and knowledge when it is given to us. I have seen many people bitterly disappointed when Mr. Sung failed to heal them. Some have lost their faith in their disappointment. I wish he had not added healing to his wonderful preaching ministry."

She never asked me for help in filling out the questionnaire. I have since seen the book; it seems to me, John Sung was an extraordinary Christian. I shall speak of him later.

* * *

Elizabeth was in Peking in October of 1911. For her the sense of crisis, which hung over the city as palpably as the autumn dust, was personal as well as political. For more than a year, her right eye had been giving her pain. Treatment had been received during a curtailed furlough to America the previous year, followed by medical aid in Shanghai. In October, she had been advised to seek more extensive attention in Peking. The verdict was dismaying, blindness in the right eye. Her daughter, Mary, has told me that one of her mother's early nicknames was, "The girl with the navy-blue eyes."

I have never seen Elizabeth without an unsightly, thick, gray membrane over that right eye. I can imagine with what sorrow she received the doctor's verdict. An important part of her work was translating into Romanized text, hymns and books for beginners and the voluminous correspondence with Americans who supported the work of the mission. More than that, she has always liked to look nice, Elizabeth with her Sweetheart Soap routine, her night-cream and pin curls netted for sleep, at 95!

She was sightseeing with friends at the Great Wall when news of the mutiny of the imperial armies arrived. Peking had been waiting for some such news for days. But to receive it while viewing the Great Wall for the first time, furnished a historical setting significant enough to dwarf her personal crisis. Standing on the wall is an awesome experience at any time.

Someone in your party is sure to know the statistics—length two thousand miles, stretching from the great "Pillar Bridge of Heaven" in the eastern ocean off into the wilderness in the far northwest; thickness twenty-five feet, height up to fifty feet, a highway interspersed with enclosed watchtowers all along the top. To westerners, it has always seemed the symbol of China, the invisible dragon brought to earth, as it coils around bare, brown, mountains, is lost to sight then rears up to crown another peak farther on, winding on forever to the beginning and the end of time, visible to men when they stand on the moon.

On that October day, Elizabeth wondered if a period of political eclipse were over. The question Will had been asking for so long was at least answered. It was to be revolution, not evolution for China.

The Dowager Empress and the weakling Emperor had both died in 1908; since then, a regent had ruled for the infant emperor. The first evidences of the promised constitutional government, the provincial assemblies, had met and demanded more democratic rights than the Prince Regent was willing to grant. The secret societies had been calling for revolution, and it had come with the mutiny of the imperial armies. The question remained whether the vast, loosely bound Empire could respond to its new responsibilities, or whether it needed a strong man with a lash to hold it together.

That was the way the Great Wall had been built, not by the labor of free men working together to protect themselves against a harassing, common enemy, but under the lash of a cruel tyrant, driving them to defend themselves. Assignment to work on the wall was the Siberia of its day. The moment of Christian missions had been very brief, measured against the life of the Empire. Had it been long enough to provide leadership, or must China still remain, politically, a cipher? With the foreign Manchu removed and a revival of government by the Chinese people, would the vast population be loyal and patriotic? How would lack of roads and railroads affect the unity of the Provinces? How could 400,000,000 people unable to read be taught to use the ballot?

Like all other visitors, at the wall that day, Elizabeth forgot her sobering questions, trying to stay on the donkey which took her down the hill. Transportation back to Peking was equally hilarious and about as comfortable—a seat on a pile of coal covered with gunnysacks in an open railroad freight car.

When she reached Hinghwa, she found the city in turmoil. Revolution was the talk of the streets. The provinces south of the Yangtze were seceding from the Empire, and Hinghwa itself was gathering up courage to drive the Manchu soldiers from the military camp which had been there for two hundred and fifty years.

Once again as in the Boxer days, Will was besieged by people needing help and advice. The Manchu magistrate sent his family and treasure to him for safety. The revolutionists set up office across the street from his house. Both parties used his study for committee meetings and asked his advice. The literati, accustomed to his leadership through years of forums and current event discussions, came asking for instruction in the forms of democracy.

A blind eye could not restrain Elizabeth from participating in the excitement. When word came from one of the country mission stations that looting was sure to break out with the withdrawal of Manchu authority, Elizabeth went up to the mountain city to share her courage and confidence with the people. On the way up the lovely valley, she passed a likin[3] station which had already been looted. It looked as if the situation might be serious. Not wishing to be absent from her school for any length of time, she sent back for her oldest son, then eighteen, to come prepared to stay until danger was over.

That was my husband, who had gone back to China after finishing high school to spend a year as secretary to his father. He was delighted to accept the assignment. Collecting some men, he divided them into watches and instructed them in their duties. Ordinarily in those days, night watchmen in China walked through the streets at stated hours, shaking a sort of rattle, to warn any evildoers of their approach and assure the timid that all was well. Francis told his newly formed guard to watch for anything unusual and notify him at once. Then he went to sleep. One night he was awakened by the panic-stricken men, who announced a strange flashing light on the city wall. A devil was abroad, they insisted, all ready to run for cover. Francis came out, watched the light for a while, and decided it was someone deliberately trying to frighten the guards away, so that looting could begin. He had the men shoulder arms and march up and down in response to his loud commands and the night passed safely. Nothing even remotely exciting happened after that, he says, disgustedly.

He loves to recall what seemed to him the most interesting sight of those revolutionary days. On the streets, and especially at the city gates, an ancient cry had been revived. His own blond curls safe on his head, he laughed heartily as the young patriots "offered" to cut the queues from literati and coolies, old men and boys, to be greeted often with the old cry, "My head, but not my hair," as young and old tried vainly to save long, glossy braids or mere pig's tails of thin gray hair from the shears. No one seemed quite sure where loyalty to Chinese customs stopped and the sign of the hated Manchu slavery began, but the shears sheared and the hair fell.

---

3 Likin was a tax collected on merchandise carried between points in the interior of the provinces, a source of revenue the Manchu originated to pay for the Tai Ping Rebellion. It was handled by Chinese employees, and was hated by all merchants because of the inevitable "squeeze," which made the tax so high as to restrain trade.

It seems that for ages Chinese men have worn their hair in a long braid wrapped around the head. Long hair was no crime against Chinese customs. In the age of the conquering Khans, Chinese were forced to wear it in two braids hanging down their backs like their Mongol masters. When the Chinese again owned their country, up went their hair in a coronet around their heads. When the Manchu invaders took over, they decreed two changes, the women were to stop binding their feet, and the men were to shave the front half of their heads and wear the back hair in one long braid down their backs. The ignominy was really the unsightly shaving of the head, not the wearing of the queue.

The women somehow resisted unbinding their feet, but the men were challenged everywhere about their hair. With the cry against tyranny, "Our heads, but not our hair!" they lost their heads, until finally they bowed to the edict. Perhaps to comfort themselves for the shaved front, they took great pride in the long braid behind, having the barber comb and pomade it and braid red cord into it; and for the gentry, hang a tassel from its end.

In more than two hundred years, the source of humiliation was confused or forgotten. So when the raucous revolutionary youths attached Manchu-stigma to the braid, off it had to come. My husband says men went off wailing like women for their lost hair. Time seems not only to make ancient good uncouth, but to confuse the issue so that the ancient uncouth becomes the mode, and men no longer know for what they should die. In Hinghwa no heads fell.

One day, Will received word from the Consul that the revolutionists had taken Foochow, had killed the Manchu governor-general and were marching on Hinghwa. He knew that among them was a young man who hated the Hinghwa magistrate because he had failed the boy in the prefectural examinations. Will doubted that the boy had the courage to harm the magistrate himself, but under the cover of patriotism, he might persuade the rabble army to do so.

Calling upon the magistrate, he advised him to wire revolutionary headquarters in Foochow, offering his services to the new regime, and post placards of the government turnover in Hinghwa. Understandably, the Manchu magistrate was reluctant to take such advice, preferring, he said, to wait at least a day to see if the revolutionists still held Foochow.

When Will told him about the rabble army on its way, he wired Foochow, received his temporary appointment, and placarded the city with proclamations of the Republic of China. As it turned out, this saved his life, for the revolutionists had, indeed, planned to kill him.

His service under the republic was brief. The literati, wanting to apply the principles of democracy Will had taught them, quite properly insisted on the election of officers from the Chinese population. When the Manchu magistrate and his family left for their ancestral home in the north, they gave Will and Elizabeth a magnificent vase, white hawthorn blossoms on a bottle-green background. This was their chief treasure, and it became so for the Brewsters, too. Not one of the art connoisseurs in Hinghwa had ever seen one like it.

When I first heard about the vase, in the early days of my enthusiasm for porcelain, I wanted to start right out on the sixty-mile trip by boat and chair to Hinghwa to see it.

"Oh, that was broken years ago," my husband said, "when we were at school in California. One of my younger brothers was sitting in a rocking chair in the parlor. Without realizing it, he rocked right up to that beautiful vase and smashed it to bits. I have hated rocking chairs ever since," he said.

I could understand his sorrow for in those days there was an active market for rare Chinese porcelains. A green hawthorn vase was like money in the bank, a commodity rarer than porcelain with missionaries.

Will and Elizabeth had another interesting, though vicarious, link with the Revolution through one of their orphans. The handsome child, whom they had "purchased" to save him from being sold into the slavery of a theatrical troupe, had returned from college in America to accept a position in the National Treasury department. In October of 1911, he had received shipment of a huge number of silver dollars from the mint for his inspection. He found them not up to standard weight. This was the usual state for dollars in circulation, which were bitten, rung, weighed, stamped and gouged to determine their weight or subtract a fraction from it, and to determine whether they were lead or silver. Mr. Sang thought new dollars should be up to standard, and, refusing a generous bribe for accepting them, returned the lot for reminting. Rumor has it that this money fell into the hands of the revolutionists and helped finance the Manchu downfall.

For a short time, China was divided as the result of the election of Mr. Sun Yat-sen of South China to the presidency. Having no ambition except for China's welfare, he soon yielded his office to Mr. Yuan Shi Kai, who represented the Northern provinces.

The custom of centuries inclined the people to authority from imperial Peking, which was again to be the capitol of China. The new republic limped along. "No revolution succeeds immediately," the politically informed pandits said. A change from the tyranny of the Manchus to a republican form of government will take time.

It was soon obvious that Mr. Yuan Shi Kai had served the Manchus too long. It is certain that like many others, he sincerely believed that only a central government through a strong-man could hold China together, and this parliament would not allow. When Yuan startled the world by announcing a new Empire with himself the emperor beginning with January, 1916, the mutinous southern provinces revolted and Japan declared her firm opposition. The double threat proved too much for Mr. Yuan who died in June of 1916.

The following November, Elizabeth was on her way to a conference in Foochow. The missions and the people pursued their day-to-day work while governments rose and fell around them. Hinghwa had just completed its own conference, and Elizabeth was overjoyed at the forward looking program it had adopted. Will had been sent to the General Conference in America earlier in the year. He had been detained for some months to receive medical aid for the headaches which had plagued him for many months. She had received letters saying that he was at last on his way back.

Spurred by gratitude that their senior missionary was returning in good health, Hinghwa Conference had voted a program which comprised his whole dream. There were to be five years of intensive evangelistic work and Bible study in all churches; there was to be an earnest effort to win the pagan members of every family represented in those churches; they were to strive for self-support, instead of depending upon gifts from America; they were to become Bible-reading churches in ability and fact; and the most important goal of all, every member, missionary and Chinese alike, was to become a Spirit-filled Christian.

Elizabeth could hardly wait to tell her husband about the magnificent program for the years ahead. She could hardly wait to see him, in fact. As her chair bounced along the familiar path, she planned her message of welcome. He would be in Yokohama on Saturday, so a cable from Foochow should reach him in time.

I asked her teasingly one day what the cable said. With her endearing chuckle, she replied, "What did you say to Francis each time he came home on leave from the army?" So we laughed together, at one in our love for our Brewster men, as in so much else.

"I can tell you, though, I sang my own Hallelujah Chorus all the way to Foochow. Will and I had been separated over and over through the years, through the demands of our work, illness or school for the children. Harold, the youngest, was now in school and the oldest was married. Will and I were free to start again. My heart was filled with praise to God for bringing us safely all this way. Will's letters were full of love and hope for our work. How happy I was that Thursday!"

"Whenever the chair-bearers stopped for tea, people crowded around to catch up on the news. Where were the boys now, and when was Mr. Brewster coming back? Was it true that the firstborn was about to give birth, and was "little brother" really old enough to go away to school? Well, well, it certainly was interesting! The family travelled about the world so much it was almost more than a person could do to keep track of them.

"I told them they spoke more truly than they knew. Why, when Mr. Brewster came home to join us in America in 1912, he didn't even recognize the third son, who had been away from home for three years! He thought Raymond was a friend the family had brought along to meet him. So you see, it is possible for even a good father to lose track of his children when they are away so much.

"But for everyone, the good news was that Will was coming back, and that I was on my way to meet him. Everyone rejoiced with me.

"How I counted the days. Thursday, the twenty-third, Friday, and then Saturday, the twenty-fifth, when Will would be in Yokohama reading my cable and sending one back to me. I thought about going on to Shanghai, but, because I had to speak at conference in Foochow, I doubted if I could make it in time. It would depend too much on whether there was a boat or not. Anyway, it seemed silly to be impatient, now that all our long separations were behind us."

From our mutual notes, I have made a summary of those family separations. I have no doubt Elizabeth with her phenomenal memory could have given them to me at one sitting if it had occurred to me to ask her. I have assembled them here with the scattered comments that identify each.

"1895 – While waiting for permission to return to our work after the Hua Sang massacre, Will and I took a trip north to rest a bit, and visit other stations. Mary and Francis remained at Sharp Peak with friends. We took the new baby with us.

"1897 – The family went to the States for a short furlough. Mary got whooping cough and was so frail as a result of it that we had to go back to China without her. My mother took care of her until after the Boxer trouble. She was gone so long, her brothers hardly remembered her.

"1904 – This was our next furlough. Will stayed in Boston for some months to give a course of lectures on missions. I went back to our work in Hinghwa with the children.

"1907 – Mary and Francis went off to school in Ohio. Dr. Leonard of the Board in New York accompanied them. He was the one who came out to investigate reports of luxurious living. The trip he gave those children! It was all strictly first class! I guess he tried to make up for some of the luxuries they had lacked all their lives.

"In 1908 – Will and I were sent to the General Conference. We took the two youngest with us, leaving the middle three with kind friends in Hinghwa. The two oldest were away at school. That time we were gone for only a few months.

"1910 – I was secretly troubled about my eye. It was time, too, for William and Raymond to be in school somewhere, so I took all five children home. Will stayed in Hinghwa. I had some medical treatment for my eye and had just found an inexpensive church boarding-school for the two boys when Will cabled me to come back at once. Because of illness in the mission staff, he needed me. I left Mary at school in Pittsburgh, Francis at Ohio Wesleyan, William and Raymond at Wilbraham in New England. When we got to Shanghai I put Edward in the American School there. The two youngest children, Karis and Harold, went back to Hinghwa with me.

"1911 – Francis had graduated from High School. He had been away for four years, so we brought him home to Hinghwa to be his father's secretary for a year.

"That fall I had to go to Peking about my eye. I took Karis, then only eight, to Shanghai and put her in school with Edward.

"1912 – I was sent home again as a delegate to the General Conference, partly because I had to have eye surgery. Fortunately, the eye did not have to be removed. I was still very ill and in much pain. Will cabled me to stay home. He said he would send the three youngest children to me in care of Francis. The Bishop had a plan for temporary work for Will, too, in the states, so he would probably join us soon.

"1913 – Will came home, not to the work on the Pacific coast as we had hoped, but to lecture again in Boston. I could not endure the cold there, and it was decided I should remain in California where all the children, except Mary, were in school. She went to Boston to get acquainted with her father, keep house for him and act as his secretary. She had been away from us for six years that time.

"1914 – Will had just come to California to rest and enjoy his whole family for a few months before going back to Hinghwa, when the Bishop asked him to return at once. Illness in the mission staff separated us again. I was too ill myself to return with him. I stayed with the three oldest boys and the youngest in California, while Mary, Edward and Karis went to China with their father.

"By December I was well enough to travel. Leaving Francis

and William in college, I went back, accompanied by Harold and Raymond. We felt so awful about Will's failure to recognize Raymond, that we thought a year with us in China was more important than the school he would miss.

"1915 – That was our happiest year as a family. All of us were together that summer on the mountain, except Francis and William who were still in school in California. Karis and Edward had brought home guests from the Shanghai School—two children whose parents lived in a remote northwest China mission station so far away they couldn't go home for vacations. We weren't the only missionary family separated for years at a time, you know.

We rented a second house on the mountain to make room for all of us, and what a wonderful summer it was, marred only by a siege of paratyphoid for Harold. All my happiest family memories are there on the top of that mountain. You have seen it too, my dear. You and Francis were there on your honeymoon, I know. The hot sun, the cool breezes from the blue and green ocean, the endless hills, the sunsets, the lighthouse!

Through all my summers there, the greatest joy of everyday came just after tea, when all of us hiked down to the lookout rocks to watch for Will. It was always a game with us to see who could spot him first. Far below us on the plain there was a dark green patch, a longan orchard, and near it a temple. The road from the city was first visible to us there. Watching that spot, someone would see either a sedan chair or a man carrying a white parasol, and shout, "There he is! There is papa!" The bigger children would go bounding down to meet him; the little ones stayed on the rock with me. About one third of the way up the hill, the path swung out into the open so that he could see us. What joyful waving then, he with his white pith-helmet, I with my handkerchief, the babies with sticks or whatever they had.

"At the resting place at the foot of the last long climb, a spring bubbled up and made a little rocky pool. Wild orchid lilies blossomed in the cold waters and Will always stooped to pull one or two for me. He never liked to come home from a trip empty handed—he always brought some small gift.

"That year was our twenty-fifth anniversary in Hinghwa, and everyone made much of it. There were parties and commending speeches, red satin banners and gifts of all sorts from loving friends. That was the year Will made his wonderful report on the Indigenous Church, too. Raymond was there to help buy the stone and do the surveying for the new orphanage and industrial plant out at Yellowstone. Will wanted to live in the country, where he could personally oversee the work of training farmers on the recently purchased flat, plantation fields so that they would be ready for farming in Borneo. Mary and George were married that year, too. Such a happy, beautiful wedding!

"1916 – Will was elected to go to the General Conference at Saratoga Springs. This time he was the one who needed medical attention. Raymond went home with him and stayed with him the whole time. I remained in Hinghwa as appointed acting missionary in Will's place. In San Francisco, Will saw William and Francis, and asked William to go back to China for a year or two. He wanted the industrial machinery brought down from Shanghai and someone to help install it, both of which William could do. About that time Mary and George, who had been stationed in West China, were transferred by the Bishop back to Hinghwa. How happy we were over that! How providential it proved!"

These were the comings-and-goings to which her Chinese friends referred. No wonder they could hardly keep track of the family! Small wonder, Will hardly knew some of his own children! This is the sacrifice missionaries made in the days when it took a month to cross the ocean, for letters as well as people. Fortunately, the years are long to a child, and the happiest, most enduring memories are made in moments.

Watching me make his favorite strawberry jam one day at our farm, my husband said,

"I remember watching my mother make jam. I can see her in her blue-and-white striped apron stirring the stuff so it wouldn't burn. She skimmed the foam off into a saucer and gave it to me to eat."

"I thought the Chinese cook did that work," I replied in surprise, as I skimmed the foam into a bowl, noting, with a smile, that now the pink stuff had no appeal to him.

"She did, but mother had to teach her American cooking, and often helped make the things we liked."

"Were you children happy? I remember hearing that your mother spent a month with each of you when you were born and then turned you over to the Chinese amah and went back to her work."

His face grew thoughtful at the implied criticism.

"That's true, she did. But I never realized any lack of attention. You know yourself the amahs took better care of our own boys than you could have done. When we got older and began to roam the country, Mother hired a young man to stay right with us. Sure, the work came first. We all knew that. Maybe that was what held us together, scattered as we were all over the world. One thing I knew from the time I was a little kid—how much my father and mother loved each other."

On Saturday morning, November 25, 1916, as their houseboat approached Foochow, Elizabeth watched again the long familiar pageant of serene russet mountains and tawny river. As usual the Min River was seething with watercraft. Suddenly, there was a loud hale, and as Elizabeth's boatmen answered, another houseboat pulled away from the tangle of boats and approached hers. A white clad figure came out of its cabin and waved.

"Why, it's Pa Miner," exclaimed Elizabeth to the Hinghwa friends with her. "Wherever can he be going at Conference time?"

When the boats were alongside, Mr. Miner jumped aboard, and, hat in hand, came to stand silently before Elizabeth.

Several days earlier, on the deck of a ship steaming up the Yangtze, Bishop Lewis, a beloved friend and advisor to both Will and Elizabeth, was visiting with some shipmates. In the midst of a sentence, he stopped. Then in trembling awe he said, "I hear bells. I hear the joy-bells of heaven. They are welcoming Dr. Brewster."

Some days later when the Bishop arrived in Chungking, he received the cable which told him what he already knew. On November 22, enroute to China, Will had become ill and died in a Chicago hospital.

The cable, unaccountably delayed in Hong Kong, reached

Hinghwa after Elizabeth's departure. Her son, William, travelled through the night trying to overtake her, but did not reach Foochow until Saturday afternoon. He found Elizabeth, almost frantic with grief, at Hua Nan College, watched over by two dear friends, Miss Lydia Trimble and Miss Ethel Wallace, whose names she has gratefully recorded.

On Monday night, she and William began the trip back to Hinghwa. In the villages along the way, sorrowing people came out to walk beside her chair. The reason for William's hurried trip through the night had spread into the remotest mountain villages. A man from one of them, who had come down with a load of charcoal, told her that his whole village had wailed as for a father.

From the Chinese Christians, too, who had come to weep with her in Hinghwa, came the endlessly repeated words, "My father! Oh, my father!" In a memorial service held by the non-Christian gentry and literati of the community, one of his discussion group members cried out, using the special name they had given him as a mark of honor and acceptance as one of themselves, "Oh, Sui Dong, Sui Dong, why could you not leave us your vision? We need guidance, and there is no one who has your vision!"

For Elizabeth, in that despairing hour when she felt she had lost both God and Will, there came the healing assurance, "Why, I am right here! Love like ours cannot die. I am right here, watching beside you!" She accepted it as from both God and Will.

For me, there are Father Brewster's own words, "The first duty of a Christian in any land is not to make converts to a church, but to represent Christ. All his doings should remind others, or illustrate to them, the life of Him of whom it was said, "He went about doing good."

Bishop William X. Ninde's visit to the Methodist Mission in Foochow, 1894

Circled: Elizabeth Brewster
Second row, left to right: Ruth Sites; Mary Ninde; Bishop William X. Ninde; Elizabeth Ninde, wife of Bishop Ninde; Mrs. Ahok; Lydia Trimble.

Elizabeth Fisher Brewster

William Nesbitt Brewster

Elizabeth with children, possibly from the orphanage

Mountain cottages for vacations during the hot summers.
Four miles from Hinghwa City.

Missionary woman in a sedan-chair, ready for a country trip,
carrying all her own food and bedding.

Bible Women

Fuzhou (Foochow) Harbor

Bridge of Ten Thousand Ages

Guthrie Middle School welcome banner for the Brewster Family during their 1984 China tour on the occassion of the 100-year anniversary of the founding of the Mission work in Hinghwa (Putien) in the Fujian Province.

Union Hospital in Fuzhou, founded by Dr. George Hollister and the Methodist Mission. (1984 Brewster Family China tour)

Brewster Family being welcomed at Guthrie Middle School. (1984 Brewster Family China tour)

Karis Brewster Manton, daughter of Elizabeth

Brewster Family and Church congregation in Hinghwa
(1984 Brewster Family China tour)

Elizabeth in Oroville, California, after being expelled from China by the Communist regime in 1950.

Back row, from left:
Katherine, Mary Brewster Woods, Barbara B. Ward, Phillip Ward, William Fisher Brewster, Jr., Nathaniel Brewster, May Douglass Brewster, Mary Hollister

Front row, from left:
William Brewster, Jr., Elizabeth Brewster, George Hollister

CHAPTER EIGHT

Part of the Answer

It is characteristic of Elizabeth that she says little about her own personal suffering. Heroics have no place in her life. Even the loss of her husband was subordinate to her own complete obedience to God's plan for her.

When she was appointed to carry on Will's work, she accepted the task and gave her best to it. Elizabeth's best has never been inadequate.

All China was in turmoil. The province of Fukien was involved in the political aspirations of northern and southern Chinese rivals for power. Overseas, World War I was tearing up Europe. Elizabeth's older sons were heading into that conflict. From her home in "Yellowstone," the new country site of the Orphanage and Industrial School, she kept her eyes on the political and military situations, her heart on her work. Her safety and that of her scattered children she trusted, as always, to God.

In one of Harry Emerson Fosdick's penetrating sermons, he asks us to consider whether we are a part of the problem or part of the answer. Elizabeth is always part of the answer.

Out of those days, when her grief was new, comes a little story given me by one of her sons. From her desk in the Yellowstone home, she looked out one day to see a child leading an obviously blind woman toward the house. Meeting them at the door, Elizabeth was startled to hear the child ask, "Is this the place where they have the love of God?"

Touched, both by this description of her work and their pitiful condition, Elizabeth invited them in to hear their story. The mother, a widow without family or sons, had tried to support herself and daughter by working the tiny fields belonging to her husband. When blindness overtook her, she rented the spots of land to a farmer who failed to pay for their use. Sick, blind and starving, she was discovered by a Bible woman who told her, "In spite of your experience, there are people in this world who practice the love of God. Go to the school in Yellowstone. You will find such people there."

This love, which the two helpless ones had visualized as rice in a bowl and a place to sleep, was realized when Elizabeth received the mother in the School for the Blind and the child in the Orphanage. The mother learned to weave the smooth mats for which there was always a market; the child was educated for useful living.

Nowhere have I described the work of those wonderful workers known as Bible women. In the *China Christian Advocate,* for March 1917, preserved because it contains a memorial to William Nesbitt Brewster, I find the following description of a Bible woman written by Miss Althea Todd, cherished friend of all the Brewsters:

"In the Hinghwa Conference there are ten Bible women employed by the Woman's Foreign Mission Society. Each woman is in touch with three times that number of preaching places and ten times as many villages.

"Who are these women? All have been idol worshippers. Most of them have been brought to Christ through suffering or through failure of the idols to help them at some crucial time. Few received any education as children. One tells us that she heard the Gospel at 32 years of age. She was a widow with three children to support by making hats. As she worked she learned to read the Primer, one word at a time. Later she entered the Hinghwa Woman's School. Her son is now a preacher and she is a Bible woman. Another Bible woman has a husband and two children to support. While the baby was small she carried it on her back when she went out to preach. Nearly all the women have from one-to-three women dependent upon them.

"Women are supposed to spend five years in the Women's School before they are appointed as Bible women. Some preacher's wives, with less training, go out to help their husbands. Others cannot complete the course, but can go out and invite women to come to church. One such, was an ardent heathen. She heard the gospel from a preacher's wife. Then she was carrying a heavy load of wood to market. Now, with her straw sandals, a picture roll, hymn book, Bible, quinine and santonine (worm medicine), she travels, hither and thither through the mountain regions. On these journeys, she calls upon the people to cast their burdens at the foot of the Cross and be saved.

"What is the work of the Bible woman? First, and most important of all, they live Christianity in a heathen environment. The neighbors soon know that a different kind of person has come among them. She tells them why she is different.

"When sorrow comes, she goes to comfort. She helps make the burial clothes and buy the coffin for the anxious aged one. She ministers by the sick bed, comforts at the funeral, makes merry at the wedding, rejoices at the birth. She teaches the mothers how to care for their babies and their homes. She advises the women not to cast out or sell the baby girls, or bind their feet. A heathen mother praises her child for scolding, lying, stealing successfully.

"The Bible woman calls the children together for meetings and teaches them to sing and pray and obey. She helps the mothers and daughters-in-law to live in peace. She teaches the women to read and to pray. She prepares them in their studies for admission as probationers. She tells them not to fear the evil spirits.

"One woman had been told by a fortune teller that she would certainly die within the year. She wept with terror. She grew weaker and weaker. The Bible woman told her that God controlled life and death. She believed and is well and happy in the church.

"As the result of an afternoon meeting, an opium user confessed her sins and with confidence trusted God to deliver her. She is now in the Hinghwa hospital. She helps to solve the problems of the women. They are her sisters.

"How many women are reached in a year? In meetings conducted in 286 villages, the missionaries talked to 24,744 people. The Bible women follow up this work. They talk to the ever busy women in the fields or in their homes.

"A woman of 83 years of age was met by the roadside. She had worshipped Buddha at nineteen places and had received no rest for her soul. Another old woman was seen walking and weeping because her only grandson had died. Another woman was seen running away from her husband, because he was not good to her. The Bible woman accepts all these situations as opportunities. She administers reproof or teaching and tells each of the true and living God whom she serves."

Reading this definition of a Christian woman and her activities in China forty years ago, has been a salutary experience for me. I wonder what would happen in our country, today, if the millions of church women were freed from their boards and committee meetings to do this personal, Christ-like service in families and community. I wonder.

Like their American sisters, these seemingly inexhaustible women had their limitations. Elizabeth's notes record sadly that one of the great evangelistic campaigns she helped conduct in 1918 would have had spectacular results if there had been adequate follow-up work. This resulted chiefly because several Bible women implored her not to urge the handing-in of names by those in the audience interested in having a Bible woman call on them.

"Just leave it to those really interested to hand in their names voluntarily. We simply cannot get around to all these multitudes of people who, unthinkingly, give their names to the ushers."

Nevertheless, the inspiration of that revival made 1918 memorable for Elizabeth. A Miss Cora Brown was in charge of the campaign. Elizabeth was assisting her with teaching and hymn singing. Dismayed by the lack of response from the audience, Miss Brown said she wished she had a chorus containing a vital Christian truth to teach them. With some detail, Elizabeth records the rest of the story:

"If we do not have one, we will make one," I told her.

"So I stayed in my room until, after much prayer and thought, I had composed the following chorus:

Li ning Siong- Da'
Ui du Teng-hu:
A- So chia duda li!
Du li keng ning

Come, acknowledge God
For He is your Heavenly Father.
Jesus invites you now,
Come, willingly, acknowledge your Heavenly Father
He acknowledges you as his son.

"'God our Father, Jesus our Mediator,' became the great theme and central thought of that revival. This chorus initiated the use of choruses in such meetings all over China. Tens-of-thousands, who could not read, learned to sing it; its power was great.

"On Bi Ciu Island, we encountered fear, tension and closed hearts. We began using the chorus, and finally hands began to beat time, lips seemed to be forming the words. One day, I heard an old man working alone in his field chanting the music. The next day, a preacher began a tedious explanation, thinking the people didn't understand the message. A young man called out impatiently,

"'Don't talk. We understand. Just teach us to sing it.'

"Then the whole audience began to sing, and we had a wonderful response."

Elizabeth's concern was not in teaching singing. She was using the medium of music, which Chinese people love, to share a truth which had changed her own life.

Proof that the idea was effective, was not lacking. In one village, an elderly woman, a devout Buddhist, learned the chorus. Almost becoming rhapsodical with the import of her new understanding, she told everyone that came near her,

"I have a Heaven Father! I have a Heaven Father!"

One day she detained a group of women from her village, and, with shining face, announced her good news. Then the light faded, as she realized that the women she addressed had long been members of the Christian church in the village.

"Did you know God is my Heaven Father?"

"Oh, yes, we have known it for a long time," they replied, smiling at her enthusiasm.

"You knew, and you never told me!" the newly aware child of God reproached them.

Meanwhile, the political tension increased. In Foochow, a provincial governor, with strong north China sympathies, was in power. In Canton to the south, revolution was building up in protest against the northern government, which had not only favored Mr. Yuan Shi Kai's plan to restore the monarchy, but also Japan's demands on China. Throughout Elizabeth's area, young men were leaving home to join the southern army. Others formed resistance bands called "The People's Army," in order to stay at home. One morning, Elizabeth discovered several hundred of the latter encamped in the Yellowstone temples and in an unoccupied government school. Since most of them were men who had known her from childhood, she expected no trouble. When they began to make levies on the people for funds, however, she had to act as mediator.

Because the Christian church was often the only organization in a village and because it was known to have contacts with America, its members were subject to immediate levy. It became Elizabeth's duty, then, to advise church pastors and army officers alike that members of Christian churches should not be exempt from supporting a patriotic cause.

On the other hand, it was not fair to tax them more frequently or more heavily than other citizens. Pastors should not be asked to collect taxes from their parishioners, nor should they try to protect them from their civic duty. Often she was called on to testify as to the ability of church members to pay, especially when the levy on them had been ruinous.

By such careful, prayerful efforts, the local churches as such, were kept out of the civil war. When fighting began, Elizabeth had the Orphanage property boundaries clearly marked and received the pledge of local troops never to violate that neutral ground.

As usual she kept up itinerating far into the country. Because she was frequently seen travelling the roads alone and unharmed, the northern general who had taken Hinghwa City, called her in for questioning on her relationship to the People's Army.

"I have no relationship with it, except that I have known most of the troops since they were babies. My husband and I have traveled this territory as friends of the people for twenty-five years. That's why I am safe at all times on the country roads."

Impressed by her reply, the commanding general gave her permission, in writing, to remain at Yellowstone to care for her orphans and refugee women, asking only that she promise to keep the property neutral.

Some time later, one of his subordinates attacked the local troops, and was driven back. During the fighting, Elizabeth scouted her property, while shells were falling on it, to see that no local troops were violating its neutrality. A few days later, the irate field officer wrote her a letter saying if she persisted in staying at Yellowstone, he would not be responsible for what happened to the orphanage or the village when the main army arrived.

With her two letters in hand, Elizabeth went in to see him. Still sore from his defeat, he received her with less than cordiality. Among other things, he scornfully referred to an earlier move by the People's Army and asked Elizabeth why she had ordered such foolish strategy.

This stung her pride. "If I were in command of the People's Army, I assure you, I would have avoided such a foolish move. Since I have no connection with it or its command, I will not accept credit or blame for their strategy."

When he demanded that she leave the orphanage and go into Hinghwa, she asked him if he would provide quarters for her hundreds of orphans and refugees.

"We are not concerned for their safety," he replied.

"Then," replied Elizabeth, "Since you try to coerce me by

threatening to give the army freedom to burn and loot our village, the city where you are is the last place I shall seek refuge. I have your letter and also one from your commanding officer, which gives me permission to remain at Yellowstone. I am a citizen of a country which maintains friendly relations with your government in the north. If necessary, I will send both letters to my Consul in Foochow." So saying, Elizabeth left his headquarters.

When the People's Army was finally beaten and dispersed, the Northern army burned and looted nearby villages, but Yellowstone was not touched. Its people gave Elizabeth full credit for having saved them from both armies. Two years later, when she returned from the General Conference in America, she arrived at Yellowstone after dark. Every house displayed candles to light her way. A fusillade of firecrackers accompanied her through the streets. This is the Chinese way of showing respect and affection.

This is one of Elizabeth's favorite stories, one she has told me many times. The memory of that joyous return always accompanies her narrative of her last ride through the street, when she left China in 1951, under such different circumstances.

One of my own favorite stories took place during that period of rivalry between the north and south. She speaks so often of receiving guidance from the Holy Spirit, that I asked her one day to give me an example of such guidance. She sat looking out the window for a moment, her eyes narrowing, as if to focus on the picture emerging.

"We were to have a district meeting for women in the city and I was on the program. Word reached us that the Southern Army was retreating toward the city, pursued by the Northern Army. On the day of the meeting, women came in from the district, in spite of the fact that the Southern Army had reached the city. The small missionary staff withdrew from the danger zone and begged me to accompany them, saying, 'What shall we tell your children if harm comes to you?' My children know I move as led by the Spirit. I have received no guidance to leave, I told them.

"As I have told you before, my dear, it is often necessary to go quietly on with the work at hand, knowing the Spirit will speak when it is necessary. It was so that day. I sent my missionary friends on with my blessing and went to the meeting. The Chinese women, with their innate courtesy, neither urged me to stay or to go. At four that afternoon, as the program closed, they crowded around me.

"Are you leaving for Foochow now?" they asked. And suddenly I was able to answer, "No, I am not. I have a sudden strong conviction, I must stay here."

The women laughed, in relief. "Here we are, like a flock of baby chicks, wondering if our mother hen is going to leave us!"

"Just a few moments later, the Chinese pastor and his wife came in great haste, looking for me. The Northern Army had arrived, asking the use of the church for their general and staff that night, and the grounds for the troops. Only one missionary staff person had the authority to give this permission. The pastor also brought word that our own army was camped outside the city—eating supper, not knowing their pursuers had overtaken them.

"Don't ask me where their scouts were; you know the armies of those days! I told the pastor to hurry back and open the doors for the general and let the troops use the grounds when they arrived. Then I sent a messenger to the Southern Army to get going."

"'You mean, God was on the side of the Southern Army?' I asked in amusement. She considered this.

"No, I wouldn't say so, even though I was! I do know that He is on the side of all people alike. As the result of that guidance, the Southern Army was well on its way the next morning when the Northern Army moved out, and only minor rear-guard fighting took place.

"The general sent an officer to thank me for the use of the church and asked what he could do to show his appreciation. I asked that he forbid his soldiers to loot, promising that if he would do this, the city and village would gladly meet his demands for provisions. The suffering of the people from looting in those days was appalling, as you know. He not only sent me word he would forbid looting, but he kept the promise. Our whole area was spared that calamity.

"That was one time when guidance saved much slaughter and unspeakable horror and hardship for our Hinghwa people.

"Sometimes, during those troubled years, there was no time to wait for guidance. One day, I opened the street gate just as a group of Northern soldiers marched past. To my dismay, I saw that they were escorting one of our Southern men to his execution. He called to me, begging me to intercede for him. I stood there not able to say a word. I knew him as an inquirer in Christianity, but more as one who had levied cruel taxes on our people. At the moment, I was harboring deserters from the Northern and Southern armies who had come to me for sanctuary, in addition to all my orphanage children, blind women and the refugee women and girls from the town.

"I was already suspected as being too friendly with the Southern troops. I dared not risk all those dependent upon me by recognizing the boy who called to me for help. He went on to his execution when I shut the gate. That night I lay awake longing for Will and his wisdom. Dealing with war and armies was not my special ability. I wondered if I was capable of doing God's work in our war-torn province. When no sign of any kind came to comfort or correct me, I knew I must carry on."

The Chinese name most frequently given to Elizabeth is "Shepherdess Mother," a very appropriate description of one who saved hundreds, while mourning the one gone beyond her love.

CHAPTER NINE

A Daughter-in-law for Elizabeth

Two years later, in October of 1921, I was discovering China myself. On the night I arrived in Foochow, all the schools were marching to celebrate the tenth anniversary of the revolution. I stood at the window of my room in a house high above the river watching the parade cross the Bridge of Ten Thousand Ages. All I could see was a long wavering line of colored paper lanterns and their flickering reflection in the black water.

Leaning out the window, it was my turn to hear for the first time the hum of multitudes of people living outdoors, rising like a cloud. I had been told to expect strange sights and sounds in China, and I had found them on the earth, below, and in the heavens above. Even as I listened to the sound of the Orient, I watched a crooked, red-crescent glow against the eastern sky with misgivings.

"Is that the moon?" I asked in amazement.

"No. That's a charcoal pit high on the mountains. They are burning charcoal up there tonight."

So began for me, the nine most wonderful years of my life. I had been sent as a missionary teacher to the Anglo-Chinese College in Foochow. On the little coastal steamer taking me to my destination, I had met a young man named Francis Brewster, who was the eldest son of Elizabeth and Will. It was a brief encounter. We were two individuals without beginning or end, interested in the present moment in a world of our own making.

Three years later, we were contemplating marriage. Elizabeth, in Foochow for a series of meetings, had sent a note asking if she might call. According to custom, I invited her to tea. We sat on the wisteria-curtained veranda, making polite conversation, measuring each other, as people will when meeting for the first time. How I appeared to her, she has never said. I saw a short, stout woman with limp colorless hair, who wore glasses with one frosted lens. On the cheek bone under the visible deep-blue eye there was a large wart out of which grew another smaller one. As I listened to her low rich voice, I tried not to stare at this blemish. I had heard that she was an outstanding missionary, but I had no idea what that meant. I was young, absorbed in the enchantment of China. Being a wonderful missionary, doubtless, would come later.

"Isn't it interesting," I heard her saying, "that the girl Francis is courting should live in the same house and the very room which I occupied when his father courted me more than thirty years ago?"

To me it seemed downright improbable. Looking at her with disinterested eyes, I could not imagine her as ever having been young and desirable. To the young, the old have always been old. I knew nothing about all her marvelous years of service in Hinghwa, or the great love between her and Will. How could I know how much glory had departed from her with his death?

She was in America on furlough when we were married the following year. Because inland travel those days was by sedan chair, we used the week my husband's business allowed, to take a tiny steamer down to Hinghwa. There was no time to go farther. He showed me his city home and then took me up to the summer house on the mountain, to visit his sister and her husband. One night as we stood on the open veranda watching the beam from the lighthouse sweep its great circle over the dark sea, I was startled by a strange, guttural cough from the enveloping night.

My husband laughed. "What's the matter? What are you afraid

of? It's only a tiger up on the hill behind us. They always sound closer than they are."

If I had known then, what only much later I was to learn about his father and mother, I should have been better prepared for his lighthearted disregard of all danger, be it flood, typhoon, war, pestilence or bandits. Even with a live tiger just around the corner it was still, "What's the matter? What are you afraid of?" Literally, I was afraid of being eaten, but already, I had learned to be ashamed of admitting such a concern to this "Daniel" I had married.

We travelled back to Foochow by sedan chair and boat. At the village on the river, while waiting for the launch, the people came out to talk with my husband and gaze at me, his bride. Among them, was an unkempt woman carrying a plump baby, naked except for an elongated bib. The mother came close, smiled, and held the dirty child out to me, saying something in a dialect I did not understand.

"What does she want?" I asked my husband, anxiously.

"She wants you to bless her baby so that she can go to school and be lucky in marriage like you," he reported, grinning at the obvious self-flattery.

"But I'm not a minister," I protested. "Tell her I will ask God to bless her child." I spoke the necessary words, and the woman drew back into the murmuring crowd.

"They are saying my mother would have taken the child in her arms," reported my husband, then called out something which made the people laugh. In my heart, I knew I had been compared to his mother and had been found wanting. This, I uncomfortably realized, was serious. Traditionally a bride is unhappy because her cooking cannot compare with that of her mother-in-law. To consider a clean white dress more important than fondling a baby, was to be found wanting in the expression of love, and that in a country where a smile or a friendly word is so greatly appreciated. I was too new in China to realize this fully, but my husband knew it and tried to cover for me. It took years of living before I learned that words spoken without such love are no blessing, even when spoken from a pulpit. Elizabeth would have held the child in her arms and blessed it herself with love!

It would be false to convey the impression that from that moment I accepted Elizabeth as a saint, only slightly lower than the angels. Nothing could be less true. Elizabeth is no saint, and I have never thought of her as such. Added to the natural suspicion between a man's wife and his mother, there was one incident in those early years which aroused hostility in me and turned my heart from her.

To begin with, we saw very little of each other. A trip of two days and a night by sedan chair is something to reckon with, especially with small children. She had been in America until the birth of our first son. After that, I visited my people in Madison, Wisconsin for another year. After my return, Elizabeth made our home, headquarters, when she came to Foochow on church business. There was very little time on such occasions for becoming acquainted.

Finally, the opportunity came for a visit from her. To celebrate, I planned a tea to which I invited her oldest friends. Most of them were my friends, too, the charming white-haired aristocracy of all the missions. To honor them, the cook, houseboy, gardener and I planned a beautiful party. Since we all followed the European custom of eight o'clock dinners, teas were always ample and delicious. Cook was to prepare all the house specialties, his own three-layer, gold cake, filled and covered with chocolate buttercream; my favorite moist black chocolate cake with an inch-high fluff of white icing; the hot rolls, that were the envy of every cook in town; the molasses cookies, fragile as lace; the delicious macaroons, whose secret was still our own; all these and more were to delight my guests.

Since it was winter, we decided to serve around the open fire in the living room. When I came down at four, everything was ready. The fire was glowing, not smoking. Roses and chrysanthemums filled the sapphire-blue bowl on the mantel. The table, where I was to pour, was covered with my loveliest convent-embroidered cloth. The cups were stacked properly with their handles turned toward my left. By each chair stood a small table of gleaming black lacquer, set with silver and a beautiful Canton china plate, which in this country, is inaccurately, called "famille rose."

Everything was as it should be. Elizabeth joined me, dressed in a pretty dark-blue satin. It was said of her in Foochow that when she was young, she was always in every way next year's model. I do not remember her that way, but she was a poised, commanding little woman, strongly reminiscent of Queen Victoria.

When the guests arrived, Wong, the butler, brought me the pot of boiling water and the party began. I poured innumerable cups of tea for the others, coffee for Elizabeth, who does not like tea. Everything was easy and delightful until one of the guests asked me my nationality. I told her I was American of Norwegian parentage. Then to my amazement, Elizabeth said,

"Yes, Francis is the only one of my children not engaged or married to someone with a good English name.

I looked at her thinking it was an unfortunate joke, but when she went on to list the names of those married to her children, I knew mine was a real grievance to her.

Determined to make light of the episode, I made it worse by laughing, "What's more, my parents came from Norway third class, but then, I guess the Mayflower Brewsters did, too." This really offended Elizabeth, who replied frostily,

"There was only one class on the Mayflower!" It was clear to all of us she did not consider that class, third!

At this unhappy moment, the two starched amahs brought in our small sons, Bill and Tony. Elizabeth drew them to her, proudly displaying them to her friends. Obviously, there was no ancestral stigma on them!

When I reported this incident to my husband, he laughed.

"You are married to me, not to my mother. Besides this is China. You have given me two wonderful sons. If you had no other virtues, that alone would make you an ideal wife!"

To his everlasting credit, my husband never criticized his mother or compared me unfavorably to her. I wish he had talked more about his parents and their work. Life was so exciting for us, that years had passed before I discovered for myself the "prideful tradition" into which I had married. Since this is Elizabeth's story, my own fabulous years in China have no place here, except as they help explain her or the times in which we lived. Sometimes during her visits at our farm these past summers, something of my life emerges out of our conversations. Such an incident took place one day when a friend brought her flowers. She was charmed when Elizabeth received them in both hands, bowing in thanks.

Speaking to her friend's delight, Elizabeth explained that in China it was the courteous way to accept gifts, because the whole body inclines in gracious humility, along with the outstretched arms. "It was also polite," she continued, "to return half the gift. I hope you don't expect me to return half these flowers! Our customary gifts were oranges and eggs, of which we always refused half. In the country near us, the approved way to honor a guest was to set before him a dish of four eggs, poached in sweetened water. Of these, it was courteous to eat two and leave two." Then with a little shudder, "For me, it would have been easier to refuse all four!"

This seemed a good time to tell about my first Christmas as a bride, which made Elizabeth shudder in earnest.

"I was in my upstairs sitting room one December, when Wong, the butler, came up to announce that a man named Long Tom, a longshoreman, was waiting downstairs to see me. I told Wong I had no business with Long Tom. All shipping business was done at my husband's office. Wong, smilingly, insisted Long Tom wanted to see me; I went reluctantly downstairs to find a tall man in the hall. Outside the door was a line of coolies carrying assorted loads. I stopped in puzzled amazement. I was used to peddlers at the door, but not in procession, carrying a profusion of wares. Long Tom bowed and said,

"This belong feast time for Missy. Master Brewster make plenty business for Long Tom. Long Tom bring Missy presents." He beckoned to the first coolie, who entered and set a tall basket of oranges on the floor. I exclaimed in pleasure at the lovely fruit.

"You likee?" beamed Long Tom.

"I likee very much," I beamed back at him.

The houseboy gave the coolie a silver dollar, which he took and withdrew. This, I knew, was the custom. Sensing that something was expected of me, I peered out the door and exclaimed joyously over the load of tangerines the next man carried.

"You likee?" Long Torn inquired, courteously. When I assented, the coolie entered, set down the tangerines, took his dollar and withdrew. I now looked eagerly to see what came next, each time expressing even greater pleasure to try to erase the worried expression on Wong's face. It was an unheard of array. There were, in addition to the oranges and tangerines, a live turkey—a rare object in China—a live goose, a bamboo cage of chickens, a whole quarter of beef, a leg of mutton, a side of pork, a load of beautiful temple candles, a load of assorted imported canned-goods, cigarettes, bottles of wine, a huge pile of firecrackers and as a grand finale, a huge tiered wedding cake. I knew Wong must have handed out twenty dollars, but my housekeeping sense told me it was a bargain at that.

I invited Long Tom into the living room where Wong served us tea. "It's a good thing my husband has just built a cold-storage plant," I told him. "Otherwise those wonderful meats would spoil." I assured him, quite truthfully, that I had never received such magnificent gifts in my life. It seemed to me he lingered a long time over his tea before he finally excused himself. Just then I heard the first faraway clanging of my husband's rickshaw bell. It was lunch time! As my husband ran up the front steps, I beat Wong to the door, throwing it open, eager to tell my husband about our good luck.

"What goes on here?" he demanded as he kissed me. "Where did all this stuff come from? What's the livestock doing in our front hall?"

"Oh, darling, Long Tom brought them. They are our Christmas presents from him."

"Christmas presents! Long Tom!" Then to Wong, standing, unhappily, among the assorted food stuffs, he shouted, "You know better, even if Missy doesn't. Where is Long Tom?"

Like magic, the man appeared from the back terrace. My husband took him to the living room and ordered tea. While they waited for tiffin, they talked. From the upstairs window, I watched some time later as Long Tom went out the front gate, followed by all the coolies carrying away the turkey, the goose, the beef, the lamb, the chickens, the wine, the cigarettes, the canned goods, the firecrackers and the beautiful cake.

When they were gone, I went down to see what was left. Wong was, unhappily, gathering up some scattered oranges while my husband scolded.

To me he said, "You accepted all the gifts Long Tom had prepared for all his customers. Some of those articles, like the meat, the wine, the cake, and the canned goods weren't even his. He had just borrowed them to make a good show. We lost plenty of face and about eighteen dollars. Oh, well, let's forget it and have lunch. Just remember the rule, accept only half the gift. In a case like today, just one-half of the first."

How Elizabeth laughed at the story. "No wonder poor Wong looked unhappy! I was in the States that year or I would have heard that story. It's a good thing you had Francis to make things right, or you would have been ruined in China. Lots of Americans are, not knowing why, and usually for much less cause."

I wondered, as she spoke, if she had any idea what had estranged me from her for so long, reflecting that people don't have to be of different race or culture to offend each other, unwittingly.

It was for political reasons, however, that our happy years in China came to a close. Indignation against Japan, in particular, for her inroads on China's sovereignty, inflamed the students until they attacked all businesses, indiscriminately. My husband, who was managing an import-export company for a Shanghai bank, sympathized with China and the revolution. This did not save his business. It suffered more than most. Our lives were threatened; a home-made bomb disrupted a dinner party; people buying our American dried fish were beaten; one of our associates was killed. To add to this terror, up-country bandits set up territorial governments, which made travelling unsafe and business even more precarious. We were all at the mercy of the nearest, strongest bandit or warlord.

I came home from a morning dancing class one noon to find the gate open and unguarded. Wong failed to meet me at the front door. Uneasy, I ran upstairs. At the top stood a Chinese man, wringing his hands, urging, incoherently, that I run for help. Bandits, he said, were about to kill my husband, if they hadn't already done so. I ran first to the nursery, but the children were not there. Looking down the back stairwell, I saw all our household gathered in a tight cluster, looking up at me with scared, slightly green faces. The cook held one child, the sturdy gateman the other. Obviously our boys were going to be protected, come what may.

Wong told me the strange man was the manager of the bank of which my husband was the advisor. It seemed that several weeks earlier, one of the bandit chiefs had deposited payroll money for his soldiers at the bank. It had been accepted by a Chinese clerk working overtime. He had given a deposit receipt that he signed. Some days later, he resigned and left town, taking the money with him. When the paymaster came in to collect his money, no record of deposit or the money could be found, and so the deposit receipt was not honored. The paymaster, naturally furious, went for help. The manager called my husband on the phone, and fled out the back door just as the armed bandits came in the front. An alert clerk shoved the cash-cart into the vault and slammed and locked the tile door. My husband, if he went to the bank, was probably dead, as the bank manager feared, said Wong.

I ran the several blocks of deserted street to the bank. The word "bandit" had sent everyone to cover. Breathless, I ran up the steps of the quiet building. Everyone stood motionless in his place, except my husband who sat smiling at the manager's desk. Around the room stood the bandits with their guns in ready position. "What's the matter?" greeted my husband, cheerfully. "What you all excited about? I'm all right." Speechless, I looked from one bandit to the next. "I haven't got their money, why should they shoot me?" he said answering my wordless question. "You go home to the children. Take them over to one of the mission houses. I'll be home when I can calm these boys down. I'm waiting now for the Consul." He came home hours later, tired but exhilarated by the incident, having convinced the bandits the bank did not have their money. As a result, there was a run on the bank, which left almost empty vaults when it closed for the weekend.

In the meantime, the Canton Revolutionists were in trouble. They needed arms, but could buy none from western nations. Today, many men speak boldly about how we "lost" China. My husband speaks from personal experience, which is, of course, bound to be a limited explanation. He explained:

"When Sun Yat-sen had established law and order in the Port of Canton and a considerable part of the hinterland, he asked Great Britain and the United States for recognition of his right to declare war against the northern warlords. This recognition was necessary in order to acquire munitions legitimately, and to hire western officers and technicians to train an offensive army. Without it, Dr. Sun's Nationalists would be classified as bandits, and no respectable foreign technician would work for them, nor would merchants dare procure munitions for them. Dr. Sun naturally looked to democratic America, from whom he learned about popular government, to help him drive the warlords out of China. The revolutionists had money in those days to pay for the help they needed. But our government and that of Great Britain refused to accord him the rights of belligerency.

"In 1924, when I was engaged in export-import trade in Foochow, I was approached by representatives of the Nationalists to see if I could procure World War I surplus for them. Because I understood what they were up against, my sympathy was with them and I was willing to try. They must have been pretty desperate to come to a little business like ours. Before negotiations got very far, the American Consul, a personal friend of mine, called me on the phone, saying, 'Brewster, I hear you are dealing with representatives of the Canton Nationalists.'

"Who told you, and why shouldn't I," I asked.

"'Well,' he replied, ignoring the first question, 'if I get confirming evidence that you are supplying weapons to them, I shall have to charge you in Federal Court. The penalty is five years in prison and a $10,000 fine.'

"I thought about that for a moment. 'Is there any chance of avoiding the prison term by doubling the fine?' I asked.

"When he replied in the negative, I knew I was beaten and, if I was their last resort, so were the Nationalists.

"That same month, Vladivostok fell to the Russian Communists, ending the Independent Siberian Republic, thereby, stopping a shipping deal I had with some Russian merchants. World politics made that September a sad month for me.

"The beleaguered Nationalists then turned to Russia, who promised them help, provided the Chinese Communists, then a tiny minority, were accepted in the Nationalist party, and all men and officers be indoctrinated into Communism as part of their training. The bitter fruit of that deal has our teeth on edge today."

So with revolution, civil war, student boycotts and upset world politics, business grew increasingly difficult. The final calamity came for us when a shipment of some thirty trucks ordered for the prospective city bus-line was not accepted because of the 1929 New York Stock Market Crash. Even in China, money went underground, quite literally. Our big enclosed yard became a parking lot for all those unclaimed trucks.

Almost overnight, there was no one to buy our flour and machinery. No orders came from Europe for our tea. Our friends, representing internationally known business firms, continued their idyllic living in our Oriental Paradise. They merely viewed the future with anxiety. For small firms like ours an era had ended. We planned to leave China the following summer. As my husband began the dismal business of liquidating assets, I moved about our beautiful home, laying hands on furniture, trying to decide which pieces were indispensable treasures.

As though to accentuate the evils the year had brought, the weather turned cruel. Usually ruddy chrysanthemums and delicate roses sunned themselves through the languid fall, swelled and bloomed, faded and fell apart in the dusty golden days. That year, flowers bloomed reluctantly, if at all. One day the amazed gardener brought in roses jeweled with ice for me to see. Bitter cold had settled over our dismal city.

The customary greeting, "Have you eaten, yet?" was replaced by the exclamation "Ten coats cold today." Unhappily, often the wearer had only one.

As Christmas approached, I watched, with a strange new awareness, as the gardener massed tree-poinsettias and feathery bamboo saplings in the corners of the big entrance hall. In the sapphire-blue bowl on the mantel, pink roses and copper chrysanthemums warmed themselves above the glowing coals. These, too, I savored, seeing them as part of a life about to vanish.

Our final departure immiment, there were obligations to fulfill. It was customary for business people to give a suitable farewell gift to the household staff, who had served long and loyally. Since the cook had seniority at our house, I asked him what the gifts should be.

"For each of us a new coat," he replied, so quickly, that it was obvious the matter had already been well discussed. His choice was a brown wool coat lined with sheepskin. His wife, he said, wanted a quilted coat of sky-blue silk, which would serve her as a burial coat.

"Now that you are taking the small boys away," he explained in a matter-of-fact way, "she has no desire to live. She plans to die sometime next year." We learned later that this actually happened. All the others, the gateman, the houseboy, the laundry man, the gardener, the two rickshaw coolies and the second amah, chose sheepskin-lined coats of dark-blue wool. The order was given to our tailor. Within a week, the handsome garments were displayed on the guest room beds. Because of the cold, we gave them weeks before the New Year, which is China's great festival.

Something my husband said thrust the barb into my heart:

"It's good to know our own people will be warm for years to come. What about the other millions who must be freezing tonight?"

All through the holiday preparations, those words hurt me. Somehow, now that our own future had become uncertain, the plight of all those who had always suffered became unbearable. The thought of them pressed into me—warm and well-fed. As I went about my tasks and pleasures I carried on a conversation about this with God.

One day, I included my husband in the conversation.

"If we could give a coat to someone we never saw, who doesn't even know we exist, it would be like doing it for God, a sort of token of our concern for all the people we can't possibly clothe."

He looked at me as if he feared our troubles had unbalanced my mind.

"Do you remember how much those coats cost? How can we possibly afford to give one to a total stranger?"

That I knew, was true, but the unhappiness persisted. Apparently it affected him, too, for one day at tiffin he offered, tentatively,

"About that coat. If it will make you happy, send for the tailor. We'll get another one. But how in the world are we going to decide who gets it?"

The solution to that problem was already in my mind, where the serene face of a former amah smiled at me.

"Duai Muoi," I cried triumphantly. "She will know someone who should have it. She is a Christian and the most trustworthy person I know."

On a frosty brilliant afternoon, our rickshaw rolled out to the forlorn mud-and-bamboo village where Duai Muoi lived, bringing her back to us for tea. She was delighted to see the boys, especially Bill, for whom she had cared until her tortured bound-feet made such work impossible. As she sipped her tea, we outlined our plan. Shaking her head, she voiced my husband's words.

"How shall I choose one, when everyone is cold?"

Then, with sudden decision she exclaimed,

"Yes, let it be that one! There is an old Christian woman in my village (we had made no religious stipulation) to whom my heart turns. She has no family to look after her. How she keeps alive in such weather, I do not know. I think the Bible woman gives her rice, which neighbors cook for her. She is blind and too feeble to manage a fire. For clothing she has some poor rags. Yet, when she is able, she sits on a stool by her door telling Bible stories to anyone who will listen. Yes, let it be that one who receives the coat!"

Duai Muoi's face dimpled with pleasure at the thought.

"As for getting it to her without being seen, that is easy. She is blind and in this weather no one will be out walking at night!"

Christmas was different that year. Trouble and uncertainty drew our little community of Europeans and Americans together in simple pleasures. Seventy friends gathered in our living room for carol singing. The cook served his delicious newly-baked graham bread spread with white butter, freshly whipped from the milk of buffalo cows. Most of the ovens in our neighborhood helped bake the bread. That, with buckets of hot cocoa, replaced the elaborate feasting of other years. My family in Madison, Wisconsin, had sent a five-pound tin of marshmallows in our Christmas box. These added the crowning touch to our midnight supper.

On Christmas Eve, our own family rode out to Hua Nan College to watch the girls present a pageant of the Nativity. It was presented with such moving beauty, simplicity and dignity, that I left the chapel with a tear-wet face.

Awaiting us was a sky of glory. Instinctively I raised my arm to shield me from the pulsing brilliance of those low-hung stars. Like shepherds of old, we stood there stupefied by great and unexpected light. The sky had depth that night. The stars were separated in space like balls of fire suspended from a gigantic ceiling on strings, some long, some short.

"Just look at them," I gasped to my husband. "How did they get so close?" To this inane question, my husband made a sensible reply.

It may have been as he said, that the finger of crisp, dry cold reaching down from the North had snatched away the moist haze that usually blanketed our southern sky, thus revealing the stars in such awe-inspiring splendor. It may have been so, but it seemed to me, the heavens were astir that night. Any moment, I expected to see hosts of jubilating angels come swinging down those airy aisles to sweep in rapturous formation before our wondering eyes. Surely, that celestial stage must be set for some purpose!

On Christmas afternoon, Duai Muoi arrived. Her face was tender with joy as she watched the boys playing around the tree, which glittered with tinsel and quaintly shaped lights. We could see that she was alight from within, and wondered what had happened to compensate for the long painful trek from the country. Courtesy restrained our curiosity. At last, pointing with her chin, she spoke.

"That is truly a heaven tree." Then, hurrying on, "I have to tell you about last night. I must tell you about the old Bible teacher and the coat.

"The package containing it arrived, unnoticed. Packages of mending are often delivered to my house, so no one asked any questions. It must have been ten o'clock when I ventured out wearing those sheepskin slippers you once gave me, so that I wouldn't disturb the village dogs. I left the coat in the box, wrapped in the sweet smelling tissue paper as you sent it. I wanted to leave it there until the last moment, to hold the fragrance. How I was going to deliver the coat, I did not know. I should just have to wait and see. It is a wonder I did not stumble for looking at the stars. Never have I seen such a sky. I was almost afraid of its glory."

My husband and I glanced at each other.

"When I approached the old Bible teacher's hovel, I heard speaking. I crept along until I could see her door. There she sat on her stool, her face lifted, talking to God.

"I took the cover from the box, laying it noiselessly on the road. But a little wind caught the tissue paper, making it flutter and rustle. The old lady turned toward me, startled.

"Who is it?"

"I tossed the coat at her, watching as it fell over her head and lap. Then clutching the cover, the box and one end of the paper which insisted on fluttering and rustling, I hurried away. I was almost crying, angry with myself for being clumsy; hoping that the noisy paper hadn't spoiled my plan.

"This morning, I got up early, thinking I would take a bowl of rice to her for Christmas breakfast. When I approached her house, I saw other people there. I was afraid something was wrong. Maybe the gift had been too much for her! But no, there she sat, wearing the lovely new blue coat, her hair combed, her face shining like one of last night's stars. She was talking about God, how he really cares when people are cold and hungry, lonely and afraid. Now at last, the people were listening."

"'I have been cold and hungry many times,' she was saying, 'but last night I thought I must surely die. I sat out here calling to God, when suddenly I heard a fluttering and rustling as of wings. Then something fell on me, something wonderfully warm and soft and fragrant as flowers. Then I knew. Out of the cold night, God had sent His angels with the coat you see me wearing.'

"The people were astonished, touching the coat and exclaiming. I set the rice gruel down, putting her hand on the warm bowl. She smiled and thanked me. 'But maybe it came from someone in the village.' I protested. She knew my voice. Patting my hand she laughed and said,

"'Who in this village owns such a coat, Duai Muol, much less has one to give away? Be that as it may, I have proof now that God is not far away. He is with us. Near enough to hear my prayer and send His angels to answer it.'"

Duai Muoi indignantly wiped at something wet that slid down her cheek, then laughed, apologetically.

"I have never been used to answer someone's prayer before."

The same thought sent little shivers of awe through us, too. God had come very close and used us unaware.

Starlight, angel wings, and the breath-taking certainty that God was with us! That was our last Christmas in China. What more could one ask for any Christmas? Anywhere?

* * *

Our last months were brightened by the unexpected kindness of our Chinese business associates. When the lease on our house expired, we were dismayed to learn someone else was waiting to occupy it. A non-Christian owner of a theatrical troop called on my husband, inviting us to be his guests until it was time for us to leave. He had a summer house in a nice garden, which he wanted to make comfortable for us. It was he, too, who took over various slow-moving merchandise in the warehouse, providing enough money to buy passage to America for all of us. He brushed aside gratitude, saying he could afford to wait until merchants were ready to buy again.

It was the curio dealer, Talkie True, who encouraged and assisted us most. Although Elizabeth had wakened my interest in old porcelains, a hobby my husband shared, Talkie True was my self-appointed guide through that hazardous pursuit. The sapphire-blue bowl on the mantel was a case in point. When he brought it to me, I had rejoiced in its gorgeous color and exclaimed triumphantly over the five-toed dragons disporting themselves on its surface. Talkie True was tolerant, but amused. Dropping the Pidgin English we found so enchanting, he spoke in Chinese.

"You love the color, yes. But let me show you something. The potter did not love his work. See how unevenly the glaze is laid on, making unsightly streaks. Look how the drops have formed at the bottom. He didn't even bother to clean them off. Examine the drawing; it is very coarse. You have heard it said that only porcelains intended for the Imperial Palace could portray five-toed dragons. This is just one piece of many, to prove that saying wrong. It is not difficult to draw an extra toe to fool the uninformed. It takes more than five toes to make an imperial porcelain. This was made for foreign trade."

In spite of its streaks and toes, I bought the bowl. Probably because of them, I still have it. Because of its color, I love it.

When our Canton dishes were sold, I asked Talkie True to find me one perfect piece of Blanc de chine, preferably in the form of a lovely Quan Yin, the Buddhist goddess of mercy. He was gone for five days. On the sixth day, he appeared on our back veranda accompanied by three strange men. When I appeared, he squatted down and untied the dirty cloth he was carrying. Out came a most exquisite little figure. I was not allowed to hold her. For several hours, I listened as the four connoisseurs examined her, passing her back and forth, scrutinizing her under glass. The three men were also porcelain collectors, I gathered.

Suspecting it was all a game, though new to me, I was properly indifferent. Finally, one of them announced that, except for her right hand, she was an exquisite example of late Ming and offered to buy her from me. The hand, he said, must have been broken and was replaced. Then, I was allowed to hold her. She was so lovely, I could only sit and wonder at her flawless perfection. Until I had to give her up to be packed, it was my delight to carry her from window to window. She was like a white rosebud with a hint of pink in its heart. I was sure if I could find the right light, she would blossom into the palest rose.

Having sold us most of our porcelains, carved screens and rare old furniture, Talkie True offered to undertake the arduous task of packing them. He ordered the building of thirty huge packing cases. He found mountains of shredded paper. For these he allowed us to pay. Finally, he moved his own workmen up to our garden to do the packing free. An American freighter was calling at Pagoda Anchorage in June. Talkie True had everything packed and stored in an unoccupied wing of the house several weeks ahead of time.

One morning, as I walked among the cases checking the newly painted addresses, I saw, to my horror, the tell-tale mud tunnels of termites disappearing into the cracks of all but three of the cases. Fortunately, those three were the ones which contained our carved screens. When Talkie True heard of the disaster, he brought his family as well as his employees to the rescue. The cases were hauled out into the garden, again, where they were opened and emptied of all the sticky mass to which the paper had been reduced. Every piece of porcelain and furniture was cleaned and repacked in fresh paper, just in time for Long Tom and his men to carry the cases to the lighters on the river.

This kindness was done in spite of a coolness on my part toward Talkie True. A few weeks earlier, a friend advertised a showing of porcelains at her house for one of his competitors. With the money from the sale of my dishes in my purse, I hurried down the road to her house. I knew I shouldn't buy anything, unless, of course, there should happen to be a treasure there! Like all antique collectors, I couldn't bear to miss such a chance. Talkie True was standing at the gate. He hurried toward me talking as he came.

"Missy, inside have got very fine pair Sung-shape Ming bowls. Belong white color. You buy for me. You sign chit. I pay master."

This as any collector knows was an inexcusable request. "What if I want them myself? If you wanted them, why didn't you buy them?"

It appeared he would lose face buying from a rival. Moreover, since he had sold us many things he treasured, he felt justified in asking this favor.

The big living room was crowded with the jewel-toned, monochrome-glazed porcelains for which China is famous. Like Talkie True, I could see only the pair of Ming bowls. I took one of the fragile beauties to the window. It was eggshell thin, hardly more than two thicknesses of glaze. The clay slip between was just heavy enough to permit an exquisite etching of peonies and dragons, which seemed to be drawn with pale fire. I bought the pair and delivered them to Talkie True with more than reluctance.

On the day before we left Foochow, there was a steady procession of friends coming to say goodbye. Guided by his own sense of what was proper, Wong ushered tradesmen to the back veranda, friends to the front hall.

About noon, he announced that someone was waiting there to see me. Wearily, I went down. Talkie True, dressed in the silk gown and skull-cap of a Chinese gentlemen, stood by the front door. The usual dirty carrying-cloth swung from his hand. He began to make a speech, gave up, squatted on the floor and untied his bundle. Out came the white Ming bowls.

Holding them to the light so that I could see the lovely design, he announced, proudly,

"Belong imperial," and placed them in my hands. "For Master and Missy! Belong my friend forever!"

And so we are.

CHAPTER TEN

The Legend of Elizabeth

The following September my husband, carrying the precious Sung bowls as hand luggage, left us to look for work in New York, which seemed the logical place for bank openings in foreign exchange. We hoped also that the crushing weight of the depression, brooding over the entire world like a malevolent spirit, would be less noticeable there.

He joined the hordes of job seekers in New York, trying first to find a bank that could use his special training. The time soon came when he, like the rest, just looked for work. In December, he wrote me that no one seemed to need him, but that one of the big stores had bought enough of our porcelains to keep us for several months. We had anticipated this possibility, deciding in advance which of our treasures were indispensable.

We agreed that we could not part with the Sung bowls or the Quan Yin. The blue bowl with the matching birds and a little periwinkle blue vase with the lip folded in were two other pieces I designated. My husband spoke for a reticulated bowl on which rested a graceful vase. Talkie True called this interesting piece a *hu-lu.* It had been taken from a monastery in Canton by the crusading Governor Lin, who bore down hard on opium users and moral offenders. The Buddhist monks housed in the monastery had been guilty of both, and so their order was dispersed, their house destroyed. My husband, who had a great admiration for the courageous General of the Opium War days, prized this memento of him.

There was also a satin-smooth, beige ginger jar decorated with blue peonies and the mythical phoenix which he wished to keep. In addition to its lustrous beauty, it had a deeper significance. The day he closed his office door in Foochow for the last time, a beloved old Chinese friend brought him a scrap of paper. It was my fortune, which his old friend had paid the city's foremost soothsayer to prognosticate. We still keep it in our safe deposit box. It reads:

"In the autumn the phoenix will fly higher than ever bird flew before." According to legend, the phoenix is a bird which rises above the ashes and ruins of life and time to fly again—hence an emblem of hope and immortality. I think my husband felt that he too was leaving all his life and plans in ruins behind him, and so he cherished the bit of paper and the lovely jar with its symbolic meaning as talisman for his own future.

His letter also said he had rented a house at $80 a month in a good suburb. We were to come at once. We arrived on the twenty-third of December, 1930.

Manhasset was then a quiet little village surrounded by woods and open fields. As we walked through the main street to our house, my husband assured me I would love the town. How right he was! The house he had rented was a gaunt wood and stucco affair, which always seemed more like a miniature museum than a home. Our beautiful Beijing rugs and carved furniture were oddly at home in its small rooms. Like a museum, we had priceless carved screens and exquisite old porcelains, but only two chairs and no curtains at the windows. The kitchen, happily, had a breakfast nook with table and benches so that we could sit down to meals together.

My husband had food in the refrigerator and what he considered the minimal cooking equipment consisting of a frying pan, a tea kettle, several sauce pans, a few cooking forks and spoons, a bread knife, a dish pan and a tinsel ornament for the top of the Christmas tree. There was no tree because they were too expensive. So, for the second time, my kitchen was equipped by a man.

On our wedding day, our Chinese cook had gone to the street to purchase the necessities, which he listed in a little notebook. Now, thirty years later, the items recall that faraway magical time. The prices are given in cash which then were figured at one thousand to a Chinese dollar, which in turn was worth about fifty-cents gold.

1 charcoal oven--------------------------2700 cash
1 frying pan-----------------------------------1500
1 deep pie tin---------------------------------- 700
1 round pie tin---------------------------------550
1 4-qt. cooking pan---------------------------3000
1 3-pt. cooking pan-----------------------------400
2 tin bath tubs---------------------------------8800
2 dish washing pans---------------------------2200
2 charcoal flat irons---------------------------5800
2 wash tubs-----------------------------------3000
1 set buckets for carrying water--------------1000
1 bucket for washing floor--------------------1000
1 hot water cooker----------------------------2000
1 pitcher---900
1 dozen glass pickle jars-----------------------576
2 tin bread boxes------------------------------ 1300
1 small water bucket----------------------------260
1 clay jar for canning---------------------------250
2 drinking water jars----------------------------600
1 pair charcoal tongs----------------------------180
1 charcoal dipper--------------------------------180
1 washing board--------------------------------1200

Subtracting the articles which modern plumbing and cooking appliances make obsolete, the lists are not greatly different.

We did not miss a Christmas tree for we were invited to spend the holidays with my husband's younger sister and her husband, Mr. and Mrs. Frank Manton, then in theological school at Madison, New Jersey. For three wonderful days, we lived free of the depression. Those delightful young people filled us with good food, took us with them to the churches they served, and introduced us to the enchantment of a Christmas matinee at the old Roxy Theatre. All of us, even our two small sons, were transported into a happier world that afternoon by the dancing, music and pageantry. Snow fell softly on red-cloaked carolers singing under the window of a house in Merrie England; dazzlingly costumed skaters sped over ice where a moment before wisemen had followed a star; fairies danced up and down a huge pine tree, and finally Santa Claus himself, a tiny elfin figure far below us, lifted his arms and shouted "Merry Christmas," even to us against the wall of the top balcony.

As soon as we returned to Manhasset, however, the problems of living presented themselves. The first one to be solved was how to turn the pile of soiled clothing on the laundry floor into something clean to wear. For my husband, this was a new thing. Having lived in China so much of his life, he had given little thought to the miracle by which clothes dropped on the floor at night were always replaced by clean ones the next morning. He had provided no wash tubs, no wash board and no iron for our household, as our cook in Foochow had done. The sensible thing to do was to call the laundry, he said.

When the clothes came back they were accompanied by a bill for $7.28. I sat down then with my husband and tried to figure out how long our small bank account would last, at eighty-dollars-a-month for house rent, seven-dollars-a-week for laundry, an unknown amount for fuel and light, and a-dollar-a day for food. Without any extras, we could manage for four months, we thought. Our neighbor, stopping in that morning, suggested that we buy a wash machine for $5-down and $5-a-month. It seemed improbable that anyone would sell us, unknown and jobless, a wash machine on such terms, but they did, to my astonished relief.

Needless to say, my husband continued his search for work. Every morning he took the train to New York, and every night came back along with scores of other tired, worried men.

On one such day, I found time to look at our porcelains stacked in their wooden boxes on the sun porch. I wanted to see my little Quan Yin again, and planned to set the blue birds and bowl on the carved cabinet in the dining room. I opened every box. When they all were displayed on the living room floor, I sat down among them taking stock. Our best loved pieces were all gone. That night my husband told me that the New York buyer had picked out twenty-eight pieces, including our heart's treasures, and offered him a price on an all-or-nothing basis. There was no alternative. We had to have money.

Some of the lesser pieces, I saw later on display in New York. The blue bowl and matching birds, as Talkie True said, were pretty, but not valuable. We still have them. The monastery piece was slightly damaged in transit and is still ours. The Sung bowls, the little Quan Yin, my husband's beige-and-blue talisman and many others, we never saw again. Oddly enough, after the first sense of bitter loss, I did not grieve for them. As nearly as one can love inanimate objects, I loved them, and so they are still mine, as exquisitely clear in my mind as though they still graced our home.

As the months passed, we sold other treasures. The chests of convent-embroidered table linens found delighted purchasers from the estates around us. My loveliest banquet cloth became a door prize at a huge charity bazaar. Most of the remaining porcelains went to an art gallery on consignment.

My husband joined the army of salesmen ringing doorbells up and down the streets, selling vacuum cleaners. I think he sold three. Ever since, people selling at our door have a sympathetic welcome from me, and an easy customer in my husband.

We who are old enough to remember those days are not entirely unprepared for the crises of today. Then, too, we looked into a future which held only menace. Men talked of worldwide financial collapse. "Science" added its voice of prophecy telling us the atom, the smallest thing in the universe, was doing very well, but that the universe itself was completely out of hand. We drew on imponderables for courage, hoping that God Himself would intervene to save us. Who else could? Newspapers and magazines were full of gloom and doom with no hope to offer.

Meanwhile I was struggling to keep four of us fed on a-dollar-a-day with my Chinese menus still fresh in mind. I soon discovered that meat was a luxury to be enjoyed but once a week. We did not know about ground beef. To us meat was something solid to be roasted or stewed. It was almost as foolish then as it is now to ask for a fifty-cent-piece of roasting beef or pork, having to ward off the butcher's sales pitch that I would do much better to buy a bigger piece and use it for several meals. I couldn't bear to tell him fifty cents was my meat allowance. I marveled at the courage of my neighbor, like myself, just back from the Orient and almost penniless, but with five young adults to feed. She would look the butcher straight in the eye and demand one pound of pork cut into chops. Finally, we both discovered ground beef. From then on, our menus were monotonous, but more filling.

In spite of our economic measures, our checking account dwindled to nothing. We lived from week-to-week on the sale of a piece of porcelain or embroidered linen. One Saturday morning, my husband and I sent the two little boys out to play and sat down to consider the weekend and beyond. There was no more food in the house; there was no money in the checking account. My purse was empty; my husband had one dime in his pocket. The nightmare had overtaken us. We had no need to look into the future for the dreaded inconceivable. It had already happened.

The mail arrived as we sat there—advertisements, several replies to job applications, and, surprisingly, one of Elizabeth's rare letters. The advertisements meant nothing to people without money; the job application replies were, as usual, courteous but negative. There remained Elizabeth's letter. We sat there looking at it, remembering. Nothing in those fabulous China years had prepared us for the starkness of our present life.

Finally, my husband opened the envelope, carefully preserving the stamps. In it was a letter and an order on the New York Mission Board for $200. The letter said, "Lately the Spirit has burdened me on your account, Francis. I hear so seldom from you. I do not know your circumstances, but when the Spirit directs I obey. I am sending you all the money I can spare and I trust it will meet your needs."

The letter had been written a month earlier coming to us by ship, as did all mail in those days. With what awe we looked at that letter, and with what gratitude. From that moment, I began to think of

Elizabeth, not as a mother-in-law, but as a friend of God. Had we not been saved by that friendship? With the old Bible woman in Foochow we said, "God is with us! He knows our need; he has heard our prayers and has used Elizabeth to answer them!" How great was the miracle of human love which prompted her to listen to the guidance and obey when she herself had so little.

After that the eerie darkness that lay over the world was less frightening. We joined a small church that blessed the community, offering our services. I was asked to make calls in the community. When the church board discovered that the curtain-less windows, not the thick rugs and carved furniture, were the true index of our finances, they paid me a little for doing it. Later, I superintended the Sunday school for 12 years.

We weren't the sole recipients of the kindness of that church. Its compassionate pastor, the Reverend Oscar Maddaus, ministered to countless people those desperate years. Men without train fare to New York received it from him; hungry people were fed in his home; hope was offered to men ready for suicide. What splendid, shining fellowship we found in that blessed community of believers!

Again on a day of crisis, a check arrived from Elizabeth to save us from disaster. Once, might have been an accident. Twice, was divine intervention, of that we are sure. So the legend of Elizabeth began to form in my heart, transcending the little earthly lady, glorifying her as one who knew God and was used by Him to answer prayers.

Our second Christmas in Manhasset was made memorable by a job for my husband. He held a Master's Degree in Education from Columbia University and so he qualified for a teaching position in the Manhasset High School. After that we began to live again.

Meanwhile, Elizabeth was alone in China, meaning, of course, that no one of her family was there. This she did not mind, except that, now and then, fear that none of us would carry on the work she and Will had started would creep into her letters. She spoke with guarded optimism about the New China. She had lived there too long, however, to burst into acclaim over the first reforms of Chiang Kai-shek's government. She told of the new roads connecting Hinghwa with Foochow and Amoy, and her hope for a used car to make shorter the distances she was always travelling.

This road work had begun before we left China. From the ancient graves thus uncovered, had come some of our most interesting porcelains and pottery. These Talkie True brought to us by the basketful, covered with the damp earth in which they had lain for ages. In my basement today, are the remnants of that pottery, two horned jars of some religious significance and a white soft-glazed ewer. The horned jars have an unpleasant association in more than one way.

I was so horrified to have the muddy things stored in our home, that I had the gardener bring a tub of water into the storeroom and help me scrub off the mud. Talkie True arrived as I was thus engaged. I still remember his displeasure. He protested that the stiff brush I was using would take off the thin primitive glaze and leave the clay exposed, which is just what happened. Today, one is naked to the clay; the other covered with a very thin greenish glaze. Perhaps someday, I shall find a museum that will be interested in them for their antiquity.

The spot from which they came was a slight elevation in Fish Street, Foochow. When the new regime of Chiang Kai-shek began the work of modernizing Foochow streets, by removing the stone steps and adding width so that automobiles could be used, the people on Fish Street were greatly alarmed. Tradition made their small hill a spot sacred to the all-pervading Dragon, who would be wounded by so much digging. When the work proceeded, in spite of their protests, an ancient burial ground was discovered, so old that the city had spread right over it. In the memory of the people, however, there lingered the knowledge that the spot was sacred, although the reason was forgotten.

When Talkie True brought us the horned jars and a pair of small squat blue bowls, he told us they were more than a thousand years old. I questioned him on the statement. He dated them by the following story.

"More than one thousand years ago by historical records, some bad people called Dong Buo made war on Foochow. They killed all the men and boys. Women fought to protect themselves with knives, but could not win. When all the men were killed, the Dong Buo took the women for wives. At that time the word for husband was "Dong Buo man." That is still the name today. These men were not all bad. As a remembrance that the women were so brave, they let them wear silver knives in their hair. Today all boat women wear silver knives in their hair. You must save these. These things I bring to you came from two layers of graves, under the first graves, where today we found hair-knives buried. So I know these jars are more than one thousand years old."

Elizabeth's letters also spoke with pleasure of the appointment of Christian and other officials on the local level who, for the moment at least, were honestly administering civic affairs. We read with amazement of the beginning of a movement aimed at the regeneration of China, of campaigns against smoking either tobacco or opium, of streets being cleaned of refuse and litter, of the revival of the ancient virtues of courage, honesty, frugality and good faith, for every one, not only officials.

This moral rearmament was the weapon by which Chang Kai-shek would awaken, inspire and unite his country against her twin foes, Communists within and Japan without. It sounded much like Father Brewster's plan, differing only by the love which was to inspire it—love of country instead of love of God. We wondered where the power to generate so much virtue would come from and how permanent it would be. That the warring governors of the provinces were finally subdued, was incredibly good news. It might well be that China's longed for new day would finally come with a Christian, Chiang Kai-shek, as its leader. Although we had felt the propaganda power of the small communist group in the Nationalist army, as they swung their whips of hate at us in 1926, we felt that the good sense and tolerance of the overwhelming majority of Chinese could not really be threatened by them. So far as Japan was concerned, we were sympathetic with her need for markets, but not with the way she seemed bent on acquiring them. Furthermore, we were certain she would not dare risk the displeasure of the other world powers by actually invading China proper.

At any rate, we Americans were too concerned with other matters those early years of the 1930 decade, to become unduly disturbed over China. Banks were closing everywhere. The financial ruin closing in on us was more alarming than the advance of Japan into Manchuria, or the flames rising from the Reichstag in Germany. These burdens belonged to others. We had our own crushing load.

Meantime Elizabeth's youngest son, Harold, had finished medical school and his internship in Honolulu. In September of 1933 he and his wife, Dorothy, and their baby daughter, Betty, arrived in China to begin a long and loving service to the Chinese people. Elizabeth and Mr. Paul Wight, missionary architect of the Methodist Church, met them at beautiful Pagoda Anchorage.

With great anticipation, Elizabeth planned for them a quick visit to Harold's boyhood home in Hinghwa. Like any grandmother, she wanted to show off her grandchild. Moreover, the return of her youngest son as a doctor was the fulfillment of her dream and of a prophecy of her Chinese neighbors.

When Harold was in his early teens, a wildcat was causing their neighbors out at the Yellowstone Orphanage and Industrial School much trouble and loss by its raids on their chickens. One day, when he was out practicing with his "22," he noticed a disturbance in one of the heavily foliaged trees in the fruit orchard across the road. Thinking it was the wildcat, he aimed into the foliage. A loud cry, most obviously not that of a wildcat startled him so much that he dropped his gun and ran to the rescue of his victim. He had shot the owner of the orchard, fortunately, without seriously injuring him.

When the people, appearing from nowhere at the sound of the excitement, saw Harold taking care of the injury, they said, '"He is one of the Jesus people. This one will be a doctor." And so he was: a doctor, surgeon and witness for God in a parish of untold thousands.

They rode with Elizabeth, in her newly acquired used car, from the river launch across the hazy September landscape to Hinghwa. From that moment, many interesting news bits were forwarded by Dorothy, newcomer in China, that Elizabeth overlooked entirely. For instance, on this first car journey into China, it was Dorothy who reported that her head and body almost parted company as they raced over the newly opened dirt road. She attributed the chauffeur's haste to the sudden appearance of armed bandits in a field as they passed, a fact which disturbed Elizabeth no more than the excessively bumpy ride.

She was already known as "friend of the bandits"—a title she did not relish, because of her "safe conduct" on the roads. Other people travelled at great risk, but not Elizabeth. The legend I was building about her and sharing with friends and the Sunday school children in Manhasset, received new stature when a woman from nearby Port Washington, Long Island, sent me a clipping, asking if the Mrs. Brewster in the story was related to us. How proudly I called to thank her for the story, and to claim the lady involved as my husband's mother.

The clipping said a party of American travelers were planning an overland trip from Amoy to Hinghwa. Elizabeth, who loves to entertain, had written to them inviting them to her home. She also offered to send her car to meet them on the new road, adding that her little flag flying from its radiator would be their protection from bandits. The Americans accepted her invitation, but, at the last moment, were persuaded that the danger from bandits at a certain spot on that new road was too great to hazard.

Sending a message to Elizabeth of their change of plans, they went by sea to a port above Hinghwa, asking if her car could meet them there, instead. Sure enough, the car with its fluttering flag was waiting for them as they had requested. On the way down to Hinghwa, they tried to visualize the Amazon who dared defy the bandits. She welcomed them at the door to her home, a tiny, white-haired woman strongly reminiscent of Queen Victoria, only more charming. They reported their delight and astonishment to their American office, which printed the story. Once more it seemed to me, Elizabeth was reaching out to help us, this time to bring us friends and prestige in a new country. How wonderful it was to have a mother-in-law whose courage had flashed around the world.

Elizabeth's account of this small adventure was reported in one of her diaries. By way of diversion from work, she had accompanied her car that day along the new road to Amoy. Stopping at the spot where she knew the bandits had their stronghold, she sent her driver up to say who she was and that she was meeting guests. The chief sent word back that her guests were as safe as herself, and that it wasn't necessary for her to take such long trips, a car flying her flag would be given safe conduct. This she knew from past experience, but notifying the bandits of her presence and purpose in waiting on their doorstep, as it were, was a matter of courtesy.

She waited all day in Amoy. When night came and the travelers still had not arrived, she told the driver to take them home. Upon arrival, she found the delayed message saying the Americans had gone by sea, with the request that, if possible, could she have them met at the seaport. "I was so angry," wrote Elizabeth, "that I didn't go myself. I sent the driver alone to fetch them. When I had time to think, I realized they wouldn't understand how they had made me lose face, and the bandit chief, too, by showing their lack of trust in us both. By the time they arrived, I was over my anger and I don't believe they guessed that they had embarrassed me."

Her comment to me on her title, "Friend of the Bandits," was as follows: "I never liked to be called that because it sounds as if I condoned bandit activities. This I never did. I knew that poverty caused by all the wars and political upheavals, made them prey on those who seemed to have a little more material goods than themselves. I never excused them for stealing to relieve that poverty, and told them so. The fact was, I had known them since they were children, watching me as I ate, sharing my cookies and oranges. For this reason, I was always safe. We trusted each other. In only this sense was I "Friend of the Bandits."

By the time she came to the 1936 General Conference, I was thinking of her as something of a heroine whose acquaintance our small community was eager to make. Typical of Elizabeth, she was so absorbed in a project of her own that we saw very little of her.

She had come to the age when family records were very important. After the conference, she spent the short months of that furlough seeking proof of the tradition that Will's family was directly descended from Elder William Brewster, of Mayflower fame.

After months of energetic travel and absorbed research, she came to visit us at Manhasset. Ruefully, she reported her findings. Tradition would have to give way to facts. Will's family and that of the famous Elder were related, but we could not claim direct descent from him. She referred to all her hard work, in the words of Jacobus, as: "The laudable desire of many descendants to claim the Mayflower Line."

That our Brewsters were directly descended from one Nathaniel Brewster, member of the first class to graduate from Harvard University, and through him to one Francis Brewster, ship owner, who came from England to settle at New Haven, Connecticut in 1641, was satisfactory to us. Elizabeth, however, felt deflated. Not even reminding her that she was part-Jefferson, a name much more precious to my politically minded husband, comforted her.

Her research, however, had turned up so many interesting facts, that when she asked us to consider a family reunion before her departure for China, all but two of her children, William Fisher, who lived in California, and Dr. Harold in China, accepted the invitation. With our children, we arrived in Delaware, Ohio to spend a few days at the lovely home of George Hollister and his wife, Mary Brewster Hollister.

This was the first time I had encountered Elizabeth's inexhaustible energy and enthusiasm. She led us through the country around Zenia, London and Belbrooke, Ohio to seek out family homesteads and burial grounds. We stood around the forlorn foundation, guarded by a lilac bush, which was the home of the Revolutionary War Brewster. He had traded his original war grant of land, where the city of Cincinnati now flourishes, for this farm, because the mosquitoes were less vicious there than on the Ohio River. In that year of depression, 1936, we wished he had been more tolerant of mosquitoes.

On another day, we carried a picnic lunch to Zenia to locate the family home of Great-Grandmother Brewster. Elizabeth had seen it with Will forty years earlier. Great Aunt Sally Murray, who was still living, told us where to go. Completely in the spirit of the past, we drove up to the door of the old red brick mansion and walked in, as if we owned it.

Someone was remodeling the place. Elizabeth caressed the beautiful cherry handrail and newel post of the balustrade in the front hall. "It's just as I remember it," she exclaimed. We rejoiced over the newly sanded floors, soaking up their first coat of wax, marveled over the thousands of pine seedlings planted around the curving driveway, and finally carried our baskets to the picnic table, so pleasantly located by a tiny brook at the bottom of the sloping lawn.

Elizabeth was filling us in on Great-Grandmother Rebecca, and her enchanting sister Great Aunt Sally, when someone noticed a very purposeful man coming over the lawn toward us. Suddenly we realized we were trespassing. Since Great-Grandmother Rebecca had died in 1920 and the farm had passed into other hands long before that, we knew it was no friendly relative approaching. I ran to meet the man, apologizing for our intrusion, explaining why we had come, and begging him, for Elizabeth's sake, not to order us off the premises. He proved to be most kind and understanding; inviting us to feel at home, which indeed we had, asking only that we refrain from walking on his freshly waxed floors. In return, we gave him Aunt Sally Murray's address so that he could consult her about the details of the original house to guide him in remodeling.

The next day, Elizabeth took us to meet that grand lady. She was then over ninety, enchanting, rotund, and obviously "family" to boast of. She was wearing a black satin dress and cap and a dainty white lawn apron, which was purely decorative. Her wonderful housekeeper did all the work. She reigned over all of us like a queen, as we filled her charming, antique-filled home with our families and their questions.

We still remember the dinner she served us that night. In those days, cholesterol hadn't emerged from the dictionary. Butter and cream were not only good, they were good for you! We were all, however, painfully aware of the depression. With what awe I watched the housekeeper prepare dinner with total disregard for expense or calories. She browned the chicken in butter and basted it continually with cream, a procedure which resulted in heavenly brown gravy. In another oven she baked biscuits high and light and fragrant. At serving time, she mashed potatoes smooth, then whipped a pint of cream into them. Into the row of hot vegetable tureens, she piled potatoes, fresh garden peas and asparagus, topping each with a huge chunk of butter. I helped refill cut glass compotes with green apple sauce, watermelon pickles and currant jelly. Dessert was a huge bowl of fresh raspberries with more cream.

The stiffly smooth linen tablecloth, the worn sterling, the cut glass and fine China were further evidences of the pleasant living to which Aunt Sally was accustomed. Aunt Sally was both charming and interesting. Her hobbies were quilting and making character dolls to illustrate her favorite books. She was working on Uncle Tom's Cabin that summer. This led us into a discussion of politics. When she learned that my husband was an ardent Roosevelt supporter, she was alarmed, pressing into his hands a book called *The Red Network*, which she assured him would set his politics straight. So far as she knew, there had never before been a Democrat in the family. She seemed to think that anyone not Republican must be somewhat subversive. She told me with great earnestness how my husband had come to visit them one hot July day when we was about nine years old.

"Mr. Murray found him out in the pasture, trying to ride the pigs. Mr. Murray said he thought the boy rode ten-pounds-a-piece off those pigs that day," she recalled, looking at my husband with great anxiety, as if this crime were somehow related to his renegade politics. For her sake, I concealed my own liking for President Roosevelt. How greatly Aunt Sally impressed us all was reflected in the astounding fact that my husband refrained from defending his political party, merely smiling, as she expostulated with him.

That reunion was a joyous time for all of us. I had never seen some of the brothers, nor had I ever known Elizabeth as mother of a family. It seemed incredible to me that, at her age, she was about to return to a blazing China. With real poignancy, we bade each other goodbye, each family carrying a picnic lunch planned by Elizabeth. When we ate ours somewhere in the Pennsylvania mountains, it was like a love feast, eaten in memory of her and her goodness. In addition to the delicious Ohio peaches and melon, she had included cake, cookies and sandwiches, which had a strange filling.

"Date sandwiches!" exclaimed my husband, his eyes misting over. "Mother remembered how I used to love these as a kid!" They are still a favorite with the men at our house, although I have never learned to like them. Equally strange to me and delightful to my husband, were the sandwiches filled with a mixture of ground peanuts and coconut. This he called "peco butter."

The California Brewsters had been introduced to this specialty by a fringe relative whose home was in Tahiti. He had planned to retire in California, but was harried back to his South Sea island by his own peculiarities. For one thing, he wore white linen shorts and sandals on the city streets, thus exposing hairy bare legs. This, California police declared, was indecent. Another offense, was his penchant for sleeping in the backyard. Adults were supposed to sleep inside in those years. He had strange eating habits, too, preferring ground up raw vegetables and their juice to cooked ones. When he left, he gave his "peco" recipe to the Brewster boys, who made it for their own enjoyment during their college years, then forgot about it. But Elizabeth remembered, and made some for my husband's picnic lunch.

So we ate, and thought with love and admiration for her, a good and loving mother. Although her life had been given to China, she was mindful of family traditions, eager to preserve them for her children, even to such small delights as sandwich fillings.

Not long after her return to China, the Japanese expanded their Manchurian invasion into China proper. At first, Elizabeth's letters were not overly concerned. She had known nothing but war from one source or another throughout her life there. Like the rest of us, she expected someone to do something about it before the situation got completely out of hand.

The most enthusiastic letters of that period were about Harold's work for the victims of leprosy in Kucheng. Through all her years as a missionary, she had labored to relieve the suffering of those bitterly afflicted people. The first official act of Will in Hinghwa, had been to build a chapel for them. Now, fifty years later, their youngest son was helping beat the disease to a standstill. No wonder Elizabeth rejoiced.

When Dr. Harold Brewster began his work of healing among the 200,000 people of Kucheng, he was immediately confronted with the misery of the "lepers" there. Their colony was a mile outside the city wall, a group of disreputable huts, with no sanitation of any kind. When the London Mission, which was doing what it could to alleviate conditions, saw his interest, they asked him to add the care of the desolate group to his manifold responsibilities. They gave him funds and freedom to work out a solution. Elizabeth wrote, joyously, that new buildings had replaced the former shambles, a trained nurse and a chaplain were in constant attendance and a garden plot had been assigned to each resident. Most incredible of all, two patients had had their disease arrested and been discharged to their homes. Somewhere, it has been written, "They shall see the harvest of their seed." For Elizabeth the promise was coming true.

One day in 1938, I opened a letter addressed in her handwriting. It was from a place called Sarawak in Borneo. A Kodak picture fell into my lap showing her dressed all in white, her hat tilted modishly, white gloves in hand. She smiled out at me quite unabashed by the nakedness of the men and women beside her. She was in Borneo, her letter said, the guest of her Chinese children who had sent her passage money and an invitation to come and stay with them. Now that she was partially retired, at 76 she was free to travel when she pleased, and was having a wonderful time among people she hadn't seen for thirty years. She suspected they had invited her down to escape the Japanese bombing. Although she had told them she was only visiting, she was being feasted and showered with gifts, until she was quite overcome with kindness. The photograph was taken on a visit to a long-house of the Dyaks, the proud aboriginal people who lived up the Rejang River. The whole letter was a puzzle to me. Who were these Chinese children and what were they doing in Borneo, I wondered.

When my husband came home, he was delighted with both the picture and the letter and gave the folowing explanation:

"Why sure, she is down there visiting the colony my father started when I was a boy. I remember he went to Borneo and bought land from the English Rajah Brooke, where he sent a lot of Hinghwa people who were hard-up financially. Some of my orphanage pals went with them. I had forgotten all about the colony, but from the sound of this letter, it must have succeeded."

As he reminisced, happily, I suddenly recalled an encounter I had some years ago. In the year 1926-27 when I was visiting in Madison, Wisconsin with our year-old-son, I was frequently asked to address church groups and clubs. That was the year Chiang Kai-shek made his successful march north and everyone was suddenly aware of China. One Sunday morning, I spoke at the Wesley Foundation of the University of Wisconsin. After the service, I was surrounded with people who had friends in China I might know, and others who wished to thank me for an interesting half-hour. After all, in those days someone who had lived for five years in the Orient was not so commonplace as today. I was on my way to the bus, when I heard someone call my name. Turning, I saw a slender, young Chinese man running towards me.

"You are Mrs. Brewster," he said, half in question, half in exclamation.

"Yes, that is my name," I replied, somewhat puzzled. He then asked me the same thing in Hinghwa dialect, using the Chinese name Bo. Again I assented, "Yes, that is my name."

"Of Hinghwa?" he persisted.

"My husband's home is Hinghwa, but we live in Foochow," I told him, amused by his repeated questions as to my identity.

Then with great earnestness, he took my hand in his.

"I want to hold your hand, Mrs. Brewster. In our family the name Brewster is very precious. A man in Hinghwa by that name saved my father from begging on the streets after he had lost his farm land. Mr. Brewster paid his way to the South Seas and helped him find a new life there. He must be your husband's father. Because of him, I can come here to study at the University and my other brothers and sisters also have college educations. My father is a rubber planter and can educate us because of a man named Brewster. I never saw a Brewster from Hinghwa until now, so I hold your hand in gratitude."

At the time, I merely added the incident to the other kind words that had been spoken that morning and forgot all about it. Now with Elizabeth's letter in my hand, the incident took on significance and I told my husband the story.

"Did you ever tell mother about this?" he wanted to know.

"I never told anybody about it. In fact I had forgotten all about it until this letter came. For that matter, no one ever told me about the Hinghwa colony in Borneo, so the incident meant nothing to me until now," I concluded, somewhat indignantly.

"Just the same, if mother ever comes home again, tell her about it. I'll bet she would know the boy's family."

Not for fifteen years did that opportunity come. One day at the farm, while I was interviewing her for this book, the rabbinical saying, "Who saves one saves the whole world," flashed into my mind, as I listened to her wonderful unfolding of all those early years in China. In immediate association came the words of the boy outside Wesley Foundation. "A man by the name of Brewster saved my father from begging on the streets of Hinghwa." So I told mother the story. With a glad little cry she leaned toward me, "What was the boy's name, Eva dear? Oh, what was his name?"

I could only shake my head, sadly. "I don't remember, mother. It was more than twenty years ago, after all, and he was a stranger to me then. I had never heard of Sarawak, Borneo, at the time, much less any connection between such a place and you Brewsters, so the whole incident just slipped from me until your visit there in 1938. I told Fran about it then."

Elizabeth sighed in great disappointment. "Oh, Eva dear, you have such a poor memory. If only you knew his name! It couldn't have been a Sarawak family. I know them all. No one there had a son who attended the University of Wisconsin. Some of our people went to Suraboya and other parts of the South Seas later on, and we lost touch. It must have been one of those!"

***

Elizabeth might wisely and conveniently have come right home to America that year of 1938, after her gift trip to Sarawak. Instead, although the Japanese crisis in China was steadily deepening, she chose to visit the Mantons in Rangoon, Burma. Mrs. Manton is her younger daughter, Karis.

Even at the close of that visit, she could have taken passage, as we all hoped, for America. Instead, she exerted every effort to find passage back to the China coast, which was under heavy bombardment. She was on the last ship allowed into Amoy by the Japanese. The very next day that port suffered a severe air raid. Elizabeth, undisturbed, was enroute to Hinghwa on a tiny Chinese coastal vessel, which she claims was providentially waiting at Amoy to take her out of danger,

When this news finally seeped through to us in Manhasset, another episode was added to my legend of Elizabeth. "The courage of that woman," we all marveled, and felt our own hearts swell with pride in her.

During her visit in Rangoon, she, too, had a moment of joyous pride when another seed, long since planted, bloomed to bless her children. In a letter expressing her happiness with her visit to her daughter's family and in the gorgeous new Burma flowers, which she was hoping to transplant to her China garden, there was a special message to my husband. She reminded him of his trip to steady the fearful in Sienyu during the Revolution of 1911, and of two boys, sons of a local minister, that he had befriended there. Because they wanted to become real soldiers who could serve their country well, he encouraged them to attend a good military school at Tiensin or Peking. He helped them get their school outfits and gave them each a New Testament. He, himself, went back to America to school that year and lost contact with the young men.

During the period of undeclared war between 1937 and 1939, Burma was full of Chinese army personnel working on the "Burma Road." One day, one of them was visiting friends in a Rangoon hospital. He found himself watching a young American woman, also visiting Chinese patients, who looked familiar to him. Somewhere he had seen those big blue eyes, the blonde curly hair, that wide friendly smile over big white teeth. But where? Then he saw that the first finger on her right hand was cut off at the knuckle. "It must be," he thought excitedly. "It must be the Brewster girl!" He remembered in his own childhood hearing that the little daughter of the Brewster's had put her hand in the mission press and lost part of a finger. He introduced himself and was received with equal delight by Karis Brewster—two people far from their beloved Hinghwa, rejoicing to find each other in a strange land.

He told her how her brother, Francis, had befriended him; and how he and his brother had gone to military school and were now in the service of their country. He was a paymaster on the Burma Road; the other brother was in the army. This incident was a joy to everyone concerned. Years later, when the Japanese war was over, this man held a position of importance in a Shanghai bank and was of great assistance to Elizabeth when she was old, as were so many others whom she had helped when they were young.

Back in Hinghwa that year of 1938, she prepared for the exigencies of the times. The small room off her study was made into her bomb shelter. In the room over it, she had her faithful man-servant stack rattan chairs. These were filled with books and papers to absorb fragments of bombs, she wrote. We shook our heads in dismay over such inflammable preparations. Eventually, we heard that she had sandbagged the roof, which sounded better to us, happily safe and far away from the destruction that flew in the day time in both China and Europe. As she herself said, preparation was almost useless. Her earphone batteries were too precious to use all the time, and there were alerts she could not hear. Sometimes, leaving her desk, she saw the servants under the tables and so she knew there was an alert on.

At her summer home on the top of the mountain, there were other preparations. We laughed in helpless amusement, as she reported, wryly, that the missionary in charge of defense required each person to prepare an outside retreat and a camouflage uniform of a grass-green hat and coverall. Whenever she was lucky enough to hear the alarms, she donned this Churchillian uniform, went out to her retreat of shrubs and trees and watched where the planes "laid their eggs," as she called them.

It seemed to us that for a lady nearly eighty, America would be a more likely spot for viewing the tragic events of those days. Nevertheless, we were very proud of her. No one else we knew had a mother deliberately choosing to stay where bombs were falling. But Elizabeth still had work to do, and China was her home.

Everyone thought the merciless bombings of coastal cities were preparatory to an invasion. Soon there began a systematic destruction of the automobile roads so recently built. Travel by car had to be abandoned. War inflation made travel by the old-fashioned, man-carried chairs extremely expensive. Their schools and industries were moved up into the mountains, their equipment carried on the backs of people, in hand carts or on the backs of donkeys. Several times Elizabeth's letters reported, sadly, that boys who had hiked endless miles from their new school sites to visit their parents in Hinghwa had been killed by bombings.

Since the United States was not yet at war with Japan, we still received occasional letters from China. Elizabeth's letters delighted us by their judicious reporting. At no time, did she resort to excoriation or denunciation. When bombs hit American or British property, she carefully explained that the buildings had not been flying their flags. She made sure her own home and Richmond Hospital nearby were properly protected by the American flag.

The fall of 1938 was the fiftieth anniversary of her first visit to Hinghwa. When conference was convened in October, Elizabeth was chosen once more to represent Hinghwa at the quadrennial General Conference, which was meeting at Atlantic City. She planned to sail on the President Cleveland, which was scheduled to leave Shanghai in February. This was the seventh time she had been elected by her Chinese colleagues to represent them at the great international governing body of the Methodist Church. On nine other occasions, she had been elected to represent them at Central Conference, which met in China. Apparently we were not alone in holding her in honor and esteem.

I hardly knew her when she came to see us that year. Amazingly, she looked years younger and prettier than I had ever seen her. The transformation was in her hair, which crowned her head in shining silver rolls.

"What have you done to your hair?" I questioned, enviously, for I, too, suffered from the same limp soft hair as she did.

"Oh," she laughed, "you see, I have a personal maid now who likes to fuss with it. She can even give a home permanent when we can buy the makings. While I am here, I shall have to depend on you to comb it, because I still can't use my arm very well."

In answer to my unspoken question, she continued,

"Maybe I didn't tell you, I broke it. I couldn't write for months, and by that time it would have been old news."

The year before, her son, Dr. Harold Brewster, was driving her back home after a visit to his family in Foochow. On the way, the steering-rod broke, causing the car to turn over. Elizabeth's arm was broken in such a manner that she had to wear it in a basketry frame straight out from her shoulder for weeks. She brushed off my concern by saying,

"It was a very lucky thing, really. The next week Harold had to make a last trip up to Kucheng Hospital before the roads were destroyed. If the steering-rod had broken on that trip over the narrow, twisting mountain roads, he and the children would have plunged to their death. This way, only my arm was broken, and the children suffered a few bumps and bruises. Besides, I never would have had a personal maid to make my hair look nice if it hadn't been for my broken arm. It's nice to be complimented at my age."

She was unbelievably young and pert for seventy-eight.

That visit was short and serious, however. She never took a full furlough, but this trip was unusually brief, because she was determined to get back to China before a clash between Japan and the United States should make departure impossible. Again we tried to persuade her to stay in America.

"No. My life has been spent in China. I want to die there among my friends—with them, if necessary.

Finally, my husband said resignedly, "Well, if you've made up your mind, I'll see what I can find out about transportation."

This nettled Elizabeth. In her haughtiest tone she replied.

"You needn't bother, Francis. I have traveled around the world since before you were born without help from anyone. I can do it still. I expect to take a freighter out of San Francisco. There will be one when I want it."

We gave a farewell tea for her so that people could catch a bit of badly needed courage from our dauntless little mother. Somehow, the menace across both oceans seemed less alarming, when she would choose to leave our broad continent to sail right into storm-black China.

Two precious memories of that short visit are still a cause for family laughter. On the day of her arrival in Manhasset, I was speaking at a large church conference in New Jersey. Dinner was over when I reached home that night. Expecting to find the family in the living room visiting, I was amazed to find them, instead, in the kitchen, where Elizabeth and my husband were busily washing dishes, an occupation almost totally strange to both of them. After welcoming her, I thanked them both.

"I have put the clothes to soak, too," added my husband, virtuously. I was afraid that I stood there with my mouth open. He might possibly have washed dishes several times during our life together, but I knew he had never put clothes to soak. For that matter, neither had I. I put them directly into the machine to wash. Hopefully, I asked, "Did you sort them first?"

"No. I was in a hurry, so I just dumped them all into the tubs together. I used boiling water though, so you don't need to worry about germs."

At this point Elizabeth hung up her dish towel and retreated into the living room. My husband followed me to the basement. As he said, he had used good, hot water. The boys' colored sox and his black ones had left their mark without prejudice and with real emphasis on sheets, shirts, table linens, dresses, towels, underwear arid hankies.

The next day I called a laundry for advice. As a result, they bleached all the large white articles, and I dipped all the small pieces and colored clothes at home in the solution they recommended to save expense. Elizabeth helped with this tedious, demanding job. In the midst of it, she began to laugh.

"Oh, Eva, don't look so tragic! I know my Francis. He was just trying to show me what a good husband he is. He wanted to make a good impression, which he did, you must admit."

This truth was so lamentably obvious, that I, too, began to laugh. We sat in the hot kitchen rocking and shrieking in shared hilarity, trying to figure out why my husband should celebrate Elizabeth's coming by washing clothes using a method from his boyhood in China. He accomplished more than he planned, bless him, for from that moment, Elizabeth, whom I had venerated as friend of God and the bravest of women, began to be my friend, too.

On the day of her farewell tea, I took down the cherished silver coffee-pot that a friend had given me. Elizabeth watched as I turned it ruefully in my hands "Isn't it a lovely thing? I'll never understand why anyone would give it away, especially since it is a family heirloom. If it weren't so badly tarnished, we would use it this afternoon."

Taking it from me, she looked the pot over. "If you would like to use it, I think I can clean it for you. I'm no good at cooking or baking fancy cakes, but I believe I can polish silver. It might even be good for my arm." So saying, she set to work. All morning, she dug into the intricate swirls and crevices with orange stick and silver polish. Finally, she handed the lovely gleaming piece to me for approval with the acid comment, "You wondered why anyone would give you such a lovely heirloom. After cleaning it once, I think I can tell you!"

How many times I have winced at the sight of that tarnished coffee-pot, then laughed, remembering Elizabeth. For us both, life has been too full to spend many mornings polishing silver!

The next day, she left us to begin the long trip back to the Orient. As we bade her goodbye at Penn Station, my husband and I were saddened by the conviction that we should never see her again on earth. For days I gloomed about in a Penelope-like mood, picturing our silver-haired Elizabeth sailing once more and for the last time beyond the sunset, wondering what final great adventure waited her in our darkling world. Like a slap of stinging salt sea, a letter came from Japan addressed to my husband, which put an end to useless dreaming.

In her usual abbreviated style, she wrote:

> Dear Fran:
>
> Enclosed is an expression of an iota of my indignation at seeing one of the largest U. S. ships loaded down with scrap iron, cotton and oil being unloaded at Kobe. Preparedness for Japan to do what? Of course in a duel, you arm your enemy and do not take undue advantage. For three years our country has been making possible this war of aggression on China, and even keeps it up when Indochina and the Netherland Islands are threatened. Hull says, 'Hands off,' but allows Japan the war materials to make aggression there possible.
>
> You are an ardent Roosevelt man. What do you make of this? Why arm ourselves and also our enemy? Why exhort Japan not to bomb Chungking, but send them the stuff to do it with? Japan says, 'Just send your Americans home, and we will use your materials to bomb where we please.' There I almost used a swear word. I cannot exhaust my indignation. Poor France, put on 'Cash and Carry,' goes down to defeat, our aid too late, while we help Japan! It is as criminal as sending help to Germany.
>
> Mother

Although we smiled at the inferred criticism of our politics, we shared her indignation. President Roosevelt had declared Japan the aggressor back in 1937, but this was small comfort to the people in China, especially in Chungking and the great industrial cities, which were being pounded into the earth. Lesser cities like Foochow were also savagely attacked. A bit of American scrap iron had missed one of Elizabeth's granddaughters by seconds, when it flew in the window where she had been standing watching the bombs fall.

In 1941, I attended a dinner in New York for Chinese missionaries and friends. At the close of the meal, we stood up in turn to introduce ourselves. Afterwards like an echo of my 1927 experience at Wesley Foundation in Madison, Wisconsin, a grave Chinese gentleman sought me out. He held the hand I offered and spoke with deep emotion.

"I have just come from China on government business. Before leaving, I was able to get to Hinghwa to visit my home. There I saw your wonderful mother. I cannot adequately explain what I feel. My China lies in dust and ashes, ruined. But in Hinghwa by a knocked-down building, I saw your little old mother. She was pointing with her cane at certain stones for the stone mason to mark. What for? For new buildings, she said, churches and schools for my China! She believes in China! She is building for our future! What this means today in my country you can never know."

At that moment, the long legend of Elizabeth was substantiated. She was remarkable not only to us but to the Chinese people among whom she had lived a lifetime. To them she was love and courage and hope. They identified her in their hearts along with their mythical phoenix. I identified her with the Holy Spirit. Otherwise, we agreed that, like Samuel of the Old Testament story, hers was no infrequent vision. When I got home that day, I dug out two testimonials she had left with me which had been given to her on her fiftieth anniversary in Hinghwa. One, I have already quoted. The other reads as follows:

"'Thy people shall be my people' has been the spirit of our beloved Mrs. Brewster, who has, in deep devotion, given herself unsparingly to needs of individuals, community and nation in her love-gift of fifty golden years of service. Fearless, optimistic, with untiring energy and contagious enthusiasm, she has enlisted the endeavors of young and old, rich and poor, alike, in uplifting mankind. All those lives that have been touched by hers, cannot but give themselves also in this service of bringing to the hearts of this people the abundant life in Christ."

These testimonials are now family treasures.

Elizabeth, however, is so delightfully matter-of-fact. On a day here at the farm, when her years pressed in on her, I told her of the New York incident. She was not pleased.

"I don't know what the man was talking about. I never used a cane. I suppose I had picked up a stick to point with. After all, I couldn't climb around among those stones. Besides, they weren't stones from a knocked down building, but from a bridge head that had been torn down. Whether they were for a church or school, I can't say. They were most likely for the Hankong auditorium, which I built with the money given me by my friends in Sarawak in 1938. I was always building something."

I laughed inside at her hurt pride. Aloud I said, "That was the point, dear. When hope was almost gone from the people, you kept on." But she was not appeased. She, using a cane!

After Pearl Harbor, the distance that separated us was accentuated by the flaming disasters of the Philippines, Bataan, Corregidor, Hong Kong, Malaya, Sarawak, Wake, Guam and the rest in awful sequence. As these faraway calamities numbed us, we wondered how Elizabeth and Harold's family were faring with the Japanese army at their doors. Letters from them were rare.

The Japanese kept the post offices open, and somehow or other, over the Hump, and by other obscure ways, a few letters did get through. Elizabeth wrote that putting a letter in a bottle and throwing it in the ocean, no longer seemed an unreasonable method of mailing a letter. Paying prohibitive postage, certainly, did not guarantee delivery.

A year after Pearl Harbor, we received a letter from her written just two weeks after that event. She spoke of going to spend a happy Christmas holiday with the Foochow Brewsters. She didn't even refer to Pearl Harbor. For her, the war was already old. The fact that we, too, were involved in it, needed no comment. The courage of beleaguered China in promptly declaring war on Japan, Germany and Italy was worth reporting. Her real concern was revealed in a later letter.

> ...We live one day at a time. Imagine paying $10 for a chicken. At best, perhaps it is less than what you are paying in Manhasset. It costs $50 to $60 a month for the most austere living. This is my greatest concern. How will our Chinese survive on their incomes?
>
> To Francis I say keep calm! In old fashioned slang, keep your shirt on, although, I confess, the daily news makes one too hot to keep anything on.
>
> Mother

Even as we were contemplating with stupefaction the possibility of enemy invasion for the first time since 1812, almost losing our national composure in the sudden shift from safety to danger, Elizabeth in her tiny area, hemmed in by the same enemy, was thinking in terms of the Church of Christ in China. She wrote us that in the city of Amoy just south of Hinghwa, the Protestant missions had merged their denominations, sharing their work. In all Amoy and surrounding areas there was only the one Church of Christ. This, she said, had been Will's dream for all China. She was strongly advocating that the great Methodist Church join the others, as it was already signifying their willingness to participate in such a union. In such a church, the Chinese should be trusted to develop their own church forms and government, free of divisions and strife inherited from us. Only a citizen of Heaven living in the world, as she had once referred to herself, could be planning and serving her country so enthusiastically, while the Kingdoms of the World raged around her. There was no doubt in any of us, where her greater loyalty lay.

Another year-old letter told us of her joyous vacation in the summer of 1941. On a day when the radio spoke only of despair, the letter arrived at our farm in Wisconsin, where we had lived since my husband joined the army and went overseas. How happy I was to read that Harold and his family had moved back up river to Kucheng and that Elizabeth had spent two glorious months there with them. At the end of that time, however, both she and her man servant were eager to get back to Hinghwa.

Travel was almost impossible, she said. In order to discourage Japanese invasion, the beautiful roads so recently completed, had been broken to bits. The one over which she had to travel to reach the river port, had 120 deep crevasses across it. The blocks of concrete torn up from the road had been thrown into the crevasses, making walking it fit only for goats. She had been told that crudely fashioned bamboo ladders were hung down the sides of some of the crevasses for the use of neighborhood people who had to move about. She was sure she could climb up and down the ladders, if she could find someone to carry her across the jagged chunks of concrete. Somehow, she was going to get back to her work in Hinghwa!

How the war gloom lifted as I read. Elizabeth, the undaunted, willing to climb up and down ladders 240 times at the beginning of a long hazardous journey. I read on. "A-Siang (her travelling man) was sick and even more homesick than she was. I sent him on ahead. He had $60, his clothes, and all my best clothes—a long coat, a short velvet coat, satin dress, flowered silk slip, etc. Well, he was captured by five bandits, robbed and left tied to a tree. He got loose and walked to the river port where a really kind person gave him $9 for launch fare to Foochow. There my mission friends gave him money to get back to Hinghwa."

Dorothy, her daughter-in-law, had written how desperate the clothing situation was. She had used up gloves and purses to make shoes for her children; drapes, for their suits and dresses; old sheets, for underwear. For her own furlough (if it ever came), she was saving her husband's tuxedo and a red linen bedspread out of which she planned to make a suit and dress. So for Elizabeth, the loss of her clothes was irreparable. Even so, there was not a single lament; no plaintive, "What shall I do?"

Instead, "I am determined to go home. I am sure there will be a way. There is another seldom used trail that leaves the main road and ends at a village farther up the river. We are going to have the crevasses counted to where that trail turns off. Maybe I can travel that way.

"I would love to hear where Francis is. Is he across the Atlantic or Pacific?"

She had written me a special word of thanks for not fighting my husband's desire to reenter the armed services.

"If you love a Brewster, you must be willing to give him his head," she wrote. "He will love you forever if you do, and never be happy if you don't. Thank you for letting Francis go into the service. There have been Brewsters in every national emergency since the Revolutionary War. Of course, he would want to be in this one, too."

Months later I heard the end of the ladder episode. There were only six crevasses to be climbed to the turn-off onto the old trail. These Elizabeth climbed safely and reached Hinghwa, untouched by bandits or war. Through all the lonely frightening war years, the memory of Elizabeth and her ladder was a strong staff on which to lean. The rest of us worried, but Elizabeth trusted and was always delivered from too great a hardship. That was the secret I needed to learn.

Upon her return to Hinghwa, she went to her mountain home for a brief rest. On the eleventh of August, she remembered our son Bill's birthday, and wrote him, among other things:

"I am writing this on our hill, Si-ga-boi, which your Dad can tell you is the scene of the joyous summers of his boyhood. My house is the highest on the hill and overlooks the plain covered now with tender green, newly planted rice, and trees in countless villages, all framed in mountains. In the distance, the lighthouse sends out its recurrent beam (circular, at one-minute intervals). Across the sea is Nang Cih Island. We can see Hankong, the seaport, where, alas, no steamers enter. This is where your cousin, William, embarked on one of the last steamers leaving after visiting me here, and just before the port was bombed and houses destroyed. Then there is the long stone bridge, guarded by big stone men, warriors brave, two of whose heads were knocked off by the bombing. Then there is Yellowstone, spread out before us, and Hinghwa City, whose great wall is now gone, only a red-earth ridge outlining its ancient borders. Well, it is a glorious view. We have such gorgeous sunsets that no artist would dare paint them, for fear of being charged with too much imagination or trying to paint a 'magical entrance to the pearly gates of Heaven.'"

Since this is the only time I have known Elizabeth to be descriptive, I quote her at length.

With her own welfare safe in God's hands and the work curtailed, she had time to think of her children scattered across the world. In another precious letter, she sent advice to our polio-handicapped son who that year was considering entering an agricultural school. "Look into Rutgers, the University of Wisconsin, and Davis Agricultural Institute in California," she wrote. "I consider these the best for agricultural training." At the time, she was sitting out an invasion threat up in the hills at Sienyu. This was of little importance. She had no access to newspapers or magazines, but stored away in her wonderful mind was concern for a grandson and sound advice on the choice of the college best suited to his needs. She was more calm and helpful than I was, safe in the heart of America.

The war was slowly turning in our favor when a letter describing her eighty-first birthday was received. Because living conditions for the Chinese population were steadily worsening, as the war approached their coast, she begged them to omit the feasts which they were planning for her. Accordingly, they arranged a church service of singing, presentation of banners and the essential oranges. Elizabeth was asked to respond with a speech. Her letter continues:

"I read Psalm 90:10. 'Our life is seventy years at most, or eighty at best. This is a span of toil and trouble soon over.'

"I said I did not agree with the Psalmist. Although he said God was his hiding place—his refuge—evidently, he found it like the refuge places we have in these years, a cave made of earth and masonry, dark and cheerless, but still a refuge from bombs. But because Jesus has revealed the Great Jehovah, also a Father, when I speak of Him as my refuge, as being sheltered in His Pavilion, I refer to one furnished by that Father's love, with all his beauty, joy and light. As I said that, the air-raid siren sounded, but the audience sat serene. I went on to say that when I walked alone in life, lo, He was with me, safeguarding and shielding me with His faithfulness. So why should I say these added years have been a span of toil and trouble? They have not been so. They have been filled with His Presence and His kindness which never fails."

In the afternoon of that day, she carried five dozen of her birthday oranges to the lepers, accepted $150 for her child-feeding program, and finally was guest at two feasts, given in spite of protests on her part. Among her gifts was a bar of Palmolive soap, which had cost $80 Chinese or $4 American money; two pints of kerosene at $50 in Chinese money a bottle. The second feast was given by two devoted friends, Misses Blanche Apple and Pauline Westcott. They paid all her expenses, including, sedan chair into Hinghwa, plus rrom and board for three days, which Elizabeth said was a magnificent gift, living costs being what they were.

Difficult as it was for her to meet the cost of daily living, it was infinitely more serious for the Chinese people. Because of this fact, Elizabeth helped work out a system of church subscriptions, using food stuffs instead of money. Such staples as rice, chickens, eggs and beans were accepted to pay church pledges. At the time this information reached me, I was trying to feed four hungry farm men with the meat and sugar allowed on a coupon book. Milk and gelatin had to be used to stretch our scanty butter allowance. Even though we lived on a farm, we were not allowed to slaughter cattle for meat or take cream from our milk cows for butter.

Elizabeth's letter, telling of the plan they were using in Hinghwa, referred me to Leviticus 27:30:

> All the tithe of the land, whether of the seed of the land or of the fruit of the trees is the Lord's; it is holy to the lord.

and to Malachi 3:10:

> Bring the full tithes into the storehouse, that there may be food in my house; and thereby put me to the test, says the Lord of Hosts, if I will not open the windows of heaven for you and pour down for you an overflowing blessing.

She said the scriptures contained a marvelous truth.

"The increase does come. I grant you it may be through an increase in ability and added wisdom in earning and using, but, for those who obey, the promise is not in vain."

Once again her cheerful good sense in approaching such great problems as collecting food from hungry people to run church and charity organizations of tens-of-thousands, put my feeding-problem in perspective. She was especially concerned for the Christian ministers whose salaries were at best minimal, causing many of them to take additional jobs to the neglect of their parishes. For these, she was asking a contribution of rice from every church family. She helped in the weighing and distributing and in keeping the books on the amounts contributed and paid out.

In those solemn days, surrounded by the malevolence of war, she could still laugh. She wrote that on her birthday she had some Chinese women in to tea. One of them had been a pupil in that first girl's school in Foochow a half century earlier. "She said I was as young as when she was a school girl," wrote Elizabeth. "I told her if that were true, she would land me in my second childhood in another year or two. We had a great time laughing and visiting together."

As the war moved back across the Pacific toward China, many people thought that Japan might make a final stand in Fukien Province and Formosa, which the Chinese consider as one. The brief interlude, when the Japanese held that island, did not sever its relationship to the mainland in the hearts of the Chinese people. This is a fact Americans even now do not understand.

If that part of China were occupied completely and became a battleground, the overland route to India would be cut off, as well as access to the mission treasurer at Chungking. For this reason, in 1944 and again in 1945, the remaining Americans were officially urged to make a speedy exit, which most of them did. Elizabeth considered the difficulty and expense of flight, how the Chinese would view such departure in the face of danger which they had to face, and the effect on the schools if so many faculty members left. Once again, she decided to stay. She could still teach if needed.

A fellow missionary, Mr. W. B. Cole, wrote in 1945 of this decision:

> Your recent telegram reiterated an earlier advice we received

from the Embassy through its representative in Fukien, Lt. Freeman. The little group has carefully thought and prayed about the matter and has decided not to attempt evacuation. There are only six of us, and it would, at best, be with considerable risk at this time to attempt the trip. It would be very hard on Mrs. Brewster and Mrs. Cole to attempt it. The situation is such in central China that one could not be certain of getting through. I think it would be hard on the work for Henry Lacy and me to move out. I am afraid they would lose contact with the mission Board. We hope, in case of emergency, to retire to a secluded place until the storm passes over. But if it comes to the worst and we get interned, it will be no more than a number of other missionaries have been enduring for months and even years as in the case of Bishop Ward. It does seem too bad for the last man to pull out. I agree that the number should be as low as possible. I have advised the women to go, but they cannot see it that way. Mrs. Brewster said that it would be the end of her sixty years in China and she did not want to die running away from her work. She prefers, if necessary, to die sticking by. Mrs. Cole could not get out without my going with her, so here we are. We hope that the crisis will pass within the next few months. So far, this little pocket has been passed by. We have expected coastal raids to plunder food supplies, but the enemy has been staid.

***

Mrs. Brewster is staying here for the present but she is certainly a game old lady. She gets restless and wants to go travelling around. However her leg bothers her and she has to keep quiet. She has varicose veins on one leg. She celebrated her 83rd birthday January 31st.

For her decision to remain at her post when escape was possible, she received the following citation.

"The Fukien Christian Educational Association unanimously voted to make grateful recognition of the sacrificial spirit and courageous loyalty of Mrs. E. F. Brewster, who, in the face of imminent danger of Japanese occupation of Fukien in 1944, chose to remain in Fukien (Province) to carry on the work for the Lord, and to convey to this honored friend the heartfelt appreciation of the Association for the inspiring comradeship and noble contribution to the Chinese cause.

We share our mutual woes
Our mutual burdens bear;
And often for each other flows
A sympathizing tear."

For her family up in Kucheng, the circumstances were different. Dorothy Brewster, who was suffering from an Oriental disease called sprue, had been kept alive for several years by liver extract flown in over the Hump by the Red Cross and marked especially for her. Dr. Harold Brewster had suffered several severe illnesses himself, and there were four young children to be considered. Elizabeth went up to visit them for the Christmas of 1943. She, who was never concerned for herself, was troubled for them. The overland route to India was extremely uncertain. Transportation was by ancient trucks and buses travelling over hazardous mountain trails. The buses were fired by charcoal engines which hung on one side making them unbalanced and extra dangerous on the miserable roads. Everywhere there was bombing and scarcity of food. The decision had to be made between such a journey and the possibility of living on the battle field between American and Japanese armies. Elizabeth was inclined to think they should stay at Kucheng.

Everyone prayed for guidance. One morning Elizabeth came down to breakfast to report the Holy Spirit's answer to her prayers. "It's all right for you to go," she announced. "While I was praying, the answer came. 'Elizabeth, have I ever deserted you? Can you not trust me to be with this family of yours all the way?'"

With implicit trust in this assurance, she bade her children goodbye and went back to Hinghwa with a light heart. A few days later she received word that they were starting out by truck with air transportation waiting for them in Kweilin to the west. The telegram included this message from Dr. Brewster to his mother:

"I feel this trip is the Holy Spirit's planning, which I did not feel earlier. Our hospital is now provided for. Union Hospital in Foochow has secured a refugee, Dr. Fischer, a good surgeon, so they, too, are in good hands. My only concern is leaving you alone with the prospect of the U.S. and Japan using this province and Kuantung for the supreme stand. You are 82 years young, but you cannot be a refugee alone, on your own two feet. Be careful, and act as led by the Holy Spirit."

How Elizabeth must have chortled over this good, but unnecessary, advice! How else did she ever act? Her diary records this triumphant comment on their departure.

"God is good. They will now have furlough while there is so little they could do here, and be ready to return when the war is over." She was referring not to lack of work, but the near impossibility of doing it because of inflationary prices which made travel and supplies prohibitive.

Three months later, the family arrived safely in Boston. True, there had been moments of terror and danger, but except for the loss by theft of small David's clothing, which required that he travel in sleeping pajamas, nothing untoward happened. As might be expected, Mother Brewster reached out to bless them. The copilot on the plane over the Himalayas turned out to be a boy she had helped educate. He showered them with kindness and gifts for her sake, making that wartime flight happy for all of them.

Left alone, she turned her energies to her Chinese children. The ministers and other Christian workers went to their tasks that year knowing, that because of inflation and scarcity, their salaries were only one-third of the amount necessary to keep them alive. They needed her courage, faith and unselfish sharing more than the vision they had mourned at Will's death. Life itself was in the balance. No wonder they begged her to stay.

As always, there were still people who had money. To these people, Elizabeth sold everything she had that was not essential to her existence. With that money she bought gold metal, rice and other nonperishable foodstuffs in preparation for the day when she might be cut off from Chungking. Although her Chinese friends had promised to care for her needs, she dreaded being a burden to them. So long as possible, she preferred to be independent, help support students and pastors' families, and pay her church tithe.

She yielded to her friends' concern for her ulcerated leg by spending much time in Sienyu. Letters written from that lovely spot sounded lonely and for the first time, wistful. They were reminiscent of the Psalmist's lament, "By the rivers of Babylon, there we sat down, yea, we wept, when we remembered Zion." She missed the stream of patients going in and out of Richmond Hospital, which she had built for the people of Hankong in 1928. The doctors and nurses were her friends, who looked after her as if she were their own mother. Their children were her "pets" and companions. The busy city streets were full of interest to her. Even when she could not travel her district, she was busy all day long advising and comforting church people, who came to her as to a "shepherdess mother."

At Sienyu she was an honored guest living in quiet and beauty, but without work to do. On March 11, 1945, she wrote: "This morning I wanted to go to church, but in addition to having no audio-ear (the cat chewed up the bone insert device), I have no decent shoes for walking. I do have one good pair, but swollen feet and chilblains make them too uncomfortable. The other wearable pair is being re-soled and mended. They originally cost $14 in Foochow. Since then I have spent $260 on them. This will give you some idea of the cost of our living and the suffering among our people. To take the place of church, I got out a hymn book and had a praise service all by myself."

She went on to say that singing had brought back such happy memories of her part in introducing music to China, that she forgot to be lonely. She recalled the Mason and Hamlin organ which she had sawed off and hinged to make it portable.

"Oh, how, even now, those visits to Kucheng and other country places and those song services, telling the gospel story, thrill me," she wrote.

She recalled her work with the blind, and their enthusiasm for every kind of musical instrument and how others had taken up this work in later years. It became so advanced, that there were two blind organists in Hinghwa who not only knew every hymn in the book by number as well as name, but remembered how many verses each had.

In another letter she spoke of the trains of pack mules that once again traversed the Sienyu hills, since trucks could no longer get fuel.

"It reminds me of how Will introduced the mule in this mountainous region to take the loads off the backs of the people. Then came the years when roads and trucks made the mule obsolete. War has now changed the picture, so that once more the mule bears the burdens."

Although the words were wistful, we at home rejoiced that she had happy memories of worthwhile achievements for others on which to feed. We were lonely, too, with my husband overseas, and ourselves living a hard new life on a farm, far from our Long Island home. The walls of our kitchen were plastered with maps of Europe and the Pacific Ocean, so that we could follow the battle lines.

How often I stood before those maps praying for everyone, wondering why the loving men and boys of the entire world should be torn from their homes and thrust into such desperate peril; wondering how the people living under bombardment carried on their daily work. Then looking at the mainland of China just opposite Formosa, I would picture Elizabeth, so close to the battle line, hemmed in by danger, complaining about nothing, except her inability to be about God's work of helping and comforting others. What a lesson she was for me to study and learn! I was always looking down the months and years asking, "What if?" and living by imagination, instead of trust.

Elizabeth might so easily be asking,

"What if the Japanese come here too?"
"What if I get sick and need a doctor?"

"What if we are bombed?"
"What if this province becomes the final battlefield?"
"What if we can get no more food?"
"What if we lose the war?"

Not once did she worry us with such fears. She continued to live one-day-at-a-time, secure in her citizenship in a Kingdom which is unfailing.

Reading one day the lovely promises in the 21st chapter of the Book of Revelations, I looked beyond the promises to the list of people who disqualify themselves from receiving them.

"But the cowardly, unfaithful and polluted, murderers, immoral people, those who practice magic or idolatry, and all liars will find themselves in the burning lake of fire and brimstone. This is the second death."

It amazed me to find fear leading the list of sins to he avoided by Christians. Once more Elizabeth substantiated the legend I was building around her. She was brave, and I was proud to have her for a mother-in-law.

On March 17, 1945, came another brief note:

"All news reports point to an all-out offensive against Formosa. Many people in the U.S. will not realize what this means to us in Fukien. To us Formosa is an integral part of our province.

"Salt is $80 a pound and matches $70 a box. Fortunately, the Youth Movement is making matches and sent me ten boxes.

"The news from Iwo Jima is terrible, but we are all looking to the final front coming nearer. Aren't we glad we didn't try to get away?"

That question rang in my ears for weeks. For her, the final victory quite obscured the peril which must come first. For the first time, I understood the ancient reply to an ancient but ever-contemporary question.

"Watchman, what of the night?
The morning cometh, but the night cometh also."

Elizabeth was prepared for the night, undismayed, because of the morning to come.

Sir Owen Seaman's *Between Midnight and Morning* might have been addressed to the Elizabeth of those days.

Ye that have faith to look with fearless eyes
Beyond the tragedy of a world at strife
And trust that out of night and death shall rise
The dawn of ampler life,
Rejoice, whatever anguish rend your heart
That God has given you for a priceless dower
To live in these great times and have your part
In freedom's crowning hour;
That you may tell your sons who see the light
High in the heavens—their heritage to take—
I saw the powers of Darkness put to flight,
I saw the morning break.

In the March 16th letter there was also a plaintive appeal for mail, a request for dozens of letters, in the hope that one might get through to her, alone, in Sienyu. "This is not a land of magazines and catalogues," she wrote, "to make the postman stop at my door. Only a letter can do that. And when packages can get through again, I do so need an audio-ear, especially the bone device; stockings and shoes, and hairnets. Well, from this letter you can see how stale and flat life is here in Sienyu."

Stale and flat with war moving in on her! How I marveled at our Elizabeth. Fortunately, the war ended without that bitter final struggle in Fukien. After months of silence, a letter came by air mail telling us that she was on her way home. She was in Shanghai accompanied by a friend, and had priority on the first transport out because of her age and severe eye trouble.

"I have been having trouble with my good eye and have not been able to use it for a month, in case you wonder at this scrawl. I can only see to read the largest headlines. I am assured by the doctor it does not mean blindness, but I must get to a specialist for new glasses before I use it. Now the Lord has been gracious. Because of me we have been put on the priority list and are getting on Army Transport about February 3,...

[Entire page 308 is missing in original manuscript]

She was quite a picture in her silk print dress, white gloves and shoes, and a pert little hat bobbing a pink rose on top of her beautiful white coiffure. I picked up her bags, happily, noting that, in spite of the dimmed vision and sore leg, she walked along without difficulty. I was so delighted to have my picture of an aged, deaf, blind cripple, wearing patched shoes and shabby clothes, replaced by this lovely Elizabeth, that I promptly told her of my conversation with the conductor. For years that has been her favorite story. By way of embellishment, the following story is always added.

At bed time, I carried her bags to her room. When she saw them, she protested, "But I had only one bag!"

The other proved to be the overnight travelling case of an army officer, obviously, what my husband would call, a "spit-and-polish" man. The shoes wore knitted jackets, the pajamas were silk, the toilet articles elegant with silver and monograms. Since we were almost thirty miles out in the country, I telephoned the depot asking if there had been inquiries about such a bag. The station master was silent for a second.

"Well, they weren't exactly inquiries, Lady! I expect the army to move in tomorrow. How can I get that bag?"

Our sons delivered it in Fort Sheridan the next day to the irate officer, who had been sitting across from Elizabeth in the train. If three bags had to be divided between them, I don't wonder the porter dropped two for our incomparable Elizabeth. I have no doubt she had been a lot closer to the war than the army officer.

CHAPTER ELEVEN

Elizabeth and Her Children

The year 1947 found Elizabeth back in China and me in Germany with my husband. George and Mary Hollister, after an absence of eighteen years, had preceded Elizabeth's arrival by several months. Harold and his family accompanied her and 600 other missionaries on the Marine Lynx, a riveted "liberty" ship, whose passengers remembered her with respect but no fondness after a week-long battle with a typhoon. Dorothy referred to their accommodations as "cattle class." They were packed into bunks stacked two and three levels high with just enough aisle room for one person to stand at a time. We had all worried about Elizabeth travelling in winter under troop-ship conditions. But it wasn't she who succumbed to flu and pneumonia; it wasn't she who was laid low with seasickness! As the ship tossed and screamed in the monotonous seas, Elizabeth climbed the ladders and stood in line by the hour for her cafeteria-style meals. She ignored discomfort for joy of going home to Hankong, where she was planning to build her first privately owned house, a four room cottage close to the gate of Richmond Hospital. There she hoped to live and die with the people who had been her friends and children for sixty years. Never again would she have to move to accommodate someone else; her next home would be Heaven. This is what she had talked about and eagerly planned for all during her furlough. She was living proof that so long as people retain their enthusiasm, age is only a word.

In her letters forwarded to us in Germany, I sensed a note of happy abdication, however. Harold and Mary were back in China carrying out the plans she and Will had laid long ago. Harold was inaugurating a public health program around Foochow which was something more than the fulfillment of a great need and his own dream. It was the only kind of work permitted him by his New York physicians after a severe heart attack almost claimed his life just after his arrival in the states in 1944. He had been given five years to live and was permitted to return to China only because it was recognized that if he didn't, he probably would not live at all. He was forbidden, however, to do surgery. The enforcement of this restriction was laid upon his wife, Dorothy. When he began to do occasional and then frequent operations because there was no one else to do them, his wife protested, bitterly. Harold's laughing reply was,

"It is much less of a strain on me to operate and save a man's life than to watch him die trying to save my own."

With this attitude Elizabeth was in perfect agreement.

"Harold is doing just fine," she wrote me. "He is busy spraying, inoculating and teaching. Among other plans, he has one which we hope will take all leper beggars off the streets and provide for their livelihood in stations where they can be treated and 'cured.' He is operating again, too, and doesn't seem any worse for it."

For both of them, life was a loan from God, and they were responsible to Him for it. One of Dr. Harold Brewster's most cherished ideas is that sin is man's defiant assertion that he belongs to himself. Recognition that she belongs wholly to God is what Elizabeth calls, "surrender." So long as Harold was doing God's work, she did not worry about his life or death.

As for Mary, she was doing the work Elizabeth used to do—supervising primary schools and directing child welfare work at the Yellowstone Orphanage, which had been taken from Elizabeth's hands when she officially retired, but not her heart. In reality, she never retired. To her last day in China, she was busy helping people.

Speaking of those years, her son-in-law, George Hollister, said:
"She was always so completely devoted to God's will and the program she and Father Brewster had envisioned for Hinghwa, that she seemed to draw on an inexhaustible source of strength. Even at an advanced age, she could travel more and do more than any average young person. We never ceased to marvel at her energy and tirelessness."

From her letters, we knew of the problems with which she wrestled. Starvation was increasing everywhere, caused by inflation which made wartime currency look like sound money. Elizabeth resented Chiang Kai-shek and his brother-in-law, the Soongs, who she blamed for the ruinous inflation. With their own tiny income, personally solicited gifts and with help sent by Methodist Overseas Relief, she fed the neediest children at a child-feeding station in her new home. These children were fed without regard to religion or lack thereof. This was of particular interest to me in Germany, where my husband and I were doing the same thing for the German people and refugee children.

Yellowstone Orphanage, too, was in dire need. A severe typhoon and tidal wave had washed away the dikes on their rice land, the "Plantation" that Will had bought for experimental farm purposes. Mary and George were desperately trying to find money for rice to keep the adjacent villagers alive and to buy materials to rebuild the dikes before there was another typhoon and the land was ruined by salt water for years to come. Since the orphanage children, too, depended upon the rice income from those fields, the situation was serious. Elizabeth had written in 1916 to one of the international relief organizations to ask for cows for the orphanage so that milk might be added to the children's diet. The children were still suffering from the dreadful scabby heads with which she had struggled so long, with no results.

"But now," Elizabeth wrote, "Mary is here," as if with a sigh of relief she could consign all these burdens to younger hands, even though all of us were middle-aged or older at the time.

We shared her satisfaction as we read Mary's letters, one of which is quoted in part:

> What can I pick out from the crowded events and incidents these past two years, the thrills and the chills, the adventures and the misadventures, the disappointments and the lovely surprise of dreams come true? To have kept up with them I should have written monthly newsletters…
>
> Journeys out to Yellowstone, six miles from the city, have at the end of them the Rebecca McCabe Orphanage, for which I am Child Welfare Director. Every visit is rewarded by the sight of children, rosy and healthy because of CNRRA powdered milk, tinned meat and soup, as well as some UNRRA flour. The children have raised wonderful cabbages, cauliflower, turnips and tomatoes from the seeds a friend of an Ohio seed-tester has sent us. Vegetables, fresh and in abundance, have surely helped to cure itch and scalp ringworm. The Chinese Superintendent tells me, for years past, those diseases of malnutrition were the Orphanage "trademark." But now, because of the loving concern and help of Christian people in America, we have been able to give the children a more wholesome and adequate diet.
>
> Many of you have asked about the CNRRA cows which we were expecting last winter. A major number of those shipped to Foochow died of tick fever. After a long sojourn in Foochow, all six of ours arrived at Yellowstone in June. One died shortly thereafter. All of them were skin and bones from not enough to eat and from their long journey. Two were giving good supplies of milk, and the poorest cow of the lot succumbed. Another cow had a bull calf. Just yesterday came a note saying, "One of the foreign cows has just had a heifer calf." In just a few minutes now we are starting to walk two miles to the canal where the Orphanage farm boat will take us the rest of the way to Yellowstone. So, we'll be seeing the new arrival. Our chief problem is the high cost of fodder. Milk for children depends on adequate food for cows. And that runs

> into money the Orphanage does not have. Anyone interested in "Relief for Cows"—and that means relief for the frailest of our children—may thus share in building health and stamina in the children.
>
> One of the happiest journeys I made was out to our Orphanage reclamation project to see the Dike that had been leveled by the 1946 tidal wave and typhoon. It was rebuilt as work-relief by Church World Service. After months of fear and anxiety, when we and the villagers feared that the dike would not be rebuilt in time to save the fields from again becoming a salt marsh, the funds came. The earth part was built in time for the spring planting. So harvest time brought rice for the long-empty bins of seven villages which work the fields, and also for the Orphanage. We must build the stone facing two feet higher for safety, and dig out the silted canals. The stone facing is halfway across now. We need at least 100 loads of rice, as work-relief to the villagers, to finish it. But the nightmare of starvation is past, thanks to a loving Father's care, and that of His faithful children.

At the time, I did not realize that Elizabeth was looking with equal satisfaction across the world to Germany where her son, Francis, now that the war over, was serving as a military governor, and I was doing my best to help him. At our family reunion at Prudence Island the previous summer, I had laughed at him as he discussed with his mother the part I was to play in his work.

"I want her to help me, unofficially, and on a small scale in Germany, as Eleanor Roosevelt helped F.D.R.," he told her. This seemed a most flagrant lese-majesty to me, a devoted admirer of that great lady. Elizabeth, however, only smiled. I thought at the time our democratic leanings were offending her, for she is as staunchly Republican as Aunt Sally. I know now we hurt her. As it was said long ago,

"A prophet is not without honor except in his own country, and among his own kin, and in his own house."

My husband might much better have said, "I want Eve to do for me in Germany what you did for Father in China."

On the other hand, he knew, as I do now, that of those two beloved women, Eleanor would be easier for me to emulate than Elizabeth. It is one thing to be a friend to people; it is quite another to be a friend who leads them to God.

Nevertheless, Elizabeth has since told me that it was as a reflection of Will that she followed my husband's activities that year. Since no Brewster writes letters except to their husband or wife, those who marry Brewsters have to keep the family informed. Once a week, I typed a long letter to our sons in Madison, Wisconsin, making copies which I sent to Brewsters around the world. There was so much of interest to report that I doubt if anyone other than Elizabeth read them.

Reading those letters across a decade, I rejoice with Elizabeth at the picture of my husband which emerges. How glad I am to have it, now that he is dead. That he had a mission is very clear. He was passionately devoted to American democracy, which he considered the political expression of Christianity. Although he was quick to point out to any Germans critical of U.S. occupation that never, in the history of mankind, had a victorious occupying army been so just and so generous, and he bitterly resented the behavior of army men and women who were responsible for the criticism and who downgraded America.

With the war behind them, many of our people were drinking too much, resulting in disregard for morality in everything. Personal indulgence was widespread. The army was trying to establish the German mark as legal tender but had set a very disadvantageous rate of exchange for Americans. To make matters worse, the German people preferred cigarettes and coffee, both because there was nothing they could buy with their marks anyway, and coffee and cigarettes gave them a false sense of well-being, which helped them through their unhappy days. Thus, the Black Market, condemned officially by the Army, but exploited by G.I. officers and their wives, came into being. One could buy anything for cigarettes, and so everyone was engaged in a vast treasure hunt.

"Don't you have anything in America?" my German teacher asked one day. "No dishes, no silver, no pictures, no shoes?"

She was startled by my indignant reply.

"Why then, do your people need ours?"

Both my husband and I had to admit that her question, however, was valid. Americans were acting as if they came from a country destitute of everything except money and tobacco. My husband, only a major, did what he could by writing to headquarters asking for currency reform and punishment of Black Market offenders. We were especially grieved when officers' wives drove into our territory to order handmade shoes by the dozen when leather was so scarce and the German people could not afford to buy one pair of shoes.

Sometimes we were tempted ourselves by the treasures available. One day at lunch, my husband said, longingly, "I saw the most beautiful thing today! A man brought me a porcelain mallard duck, life size. I never saw anything in porcelain, even in China, that I wanted so much. You wouldn't believe natural beauty could be reproduced so perfectly."

"What did he want for it?" I asked, unnecessarily.

"A carton of cigarettes."

There was nothing more to be said. The cigarettes were no problem. I did not smoke and my ration was always given away. But we did not buy with cigarettes. That afternoon at tea, I saw the exquisite porcelain duck in the home of another officer and listened to my hostess gloat over it. It seemed to me that the way of the transgressor, far from being hard, was often very easy.

There was an oil painting in Bayreuth that I wanted with equal intensity. Our happiest hours, in that end-of-an-era atmosphere that was Germany in 1947, were spent in the magnificent forests hunting the beautiful little deer, called "rei." The searing drought which had lowered the Rhine to 12 inches was driving the hungry little creatures into the fields and gardens of equally hungry people. Since only Americans had guns, we accepted invitations from neighboring game wardens to go hunting as often as my husband's duties would permit. It hurt me to see the deer killed and appalled me to watch the game warden slit and draw them even before the echoes of my husband's gun was still. But each one killed meant meat for people on a black bread, potato and cabbage diet.

On one such trip, the cook and housemaid went along for the ride. We three women sat in the car listening to the classical music coming in from Rome, while the men edged their way along the dark forest toward an open meadow where we had seen several deer playing in the sunlight. Below the music, I heard Frau Heller murmur, urgently, "In God's name, Frau Major, don't move. Just look to your right." There, not four feet from me, stood five rei, listening as intently to the music as ourselves. While our men hunted them in the distance, we enjoyed the music together, like creatures of innocence on a holy mountain. Then a dog barked and we were alone again. The disgruntled hunters, returning empty-handed, didn't believe us when we told them of our concert companions.

After that, I couldn't bear to see them killed. Instead, before going off with my husband, the game warden would install me in a high seat in some lofty tree, showing me where to watch for animals. It was where the lordly red hart (a large red stag in Europe) might come out to drink. How many enchanted hours I sat thus, often alone, watching, listening to the primeval stillness, giving thanks to God for so much unspoiled beauty of woods and wildlife. Never once, though, did I see a red hart. The painting in the Bayreuth window, which I so desperately wanted, was a frame around one such God-shared hour, with a red hart added. He stood, king-size, on a high promontory in the foreground, looking out across a lovely wooded valley where the morning mists rose to soften the vivid blue-green of the forest on the opposite hill and the rose dappled sky of dawn. How I wanted that picture! The finest wildlife artist in Germany, then residing in the Russian Zone, had painted it. His Bayreuth agent asked only two cartons of cigarettes. Nothing more and nothing less!

Kurt, our German ex-bomber pilot/chauffeur tried to help me. After our weekly trip to the Bayreuth commissary, he would drive me through the streets still smelling of burned bodies to the shop where the picture was displayed.

"Two cartons of cigarettes and it's yours, " he said. "I'll give the dealer this package to hold it for you, then for several weeks save your cigarettes instead of giving them away. That's all there is to it. The picture is yours." We went home without it.

The next week, he had another angle. "The office staff will save the cigarettes your husband gives them and buy the picture for you. How's that? Is that wrong, too?" He knew it was, so shaking his head he drove me home.

The third week, I thought his argument was good and reported it to my husband.

"Kurt says, we give cigarettes to people some of whom we know will trade them for potatoes and bread. He says this artist needs food, too. Maybe he wants the cigarettes to buy potatoes over in the Russian Zone, and since we can't get food to him, why can't we give him cigarettes which can be smuggled across the border and we can take his picture?"

"Because my dear, as you well know, you will be taking something very valuable for cigarettes, which is immoral, in addition to being against army regulations. We don't trade on the misery of people, many of whom will probably live to condemn Americans for taking their treasures under such circumstances. If the shop will take German marks, I will buy them at army rates so that you can have that picture, whatever it costs. You can give food in addition, if the artist can come and get it, but you cannot pay for the picture in cigarettes or trade cigarettes for marks, not even if the army changes its regulations. We aren't here to make personal profit out of the war.

The fourth week, Kurt and I stopped before an empty window. He swore under his breath and ran into the shop. The picture was sold. On the way home he took out his precious package of cigarettes and broke the seal.

"I might as well smoke them now. I think your husband and you are crazy. What's the use of being a military governor if you can't take a few privileges? Can you tell me that?" I didn't need to answer, for he went on. "Just the same, I am beginning to see the principle behind this democracy he is always talking about."

That comment from Kurt was worth much more than the picture, which now lives with our vanished porcelains in remembered delight.

Kurt and I were on the road much of the time carrying out my husband's unofficial business while he was busy with official affairs. We visited refugee camps, castles, schools, churches, old folks homes and the overtaxed private homes, carrying food, clothing, medicine, and what comfort we could offer.

I can still hear the heartbroken plea of an aged refugee. "Oh, Frau Major, can you not give us one tiny hope that someday before we die we may see our dear homes again?"

On Sundays we sat, often bitterly cold, in the stone church, listening to despairing sermons. During Advent of 1947, we heard the preacher tell his congregation, "There is no hope for us except the Last Judgment, whose fires I see even now reflected in your faces."

It was to bring hope and cheer to these people that Kurt and I traveled the roads summer and winter, distributing the contents of the overflow of good will that came by the tons from America.

That Christmas, when Elizabeth was providing gifts for thousands in China, her son was doing the same thing in Germany. During the month of December, he personally provided "Christmas" for 1500 refugees and children in his territory—cocoa and oranges for the hospital sick in our town, coffee and stollen for hundreds of adults, cocoa and cake for the children. The American soldiers in a nearby city also contributed wooden toys and candy for hundreds of our children. Those, too, were wonderful men!

After dark on Christmas Eve, I watched my husband plod thru the deep snow beside our furnace-man who pulled a small wagon behind him. In it were forty freshly dressed rabbits; the huge German kind. These were shot by our constabulary boys and dressed by our servants to provide Christmas meat for priests, pastors, doctors and city officials. The hospitals and refugee camps received venison, and all the poor that came to our door were given roast rabbit to take home.

I often remember the humbling words of one such recipient, who said, "Grateful as we are for such wonderful gifts, we are more grateful because you and your husband sit with us in church on Sunday. The worst fate of all is to lose faith in God, and when we see you there, we dare to believe again."

The letters record other deeds that December that were equally loving. My husband listened to a nun's plea, and arranged for her mother's body to be shipped to the family plot in Nurnberg, something no German could have managed because of the shortage of shipping space. He heard that a seventeen-year-old boy was dying of septic poisoning who could be saved by precious penicillin reserved for G. I.'s and syphilitic German women. He telephoned around until he located some, that was released as a special Christmas concession, and sent our chauffeur a day's journey to get it. He heard the pleas of a cooperative farm unit for hay for their registered Holstein cattle, that were literally dying on their feet for lack of fodder in the drought-burned fields. The army delivered trucks of baled hay to that farm on our last day in Germany, transporting it all the way from the Bavarian Alps.

As I read those letters, I smile to see another side of his father reflected in my husband. He was kindness itself to the people, but to the religious and civic leaders he could be equally stern. The Catholic hierarchy owns great palaces in Bavaria. In our territory there were several such residences. At a time when every household was required by law to take in refugees, the doors of these palaces and the less pretentious dwellings of the local clergy remained inhospitably closed. This angered my husband, who felt that those who represented God on earth should be the first to take in the homeless.

"I'll help you in every way I can as pastor of your congregation," he told our local priest, "but I'll fight you to the end on your special privileges. How can you and your superiors live like kings in a time like this and say you represent Him?"

When an entirely Catholic village sent representatives to him with a special plea, he kept his promise. Many of them had not been out of their village for five years, the rest only as far afield as they could walk. They wanted him to arrange truck transportation so that they could make a pilgrimage to a beautiful cathedral in a distant village. My husband had a wonderful idea, which army headquarters was kind enough to implement. It was a real miracle the day a train backed down the long unused tracks to take the whole village for a day's excursion, with me along as the unofficial representative of the American Army of Occupation!

Lutheran ministers who defended one of their faith, who had been an officer in the Hitler Youth Movement, also felt his anger.

"He calls himself a shepherd in the Christian sense, yet changed his allegiance from Jesus to Hitler. What kind of Christianity is that? A good shepherd dies for his sheep; he doesn't betray them or lead them astray."

Certainly to Elizabeth, it seemed that something of Will had come alive in Germany through his son. She was not, however, entirely satisfied. Devoted as she was to America, there was a higher loyalty she demanded of us all. Perhaps my joy and pride in my husband's work was too apparent even in family letters. To us in Germany, she wrote:

"My family has a big responsibility to carry on the traditions of Christian service. You, Fran, and your sons must maintain the standards necessary for such work by being all out for Christ. Without the spiritual power which comes from full consecration to Him, true Christian service is not possible."

This I recognized as true, and it troubled me. Our last days in Germany were busier than usual with friends and acquaintances coming to say goodbye. One afternoon as we sat drinking coffee listening to their grateful, loving words, I remembered what Elizabeth had said. The worry came out in the flat statement,

"But we haven't preached Christ!"

Our guests looked at me in consternation. One of them, a former Nazi party member, spoke up vehemently.

"Preached Christ! If you had, do you think we would have listened? When people are living in total blackness—hungry, cold, homeless, their country beaten to the earth—should you preach to them? Never! When we came to this house or to Major Brewster's office, the door was opened to us without question. Here we have found friendship and food and help whatever our past, whatever our sorrow. Don't worry. We know what you believe without preaching."

How many times I have remembered those words to give comfort, but never without wishing that, like Elizabeth, I could point to even a few people that acknowledged God as their Father because of me. Happily the army chaplain made witness of another possibility for us.

Several days before we left, he had sent us a box of German New Testaments. My husband donated the services of his best stenographer to make dozens of copies of a prayer written by Cardinal Dougherty. These we pasted on the fly page of the Protestant Testaments and handed them out as farewell presents, to make up for the preaching we had not done. The prayer is as follows:

Learning Christ

> Teach me, my Lord, to be gentle and sweet in all the events of Life—in disappointments, in the thoughtlessness of others, in the insincerity of those I trusted, in the unfaithfulness of those on whom I relied.
>
> Let me put myself aside to think of the happiness of others, to hide my little pains and heartaches, so that I may be the only one to suffer from them.
>
> Teach me to profit by the suffering that comes across my path. Let me use it so that it may mellow me, not harden or embitter me; that it may make me patient, not irritable; that it may make me broad in my forgiveness, not narrow, haughty and overbearing.
>
> May no one be less good for having come within my influence, no one less kind, less noble, less true for having been a fellow traveler in our journey toward eternal life.
>
> As I go my rounds from one distraction to another, let me whisper from time to time a word of love to Thee. May my life be lived in the supernatural, full of power for good, and strong in its purpose of sanctity.

We had been back in the states only a few months when Raymond, Elizabeth's third son, died of a cerebral hemorrhage. The family circle had remained unbroken since Will's death. She wrote with her usual fortitude:

> It has been such a shock—Raymond, who seemed in such perfect health, who had never been ill. He was the only one of us to be with your father when he entered Eternal Life, and now is the first to join him 'over there.' How glad I am that we had the family reunion in 1946 before death again entered the family. How much we owe Raymond, especially the three younger children, for help during college, and I for his recent gift of $150 with which I completed my little home here in Hankong.

His death brought home to all of us that we were well into middle age, a fact it was hard to realize with a mother as alert and active as Elizabeth. Dr. Harold Brewster had seemingly recovered entirely from his heart attack. He had already lived more than five years longer than the doctors gave him. For the comfort of other heart patients, let me say that at the time of this writing, he has lived sixteen very active, useful years since his heart attack and considers himself well.

Another brother, Fisher, in California, had made us anxious because of high blood pressure, heart attacks and a stroke. We knew Elizabeth worried greatly about this, he was possibly her favorite son. At her insistence he came across the country for the 1946 reunion although he was not really well. With what delight we heard that on her way back to China she had visited at his home for a few weeks, and that he was driving her all over the state. Her faith had given him the confidence he needed to drive and to go back to work.

In China, where conditions were always desperate, a crisis impended. The inflation which had accompanied the Japanese war was nothing compared to the disaster advancing upon the helpless people. Elizabeth reported semi-starvation in her area. The tremendous popularity which Chiang Kai-shek and his wife had achieved during the Japanese war, when they had suffered heroically with their people, began to wane. Rumors buzzed through the streets that the government was corrupt, even though many people thought Chiang himself was honest. The defeated Nationalist soldiers crowding the streets spoke, bitterly, and openly,

"We starve while our officers take our payroll money and fly off with it."

Elizabeth wrote us that the hungry people watched, apathetically, while the rejuvenated Communist armies took city after city, saying,

"Nothing could be worse than life under the Chiang regime. After all, the Communists are Chinese, too. Perhaps things will be better, as they promise, when all China is under their control."

There was an urgency in all Elizabeth's letters those days before the Communists arrived. There was building which had to be done to complete her dreams, a street dispensary and clinic for the Richmond Hospital, a dispensary at poverty stricken Bing Hai and a library and social hall for the city high school. With $50 gold, which she exchanged at the rate of 400,000 Chinese dollars to one U.S. dollar, she bought bricks at $4,000 a piece. Fruit for breakfast one day cost her 100,000 dollars. Mary Hollister wrote that it was not unusual to find $1,000 bills on the street. Since it was worth only one-fourth of a cent, people didn't pick them up. Elizabeth spoke of getting a great bargain on rice for her child-feeding program—500 pounds for seventeen million dollars. We shuddered at what such prices meant to the Chinese economy. Elizabeth reported that even the post office refused money. She had to bring six pounds of rice to mail us a letter.

Storms and floods added to the distress, destroying much of the summer's rice crop. In logical sequence, illness and bandits preyed upon the stricken people. In such an atmosphere, anyone promising a change was likely to appear a savior. So the people waited for the Communists to take over.

Dr. Harold Brewster described the financial chaos in these words:

In 1935, after several years of the Japanese invasion, the Chiang government called in silver and replaced it with National currency. The people, of course, who liked silver better than paper, buried a lot of it "just in case." When the Japanese blockaded the China coast real inflation began and continued quite understandably during the war. But after the war, instead of improving, it grew steadily worse.

Chiang himself is personally honest, but his government was certainly corrupt. Too much gold was siphoned out of the country and the Communists no doubt helped, too, by hoarding gold. By 1948, the people had such a poor opinion of the value of China National currency, that Chiang had to call it in. People won't trust a government whose money is no good.

Chiang then issued new money—the gold yuan, and personally guaranteed it at the rate of 5 yuans to one U. S. dollar. It was supposed to be exchangeable for gold bars at any time. It was stable for a only a couple of weeks, and, by 1949, people wouldn't accept it any longer. Instead they preferred to barter. A farmer would bring a load of rice to the rice shop. The owner would give him a receipt which he would show to the cloth shopkeeper or whatever he needed to buy. That man would then go to the rice shop and draw rice on the farmers account to pay for the cloth, etc.

People began to dig up the silver they had buried back in 1935 and used that. But they had become used to paper money, so that silver seemed clumsy and heavy to carry. Then the Central Bank of China issued silver certificates, but people didn't trust them.

Down in our province the Provincial Bank of Fujian issued silver notes which were covered 100 percent by silver in the vault, and grand, old Admiral Sah, whom you and Fran remember, was given the only key. He was one official everyone trusted, and so they accepted those silver certificates.

Chiang's gold yuans disappeared entirely. When the

> Communists came, we had to exchange both silver and silver certificates for their money. As soon as it began to inflate in value, they issued bonds and made everyone with money buy them. The Chamber of Commerce had to sell the bonds too, so surplus money was drained off. Then price controls were enforced and money became stable again. Chiang could have done the same thing, but he didn't, so he lost China.

Inspite of the political picture, Elizabeth and the Hollisters hoped to stay.

"Even though we are not Communists, we hope to be allowed to stay on our long record of service to the people," she wrote. "And we will sow beside all waters."

In contrast to the stark mood of her last letter, I quote one from her daughter, Mary Hollister, as evidence of how that sowing was being done:

> Hinghwa, Fujian, China
> April 10th, 1949
>
> Dear Comrades of the Christian fellowship:
> The rhythmic tread of bearers as they carry me in a sedan chair always starts a melodic refrain. Sometimes the words are those of Robert Frost:
>
> For we have promises to keep,
> and miles to go before we sleep.
>
> So it was on this journey from Yellowstone to Chausia by the sea, where I'd promised to visit Children's Feeding Centers made possible by wheat from Church World Service and some gifts that were sent to us for relief. Thirty miles at three-miles-an-hour is far to go indeed, before nightfall.
>
> Fifteen miles away, I stopped at De Tau to ask the pastor

about a member whose message he had delivered to Richmond Hospital, saying, if the Hospital would send nurses he would furnish the building for a clinic. The pastor at once led me to meet the man whom the whole region calls 'Head Boss.' An unlettered man, orphaned at seven, he has built himself into a place of wealth and influence in his community. The Christian motive of his service, he learned from the home of a Methodist minister years ago. His daughter has had the advantages of a Christian education he himself did not have. She is now the principal of the local primary school whose deficits are met by her father.

The Head Boss said, 'Yes, I have several buildings that are at your disposal for a Health and Child Care Center.' He led me to a long two-story building, facing a large playground.

'I built this hoping there'd be a Junior Middle School,' he said wistfully. Then he led me to two other buildings in the heart of town, now occupied by shops.

'Take you choice. When can you send the nurses?' I could not give him an answer. Richmond Hospital already has a deficit in its budget.

'When friends from America send us gifts to match yours,' was all the hope I could give him.

I started out once more for Chau-sia, but rain drove me back to De Tau for the night. Visiting with the daughter of the Head Boss, I learned more about her father's interest in Rural Reconstruction. Twenty years ago, in a time of revolution, he fled with his family to an ancient, uninhabited monastery in the mountains. There, he has brought the barren hillsides into cultivation, trying different fruits and vegetables.

He imported Leghorn poultry. The family has cows, native stock, for milking. He had heard about the Orphanage herd of Holsteins, and plans to bring his cows to Yellowstone for breeding.

Most significant of all, he has planted the naked, clay-red mountainsides with pines, persuading others to do likewise.

This was a man I want our young Agricultural College graduate, newly arrived at Yellowstone, to meet and know, to see what one man, without any education, can do for a countryside.

When I was invited to visit the 'Mountain,' I pinched myself with delight. Did I not have a whole day to reach Chau-sia, only 15 miles away, even with brief visits at Deng-gang and Chau-rang? I walked up a steep trail in the gay company of the Principal. All along the path, sturdy pines showed what could be done to prevent the erosion that throughout the Hinghwa region results from the scalping of the mountainsides for fuel, washing down the red clay into what have been fertile fields.

The terraces beneath the monastery were aglow with the blossoms of peach, pear, and plum. The fields below the high stone walls were green with beans, onions, and other vegetables. Wheat in the valley had been burned by six months of drought. Here wheat was green and flourishing from mountain springs.

In the monastery itself, at least thirty village men are housed when work is heavy. Poor folk, who would starve except for this work, sleep beside the curtained Buddha's shrine. The Boss gives them food and fuel to take home to their families. Beside the Quan Yin rock grotto in the rear, is the huge ancient kitchen and bathhouse that used to serve monks and now serves the workers.

We ate steaming green horse beans picked fresh from the fields. The vines were left in the ground for fertilizer, a new practice the Head Boss learned from the West. 'Now others of the village folk follow his example,' his daughter told me.

I left that lovely refuge with its demonstration of what even a little zeal in rural reconstruction can do, further convinced that our Orphanage program must help others to like energy and enthusiasm. Such service to human need is not only our surest hope for survival, in a time of revolutionary change, but also hope for desperate and hungry folk.

As the chair bearers swung along the wet beach, skirting the receding tide, I thought of the Master's promise of More Abundant Life. I looked at other stark red-clay hills where nobody had planted pines. I thought how much we had failed, in at least part in the promise to those who follow Him so simply and so gladly.

Across the sand-rifted fields came a red welcome banner followed by fifty children, each with a gay colored-paper flag and scores of their elders. They came from Deng-gang, they said.

'We waited all yesterday afternoon. But now you're here and we are so happy. It is over twenty years since any one from the City visited us.'

They did not reproach me for the weary miles they had trudged the day before and this day. I had expected to stay an hour. But how could I do aught but stay the night? That afternoon, I spent visiting every Christian family, some thirty in two villages. In all the courtyards, their non-Christian neighbors joined us in the give-and-take of conversation and the showing of the latest babies at the prayer for blessing.

Such cheerful folk they were, never murmuring against their hard lot. It was their pastor who told me that their dried sweet potatoes were almost gone now, and the people were already on two meals a day. We walked beside wheat, so stunted by long drought, that it could not possibly head. It was the crop upon which they depended for their next quarter's food supply.

Chau-sia, at last! How can I etch for you the picturesqueness of that town of stone houses perched in the inner curve of a rocky promontory, with amber sand and silver bay at its feet? 'The first catch coming in!' they told me excitedly, as if the fishing boats were returning in my honor. I visited in the homes of Chau-sia.

In almost every one there were women widowed by the sea. Often the men of a whole household had been lost together in one sampan. Other homes, where fathers still toil, are too poor to replace their sampans and nets lost during the war. In addition to their sorrow, they must endure the taunts of their heathen neighbors, 'Where now is your God who loves you?'

But it was Lo-cho that finally broke my heart! 'The poorest of all the villages,' they had told me. One hundred dollars from Madison, Wisconsin opened a child-feeding station here. Seeing the others, I had not believed Lo-cho could be poorer. Where other villages had sweet potato patches, Lo-chow's fields are covered by the windblown sand. Their houses beside the shore are drifted up to the eaves, like a picture of 'Snowbound' in ecru. They have no fishing boats, and only have the small nets which can be used on the beach.

Five old people died of starvation the past few weeks. Two committed suicide, rather than suffer slow, gnawing death. I stood beside the bed of straw where a wizened, tiny skeleton of an old woman lay, her hot, thin hand in mine. Her family stood beside me weeping. She had asked that I come and pray for her. 'I've been a Christian since I was 19 years old,' she smiled at me. 'Does any liturgy of the church have a prayer for one dying of hunger?'

Somehow God helped me pray words for her comfort, but I was comfortless. In my own heart I could only plead forgiveness for a Church that had failed her and so many others, and dedicate myself anew to making our Gospel function for all of life. 'For we have promises to keep.' The Master's promise of More Abundant Life for body as well as spirit—can we preach it and not help Him fulfill it?

The Rebecca McCabe Orphanage moved out to the country site of Yellowstone more than 30 years ago, in order to more completely fulfill that promise of Life More Abundant. Here were orchards, gardens and fields which would not only give food for needy Chinese children, but would give agricultural training and vocational skills for livelihood. From these fields, we hope to produce a more adequate diet for our children.

Already with one-meal-a-day of wheat and soy bean meal, the children have gained in one month as much as they did in five months on the former all-rice diet. By improving the crops in our fields and the diet for our children, we hope the Orphanage may become a demonstration center for the whole Hinghwa region.

We cannot possibly receive all the starving children around us. But as a Rural Service Center, we can do our share in preventing such starvation. We have added two fine young agricultural workers to the staff of the Rebecca McCabe Orphanage, not only to plan our production and help train our children, but also to hold institutes and, through personal visitation, help villagers improve their methods. Among the projects needed are the reforesting of the barren hillsides, both to prevent further erosion and also to furnish fuel in areas where it is as expensive as rice; the planting of grass where sand is overtaking whole seaside villages; encouraging the formation of fishing cooperatives to replace boats and nets lost during the war; and introduction of better seeds and stock.

Health is closely related to nutrition and agricultural improvement. And so our Public Health service must reach out to hundreds of villages without doctor or nurse. For twenty years the Jakway Dispensary, which used to serve the countryside with its Chinese doctor and nurses, has been used only as an Orphanage clinic. We must return it to the community service for which it was built.

Head Boss is still waiting wistfully for the nurses for his building. From the long list of applicants for the Orphanage, how can we choose between so many equally needy? We haven't enough scholarships for the children we already have. In the next few months, will we be able to save some children from the starvation I saw in the bloated, gray faces in Lo-cho and other villages? Remember the sand-covered sweet potato fields and the

> old Christian woman dying of hunger? Will you help us fulfill the promise to the hungry and needy who follow His Road with you?
>
> For we have promises to keep,
> And far to go before we sleep,
>
> You and I, together with Him we serve,
>
> Mary Brewster Hollister

Several months later, the serenity of Mary's letter was offset by the following excerpt from one of Elizabeth's letters:

> I, who have always been an optimist, am now a pessimist as to the next ten years in China. I hope the U.S. does not give aid to the Nationalist regime. The Nationalists, whom we have all backed as Christian, have sold us down the river, while they emerge among the richest people in the world. Their officials and generals have enriched themselves and starved their soldiers. Nationalist soldiers up north are flooding our province preparing to defeat the Communists on twenty-four pounds of rice a month and $2 in silver.

In a country like ours, it is well to remember that public opinion guides foreign policy, and so I quote Elizabeth's opinion, despite it being as unpopular today as it was when written. Our country, like our family, is still divided on Chiang Kai-shek and his island fortress—on whether or not we should recognize Red China, and whether it should be admitted to the United Nations. At the time, my husband agreed with Elizabeth that Chiang had forfeited our support. He had once again the faint hope that if we remained neutral in the Chinese civil war, we might be able to win China to democracy. But other voices stronger than ours reached our government, and the decision to support Chiang Kai-shek was made.

A man spoke to me almost in anguish a few weeks ago:

"How is it possible that our country, which has only one desire, to live at peace with the whole world, finds itself so attacked almost every day? What have we done wrong? You used to live in China. Could we have kept her friendship?"

I do not know, that is certain. If there was a fluid period, it soon hardened against us. Letters from Elizabeth, and others written in that period, indicate how our defense of Chiang puzzled the people and enraged the Communists. It reacted adversely on everyone connected with America or the Christian church. Newspapers and the superlative propaganda machine branded the United States, "Uncle Sam, China's No. One Enemy." Our long friendship with China was over.

Who can say whether a neutral position would have moderated the excesses of the "People's Democratic Party" directed at the Chinese population or its hatred of us? I suppose it would have been possible. I wish we had tried, and kept on trying.

In March of 1950, Elizabeth reported, with resignation, Harold's departure. When his family had left China a few months earlier, he had insisted on staying on to see "If Christians with the full armor of God, and nothing else, no guns, no tanks, no bombs, can meet the full hostility of Communists and win them over to Christ. Even under Communism people get sick and need medical care, and the health services we can give them. The Spirit of Christ as shown in loving service for all the needy is a witness which cannot be forbidden." He left with his proposition unanswered.

His mother approved his decision to leave. He had promised his wife to join her and their family as soon as conditions required it, and the Bishop was advising all missionaries to leave as fast as they could get exit permits. The time had come when Americans placed their friends in jeopardy. It was best to leave. It is interesting to note, that at this writing in 1960, the hospital he served and many like it are still a Christian witness, reminding the people of a friendly America.

Elizabeth had herself applied for an exit permit because her eye needed surgery. While she waited, she continued her child-feeding project. Months later, still waiting for permission to leave, she learned that the people of Hinghwa had petitioned the government not to grant her a permit. "They said they needed me," Elizabeth wrote, "and they did not know I required eye surgery."

With a touch of her former humor, she wrote that George Hollister, whom she dearly loved, was, like Paul in prison in Rome, reduced to writing letters to the churches. The Hollisters, Elizabeth and all Americans left in China were under virtual house arrest. While they waited for the endlessly delayed exit permits, each occupied himself as best he could. Some merely tried to "be good." George wrote booklets and sent them to every pastor whose address he could find, with the object of fortifying his faith and enabling him to answer the questions of unfriendly critics. In return, he received many letters of thanks, several of which I quote:

> Dear Mr. Hollister:
>
> I have received your publications, 'I Believe There Is a God' and 'Understanding the Bible,' two copies of each. Reading them my inner spirit was happy and joyful beyond words to express. I am thankful almost to the point of tears that you, separated from me by several thousand li distance, are in the Lord's love concerned over me, I can only praise the Lord's grace and thank you. The books you have written give great help to us who believe in God. Our religion is constantly debated. We have difficulty meeting the questions. These books solve great many problems, and also strengthen the faith of us Christians. The help we get is not little.

> Dear Mr. Hollister:
>
> May you have peace in the Lord.
>
> I have received the books and pamphlets which you sent. After I read them, I was very happy and much impressed. Because we know in this great time there is need for someone with deep knowledge of theology and science, zealous for the teaching, who devotes his heart and time and money to protect the truth on

> earth. Having the fortune to read your books overcomes sorrow and discouragement. My brothers and sisters in the church have received great benefit. Truly, we are grateful and will not forget.

With the new regime firmly in control in Hinghwa, persecution began. Some frightened man, hoping no doubt to curry favor for himself, denounced George, saying he had radio equipment in his house, which was, of course, totally false. Then began months of great anxiety, as exit permits were granted others but withheld without explanation from the five Americans in Hinghwa.

Excerpts from China during those months tell the story better than I can.

Letter from Mary Hollister dated January 16th, 1950:

> Darling Fran and Eva, Bill and Tony:
>
> Yesterday afternoon, I returned from a visit to a village three miles from where I had gone with a lovely lady, Dr. Fang, to her ancestral village, and the church where she has done so much to help. And there were three letters, one from Maude Sarvis, one from you, and one from Eleanor—all three from such beloved people. I put my feet up on the hassock and in our comfy Sleepy Hollow chair, which you may remember from our W. Winter street living room, to revel in visits with you three. I had preached at morning service, had visited in homes, and walked a still unaccustomed six miles, but I forgot my weary feet, or rather my lame knee, still feeling effects of that tumble I took when Mother's chair went down the bank last September on our trip out to the peninsula—did we tell you? Mother came up unscathed and smiling, but I fell down from my sedan chair to reach her and got black-and-blue.
>
> Mother loves to tell the joke but I still get green at the gills remembering how I felt when the typhoon wind blew her chair down the fifteen-foot bank. I could see it sliding and Mother with it but, by the time I reached her, the coolies

had braced themselves and had helped her back to the sweet potato field. I've never written up that trip and I should do so.

Mother used to visit all these village churches out on the peninsula and of course all over the Conference, but Binghai was always her first love as it was Father's, because the folk there are so poor, but so devout and appreciative and eager. She had long been planning this trip. August we were just being 'liberated.' But early September I decided we could attempt it.

We found that the soldiers too were going out on the peninsula that day commandeering boats and boatmen in the very coast towns we were visiting for island attacks. And the planes seemed to know of troop movements. But we kept on with our itinerary, changing only one overnight sojourn in a fishing village occupied by troops. That village insisted that we have our afternoon meeting there as planned. We found the soldiers occupying the church itself, but they made no objection to our service.

We had our young Agricultural Rural Director with us who always spoke, beside Mother and myself. After we had an early supper and were going on to another village for the night, the officer came out in great distress because he thought we were leaving on their account, and he insisted that we not leave, because they would not give us any bother or inconvenience. We explained that we were following a previous promise to stay overnight elsewhere, and it was not at all because of their presence in the church. (And everywhere we went, there was this same courtesy and friendly interest.)

But the planes made me very anxious when the children and people of the churches would come out to meet us with banners and firecrackers. I couldn't get them to cease welcoming us, but when the farewell processions were in the middle of the day, I could at least plead that they not go too far.

What a joyous welcome there was everywhere for the

Shepherdess Mother, and a thrilling humbling experience for me, her daughter. In one place were two former Orphanage young people, both with nurse's training she made possible, who were working in a former Station Class house which they were able to purchase through her efforts. They brought their children and one knelt to get on a level so she could hear him. With tears in his eyes, he said, 'More than to the Mother who bore me, I owe to you, our Shepherdess Mother. We dare not think where we would have been without your concern and help. Every day in our family we speak of our debt of gratitude to you and ask the Heavenly Father to help us repay you by helping others.'

Every church we visited, she delighted them all by inquiring after their families, whose every name she remembered. One old patriarch said with humble pride, when she inquired about him by name, 'By God's blessing there are 79 old and young in my family now.' She knew him when he was a young man and persecuted by his clan's folk for becoming a Christian.

It was especially fitting that our enthusiastic, winsome young Rural Director was with us, for his kind of work was an essential part of Father's dream of helping bring our Master's More Abundant Life to these underfed village folk. This trip was for him a moving experience—the barren, rock-ribbed hills, the sand inundated sweet potato fields—he'd never seen this before, coming from Sienyu's fertile green rice-producing valley. He made careful studies of their needs for a trip George is planning down to the peninsula with this young Ku and an equally eager, engaging young FCU graduate in Agriculture, whom we have added as his assistant. We hope to carry through with the fishing cooperatives and the erosion control projects we have in mind.

Today George has gone in the Ambulance up to Sienyu for a District Conference and I'm not able to go along—worse luck. But the Mutac Chapel is to be dedicated on

Friday, so Mother and I will go up Thursday for that, since I drew the plans. It is named Po-Sing for both Father and Mother, 'who opened the Church in this region and founded this school' the inscription reads. I haven't seen the building since the roof was on—the lovely up-curved Chinese roof. But people who have seen it report that it is beautiful.

Mary

Letter from Carlton Lacy dated July 31st, 1950:

Foochow, Fujian

From behind the bamboo curtain, we send greetings just this once more. Probably my letter next time can come to you with domestic postage. Yet that is one of the uncertainties of these days. We take a day at a time. Yet, the policy is clearly stated that all administrative responsibility shall be turned over to Chinese Church leaders. It seems equally clear that no new passports can be secured, and our American passports are good for only one or two years without extension—and we now have no officials here to extend them.

A third consideration is our government's position relative to Formosa, which, of course, can be regarded only as one of opposition to the plans of the regime under which we have to live and work. Until now, morale has been bolstered for months with the assurance of better times after the liberation of that last bit of China's territory. Naturally, interference in any way with that objective arouses the bitterest hostility from the propagandists and the newspapers. So long as we remain here, the Church inevitably is associated with "China's No. 1 enemy." Even the friendliest people on the street think of us as the paid agents of Uncle Sam. To be taken as a spy wherever one goes leaves him little opportunity for service or even for testimony. Even if he is able to maintain good nature it is apt to be misunderstood.

Nor have I mentioned the trigger tensions that are wont to break out in a hostile act at any moment on almost no provocation. Nor the constant caution necessary lest a casual word be falsely reported. One of our pastors recently has been in jail for several weeks because he was overheard to remark to a friend that he regarded the taxes as unfairly levied. Such remarks in a free country must be made directly to the officials concerned, not made behind their backs.

The Church and its institutions are assured liberty, and there is no intention, apparently, of taking over our schools. But they must be run (and even if we hold a Church conference it must be directed) with the objective of cooperating with and furthering the aims of the present regime. Any other position cannot be tolerated; which makes those of us who are steeped in what we have been thinking of as western democracy but which we are now taught is American imperialism, simply irritating reactionaries. Here many Christians are really being put to the test, and the presence of the missionary probably cannot help them much.

For these and other reasons I have cabled our Board of Missions recommending the withdrawal of all our missionaries from this Area. We are just across the strait from Formosa. (The rest of what I wrote in this paragraph my discretion warns me to delete and to substitute the slogan that we see and hear everywhere and to which life is geared, 'On to the liberation of Taiwan.'

I would like to tell you some stories of heroism—of seniors in high school who failed their exams rather than give an answer that would deny their Christian faith; of school teachers and principals resisting all sorts of pressures rather than be untrue to their convictions; of churches that are drawing larger congregations than ever before; of one of the most brilliant men graduating from theological college and accepting appointment to 'Podunk' with the quiet remark, 'I resolved to accept whatever the church offered me, as from God;[1] of a superintendent of nurses driven by a 'trial court' from her hospital and saying calmly, 'Don't worry: God some way has his hand in this;' of a Bible woman offering to give up her scholarship for a year of refresher study because there were those who in these crucial days felt they needed her to strengthen their faith; of the man who has already lifted much of my load of responsibility, saying of a fellow-worker, 'We cannot agree, but I will not quarrel with him;' of the college president standing up in a public meeting to beg pardon for having criticized when she ought better to have been praying for a person—and more such incidents that make us certain the foundations of the Church are firmly laid....

Carleton Lacy

Letter from George W. Hollister dated August 15th, 1950:

Hinghwa, Fujian, China

Dear Friends of the Hinghwa Conference,

With the world situation so precarious; with the Chinese press and official propaganda so openly taking the part of North Korea against the United Nations, so venomous against the U.S.A. and so loudly affirming a determination to liberate Formosa from U.S. 'Imperialistic domination,' it appears wise for missionaries to withdraw from this area if possible. Some have already asked for exit permits. Mrs. Brewster is asking to return to the States hoping expert surgery may save the remaining sight of her one eye. But no exit permits have been granted from this province for over a month, and some friends fear the long delay is ominous.

1 His hope to return to the United States was not met. He died in China months later.

Before the present international crisis (Korea) broke, the pattern for missionary work in China was becoming clearer. A group of Christian workers met Chou En Lai and other government officials in Peking. The following principles were stated as official policy:

> All church institutions such as schools and hospitals are to be taken over by the end of two years.
>
> Foreign funds for church work "bring unfavorable cultural influences" on the people. So such funds must gradually be cut off to avoid "cultural imperialism."
>
> There is to be freedom of religious thought.
>
> There is to be freedom to preach in church buildings, but not in streets, etc.
>
> Missionaries will be permitted to stay until furloughs are due or passports expire. After furlough, only a few will be permitted to return, and then only on approval by the government.

Such were the policies being shaped for church and missionary work before the Korean crisis. These do not always follow intended time tables, and may not be as liberal as some of the major leaders. Sometimes it appears to be a deliberate policy of local workers to disrupt the work of an institution so completely that chaos results. Increasingly, Christian teachers are losing their positions because they are Christians. In some cases there is discrimination against Christian students. This is not always true, but appears to be a trend.

Our Guthrie High School is in chaos. Officials are demanding that the Orphanage receive about twenty adult cripples and aged persons from the county 'home.' Our protest, that the Orphanage is for children, not cripples or adults, and that a combination of such dissimilar groups would make our program for the children impossible, falls on deaf ears. The strain in some other institutions is increasing.

I know the views of some missionaries differ from mine. But I feel we should do what the government leaders suggested, and should sharply reduce funds being put into some phases of the work, especially salaries of the preachers. Where schools become in reality anti-Christian, I cannot feel it is fair to you to use your gifts to assist such schools or help students study in them. I can't feel that you would approve help to a student who ceases to identify himself with the church, or to a school that spends a large proportion of time condemning Christianity and promulgating atheism.

So, until the situation clears somewhat and we can see the way more clearly, please hold all gifts for the work that you would normally send in our name. This applies to all funds for all institutions and purposes without exception.

There are still ways in which to serve. I believe it will be possible to continue our Rural Service program for a while. Our hospitals are still ministering to the communities, although under increasing difficulties. Emergency aid will be necessary for teachers dropped or students expelled because they are Christians. There are still hungry children. And adults also come pleading for their families. As long as it is possible to print and distribute Christian literature, that offers valuable opportunities. But until we can evaluate the needs and opportunities a little more clearly, please hold all gifts you would send in our name.

These weeks in which no travel has been permitted have been among the busiest I ever spent. I told you in my last letter that a book I wrote on 'Sin and Salvation' was just off the press. The first edition went so rapidly we rushed a second edition. Then I wrote a tract, 'I Believe There Is a God.' I thought 5,000 would be enough. I doubt if the second edition of 5,000 will last through this year. I have been working on another small book, 'Understanding the Bible.' Printing has started and I hope the book will be off the press by the end of the month.

I am sending copies of my books to almost every preacher in China whose name and address I have been able to secure. Nearly every day letters come in response. Their words of appreciation have been a real tonic. In an atmosphere where atheism is the popular style, the tract, 'I Believe There Is a God,' seems to meet a particularly pressing need. A few days ago, a request came from Foochow for 130 copies for use in a Student Institute. The other day a request came from Nanking for 200 for use in village churches.

One main reason I returned to China was to do just such literary work. The events of the last few months have made possible the partial accomplishment of this purpose. I prefer to work under less pressure. Each time I begin, I have a feeling I am racing against the hour glass, fearing the sand will run through before the task is complete. Each time there have been factors making haste wise.

I have preached nearly every Sunday at the Youth Service. When the pressure has been increasingly anti-Christian, it is not surprising that attendance has fallen off considerably. It is encouraging to see the number of students and teachers who still attend.

If exit permits are granted, we will write again when we leave the field. If permits are not granted—but isn't that the tomorrow for which we are not to be anxious? In this world, the uncertainty confronting a few missionaries sinks into insignificance. My heart is heavy for these people with whom we have been working, whose burdens you have been sharing. What their leaders hope to gain by committing their people to active participation in the international crisis, I cannot see.

My heart is heavy for our own nation, especially, for our youth. How devoutly it is to be hoped that the great catastrophe looming before us can be averted! With so little information available for fair judgment in evaluating the news, to us the hope seems faint indeed.

As each of you seeks to meet the burdens of the hour as

they fall on you, may God's blessing be with you; may His presence bring you strength and courage for the task. I'm one who by nature prefers to walk by sight. The past few years have given me much discipline of soul in walking by faith. It looks as if the near future is going to increase that discipline in due measure, for me and perhaps for you. If we go with Him, always seeking His will, uncertainty need not be fear, and questions need not be dismay.

What a sick world this is! And how long will it take blind, groping humanity to learn it is only love for God expressed in love for man that can cure this illness? Is it because we who profess this faith practice it so poorly that humanity follows so many false messiahs so blindly?

Yours in His service,

George W. Hollister

Letter from Elizabeth Brewster dated August 21st, 1950:

August 21, 1950

And now Foochow has been taken over by the Communists. We do not yet have all the details, but the march has included all areas down to Hinghwa, Putien City and Country. The Communist army found no resistance in this region. The Nationalists left from Hankong by boat or secretly.

The City Magistrate who had been responsible for killing over 200 Communists left before the army arrived with a bodyguard, but they deserted him about 15 miles on the way, for his safety or why, is not known. Probably he got through more safely without them. Even he, a faithful Nationalist County Magistrate, left with 4 or 5 ounces of gold. Of course, he had sent much more ahead.

The Communists coming in assured the other officers that they were to carry on. The large number of their soldiers went on through to take over the County towns between here and Amoy which is their objective and completes the mainland of Fujian. The Nationalists still hope to occupy the Islands along the coast. All we fear now is the bombing, which always kills citizens and not the Communists nor Capitalists. We do not know about the future, but we do not anticipate danger. We know some changes will be made and probably there will be some revengeful retaliation.

They claim to have no relation to Russia and want none with America. Preachers, they say must be supported by the people they serve, which of course is what we have urged and do not believe these men, if faithful, will suffer. We, of course, must still have help in educating other children. "Lawyers and Bankers must watch their step." Doctors, teachers, are especially appreciated.

We are concerned about our leading layman, Joseph Y. Huang. He was, during the Japanese War, appointed by Chiang Kai-shek leader of the Youth movement. In 1946 he went to the U. S. where he heard about the Goh Ming's betrayal of country. Since then, there has been no communication.

Elizabeth Brewster

And then on August 30th, 1950, this note from Elizabeth:

August 30, 1950

I have given up all hope for U. S. permit. Isn't this a glorious ending to 66 years?

Love, Mother

Subsequent letters from George Hollister:

October 6, 1950

These days the officials have all been busy with 'Independence Day.' There has been much propaganda about the 'paper-tiger U.S.A.,' powerless to do anything against anybody, can't even lick Korea by itself, but has to call all the other nations to assist it in its fruitless efforts to oppose North Korea.

News about Korea is leaking out to the people. The reports say that people in Foochow are able to listen to the radio without any interference. People coming from there seem to be bringing information with them. As a result there seems to be something of a different temper of mind in some circles about the possibility of easily taking unconquered islands of the coast....

George Hollister
Hinghwa, Fujian,
December 24, 1950

The official campaign of bitter enmity against the U S. has been stepped up. It is now against public good to have any goodwill toward any American. Agitation in the schools has increased. For quite a while I have not gone outside of this compound for any purpose whatever. The best plan seems to be to stay quiet and out of sight.

The land distribution program is being pushed. At first it was to be tried in only a few localities. But now it is to be general, all over the county. A large group of workers is now assembled to be instructed in procedure. These are then to go out and put the plans into effect.

Each day we hope against hope for speedy permits. Until they come, there is nothing to do but hope and pray.

George Hollister

Hinghwa, Fujian, Jan. 1, 1951

Dear Family:

This is my first letter of the New Year. And for once in my lifetime, I struck the correct figure the first time. Maybe that is because the passage of time is so significant to us at the moment that each day has special meaning.

The paper reports the freezing of Chinese Government funds in the States. In retaliation, this Government is taking steps against U.S. funds in China. Just what is involved for mission funds or missionaries is not yet clear. It is a horrible feeling to be caught in the rapids above the falls, powerless against the currents. I never did preach on the text, '0 ye of little faith, wherefore didst thou doubt?' But at this particular moment, I admit my personal need of the admonition and rebuke. The currents are racing and leaping, and the roar of the falls seems louder day-by-day. No, I don't blame those disciples now as I might have done some years ago. So I had better go and preach a sermon to myself on that text.

In a few villages, the division of the land has been carried on in an experimental way to guide the application of the principles to larger areas. And now the principle is to be applied to the whole county. I understand it is to be completed in three months, maybe even sooner. Just what provision will be made for the Orphanage, when most of the fields are taken, is a matter that has been referred to a special committee among the officials.

The papers tell of many students all over China volunteering for the military forces in their eagerness to stop American Imperialism. From the numbers volunteering from the local high schools, the total must be very high. Naturally, the number is higher among the boys, but it is surprisingly high among the girls, also.

George Hollister

And finally, Mary Hollister writes on February 16th, 1951:

> Dad has told you the good news. TODAY our names go off to the Foochow paper, to appear three times. Because of Chinese New Year, the Bureau of Public Safety said the Fifth of the First Moon would be the best time for us to begin our journey, since the first three days of the festivities would hold us up anywhere we were along the road, so we might as well wait here for it to be over. So the fourth day they will examine our baggage and the fifth we can start for Foochow. This date for departure is February 10th, Saturday.
>
> They tell us Mother is to come here with her baggage beforehand, on the 2nd we hope—so I can make out her baggage lists for her. For the ladies, the Bureau of Public Safety sealed their trunks, which was a great help to them since the sealed trunks were not opened until Canton. And they say they will do the same for us.
>
> Mary Hollister

The journey they had so prayerfully anticipated, was long and hard. They were to go to Foochow by truck and boat; by launch far up the Min River; then by truck over the same perilous mountain roads which Harold and his family had traveled seven years before, across country to the north and to south railway at Champlin; from there it was a two-day journey to Canton. Friends had petitioned the government to allow Elizabeth to travel directly from her seaport home by boat to Hong Kong, giving her age and infirmities as a reason. When the request was denied, she gathered her possessions and went into Hinghwa as required, so that Mary could make a thread-by-pin inventory of her baggage. This was no hardship, but very irritating to people who were anxious to be on their way.

Elizabeth has told me of those last days. On the final one in Hankong, friends slipped in and out bidding her goodbye, seeking to win her promise to return. This time there could be no return, she told them. It was goodbye after 66 years of happy association. That night the hospital staff gave a small farewell feast in her honor, promising her that they and many others would be in Hinghwa to see her off with the firecrackers and ceremonies. Others would line the Hankong streets through which the party would pass to see her begin her last journey home.

When that day came, there were no fond friends crowding the house in Hinghwa to press her hands in loving farewell. Of all the Hankong friends who had promised to come, only one family arrived. Elizabeth began to wonder what happened, but she did not want to embarass anyone with questions.

"I thought to myself, 'Well, of course, why should they walk here when we go right thru Hankong? They'll be waiting there. Perhaps they weren't allowed to come.'"

But when the party reached Hankong, she could hardly believe it was her home town. The streets were deserted. The shops and houses were shuttered and still.

"Then I knew something dreadful must have happened, something of a political nature to frighten the people. But I felt their grief and love as I passed down the street for the last time. I knew that behind all those closed shutters my friends were peering through cracks and were watching me with tears and prayers.

"I remembered my countless comings and goings, the loving, anxious concern that sent me to America, the joyous clamor that greeted each return, the lighted lanterns, the firecrackers, the people running out to welcome me home. Now there was only silence.

"Not until we were a day out of Hong Kong on the open sea, did George tell me that the evening before we left, fifty men, mostly wealthy merchants, the mayor, and my beloved Joseph Huang, were called out of their homes, tied together and marched into Hinghwa for 'education.' Mary and George heard the gunfire. Thank God I did not. That is why no one dared to appear on the streets as I passed through.

"I felt terrible about Joseph Huang. He had tried to clean up the

Nationalist party in our area, to purge it of corruption. There was no reason whatever for killing him, nor the others, for that matter. But that is the way of revolutions. I know the Nationalists had killed several hundred communists, too, and I suppose they had to have revenge.

"We traveled by truck to Foochow. The roads were filled with army vehicles and soldiers all going our way.

"When we got to the river, there was enough traffic ahead of us to occupy the ferry for three days, and we had to be in Foochow by morning or forfeit our exit passes. I prayed. I am sure we all did.

"Then a man walking past our truck recognized me. They all knew me by my white hair. He stopped to visit and we told him of our plight. There was a young family in our truck who I knew. The husband got out and went off with the friendly visitor. It was dark when they came back. They had gone up to the river and found the head officer, and told him about us sitting way back in line. He gave them a flashlight and told them to go back, pull us out of line and bring us up the river. There was to be one more ferry that night, and he would get us on it. How we thanked God and those three men!

"That man travelling with us was another mystery to me. He was the grandson of one of the first blind orphans Will and I picked up to educate sixty-six years earlier. He had his wife and two children in the truck with us, too. I knew he had joined the Communist party, and thought it strange he would care to be seen with us. They stayed close to us during our four days of questioning in Foochow and saw us safely on the launch to Yenping. After we were on our way up river, George told me the warlord had brought his whole family as guarantors for us. In case we were refused to leave, they were prepared to offer their lives for ours. So at the end, we were not forsaken. Because of a baby I had saved sixty years before, we had four people ready to die for us.

"It was an awful trip. Beyond Yenping we got into trucks for the trip over the mountains. I'll never forget those roads! George held the back of my neck for two days to keep it from being broken by the jolting. Then we traveled two more days by train to Canton. And that was the way I left China."

Out of those last harrowing months, there came another lovely story. When the Communists occupied Hinghwa, their soldiers were quartered in homes. None were sent to the Hollisters, who were under virtual house arrest. One hot summer day, a minister friend came to visit them. He said that of the four soldiers at his house, one was weak and ill with a distressing stomach ailment, probably ulcers. He wondered if the Hollisters, who owned an electric refrigerator, would make a little ice cream for the man. Since there was some already frozen, George filled a small bowl which the minister hurriedly carried away. The next day he came again. The soldier had greatly relished the ice cream, he said, as had his three companions who had the privilege of licking the spoon and bowl clean.

"Would Mr. Hollister send another bowl so those three men could have a taste of the delicious stuff?"

Through the hot weeks that followed, while the Hollisters waited longingly for permission to leave the country where they were so unwelcome, ice cream went regularly to the four soldiers. A few days after they left to go to the Korean front to fight our United Nations army, the minister came again to see the Hollisters. He brought a gold ring to George. It was a gift from the sick soldier whom the ice cream had greatly benefited. He had left money with the minister and described the ring he wished made for the American he had never seen. Inside the plain gold band were two Chinese words which translated read, "Loving Helpfulness." With this fitting benediction from such an unlikely source, Elizabeth and her children left China, but, please God, not forever!

CHAPTER TWELVE

Our Priceless Dower

Someone in California mailed us a newspaper account of an interview with Elizabeth granted upon her arrival. Surprising words leaped out at us.

"I have no enemies in China."

Against the news of the day, this was an astonishing statement. Did she mean that she hated no one there or that no one hated her? Was she forgetting the terror Chinese as well as Americans were suffering? Perhaps, we conjectured, she was just being cautious to protect those who, like Bishop Lacy, were still being detained. When her first letter arrived, our questions were answered.

"I have left my membership in the church (in China) and I shall send my tithe there as long as I live."

As she had written us previously, the turmoil in China was just one more revolution, so far as she was concerned. She was not withholding her love and faith, no matter how long and savage the struggle. Her words have had a stabilizing effect on me in many other crises. It is a fine thing to be forgiving and generous when the wrongdoer is properly punished and the injured justified and compensated. It takes the presence of the Holy Spirit to forgive when the transgressor flourishes, multiplying his sins.

Elizabeth's attitude recalled an incident from the Spanish Civil

War when so much evil was done by both sides. Several soldiers of the Republic had seized a Catholic priest, and, in an excess of mistaken patriotism, chopped off his right hand. The comment of the priest is unforgettable. Looking from the bloody stump to his tormentors, he voiced his wonderful discovery,

"I don't have to hate!"

It was as if he was saying that he might recover from the physical hurt, but never from unforgiving hatred for the men who did the wrong. Later we heard that Elizabeth was denounced by men and women under pressure and fear. If she knew it, she understood and forgave. She never spoke of it to me.

For us, the most wounding knowledge came from the information George Hollister brought us. He said the Socialists, as they prefer to be called, not only stabilized money and controlled inflationary prices within weeks, but, more incredible still, they wiped out the "squeeze" system which had corrupted Chinese business for centuries. This corruption extended from the buying and selling of public offices in all ranks to the purchase of one's daily food. Foreigners living in China suffered, particularly, from the latter sin. Everyone knew that the family cook padded the price of groceries for his own benefit. Some conscientious Americans hoped to eradicate the evil by raising the man's wages, but for the most part, the experiment was unsuccessful. The habit was too firmly fixed to be uprooted so easily.

That these desperately needed reforms were made, not by Chiang Kai-shek but by the Communists, was at least in part, what Elizabeth had in mind when she wrote us that his government had sold us down the river. We were reminded of the persistent reports of the students from China, who liked to say that the Communists behaved, in some respects at least, as Christians were supposed to behave. Men and women served together in the army with puritanical virtue. For the sake of country, young people sacrificed every possession, including life itself. The moral regeneration, for which Will and Elizabeth and thousands of others had worked and prayed, had been accomplished on a national scale, not by love for God and mankind, but for pride in country and through the fear of death.

George Hollister told us, too, of the passionate self-sacrificing zeal with which the youth of China had adopted their new cause. The questions he did not need to ask were these: would Christians do as much for God? Would Americans do as much for their country, or had the love of self become too deeply ingrained?

When Elizabeth came to visit us, we asked her whether the Chinese Christians could answer the challenge of their new government, to prove that they had something better to offer than the new god of National Socialism. Was their faith strong enough to survive? The self-supporting church for which she and Will had striven to establish was not yet a fact; the United Church of Christ was still further from realization. Could the Church survive, we wanted to know.

"The Church will survive," she smiled, presumably, at our assumption that men alone would decide its continuance, "but it will doubtless decline in numbers when American help is cut off. There will be persecution of Christians as stooges of a foreign religion, but many will hold steady."

She told us then of an old woman in the church who died some months before Elizabeth had left China. It was once more the story of one who had apparently died only to return briefly with a message. The old lady had opened her eyes to say to her sons,

"Be true to the Church; this is very important; I was sent back to tell you. Remain Christian; be true to your church. Also, tell Mrs. Brewster, I saw her heavenly home. There is a five-story house waiting for her. I saw Miss Wilson's home, too. She lives next door in a little white cottage surrounded with flowers. Her place is small because she is only one and doesn't want a big house. But the Brewster's house is five-story high, because of all their children and grandchildren."

The childlike faith of the story delighted me. I, too, expect to live in a family in Heaven.

"Oh, Mother," I laughed, "be sure to save me a room with a southern exposure!"

"I will, dear," she promised. Then after the briefest pause she continued, "so that you can see the mountains against the sunset, and look out across the ocean to Nan Cih Island, where Francis and the other boys slept on the white beach with the pirates, and straight out from where the beam from the lighthouse sweeps the sky like a beckoning silver arm!"

She had described the view from her summer home on the mountain outside Hinghwa. No doubt, Will was in her picture, swinging up the steps with flowers for her in his hand. In my picture, my ruddy-faced, blue-eyed husband walked beside his mountain chair, swinging his white pith helmet, as he came in sight of the stone cottage where we waited for him.

For both Elizabeth and me, Heaven is where our Brewster men are waiting.

* * *

It was during one of those earnest conversations that summer, following her arrival home from China, that I asked her:

"Was it worth all your effort and Father Brewster's? Would you do it again, if the opportunity presented itself? Or were all your years in China thrown away?"

How glad I was to hear her reply.

"I would do it all again, gladly. I have seen my joy shared too many times to be discouraged. I have known too many full of the knowledge of the presence-of-God, to despair."

I wish she had told me then about John Sung, a man so full of the joy and knowledge of God that he became China's greatest Christian evangelist. I had never heard of the man, until the day at the farm, when a letter came from England containing a questionnaire from someone planning to write his biography.

"Do you know such a person?" I asked

"Yes, I know him," she replied. "He was a great Christian and evangelist, but he went off on a faith-healing tangent. I wish he hadn't done that. I have known people to turn against Christianity because John Sung, Siong-ceh, as we called him, "healed" them at a meeting. Afterward when their sickness was found to be with them as before, they would become bitterly reproachful against all of us."

Several years later, when I was going through some of her letters to Harold, dated 1927 to 1931, I found frequent reference to one Siong-ceh Sung. She spoke of accompanying him on evangelistic tours, of his great earnestness and of his ability to win young people. She spoke of the birth of his first daughter, whom he named Genesis.

"We're hoping to tone the name down to Gene," she wrote. Not until I read Leslie T. Lyall's book, *John Sung*, did I realize that this young man, who had swept through China like a modern Paul, was the Siong-ceh in Elizabeth's letters. In the fifteen years before his death, in 1944, he had preached Jesus Christ from North China to Borneo with power and conviction rare in our day. Perhaps his attacks on dead churches and people who used the Christian ministry as a profession caused her concern; perhaps his dramatic and often emotional preaching offended her. Perhaps her own desire to see the Church of Christ unified in China was disappointed when John Sung went to work with one of the "splinter denominations." Nevertheless, he preached God into the lives of countless people living in China today, blessing them with his own faith even as Elizabeth did with hers.

His father was one of the "bright boys" that Will found on one of his country trips. Later, he arranged for the boy's education in Hinghwa. He became a Christian minister to whom Elizabeth often referred as "silver-tongued." His sixth child was Siong-ceh, later known as John Sung. This child was present at the revival meetings in 1909 when, as Will wrote, the Holy Spirit visited the Hinghwa area Church with extraordinary grace and power. Among those so greatly blessed were Siong-ceh and his father. Together they prayed for the church, for their country and for their family. Privately the boy prayed for help to study in America, promising to spend his life preaching in China if God saw fit to grant his desire. Miraculously, passage money and free tuition at Ohio Wesleyan College were provided, but not his father's approval.

He proved to be one of the most brilliant students Ohio Wesleyan had ever enrolled. He specialized in mathematics and chemistry, earning his bachelor's degree in three years, his master's degree in nine months, and his doctor's degree in the chemistry of explosives a year and nine months later.

Refusing all the flattering offers made to him, he then enrolled at Union Theological Seminary in New York. He had lost the precious awareness of God he had found as a boy, and was determined to recover it, if possible. It was at Calvary Baptist Church that God spoke to him again, through a fifteen-year-old girl evangelist. In gratitude for that message, John Sung renounced the brilliant career open to him, and went home to keep his promise to preach the reality of God and His forgiving-love to the people of China. On the ocean he threw overboard all his diplomas, medals and offers of jobs, saving only his doctor's diploma to please his father. Devoted Christians though they were, his parents were also true Chinese, revering education. They could neither accept nor forgive his decision to discard all benefits of his education, especially when there were several children in the family waiting for the opportunities a preacher's tiny salary could not provide. John steadfastly kept to his promise, accepting poverty as bitter as their own as his lot in life. Out of this great renunciation, God fashioned an Evangelist without equal.

In that capacity, he travelled all over China, Malaya, Borneo, the Philippines, Hong Kong and Singapore, changing people everywhere, producing many preachers and individual evangelists. Dr. Harold Brewster has told me of the man's compelling message; of his ability to move an audience; of the hundreds of young people who managed at terrific sacrifice to attend his Bible study camps for weeks at a time, even in the sweltering summer, and how they chose to remain in their seats from service-to-service, lest leaving, they might miss John Sungs's next appearance. Whole churches were revived to living Christian witness. That the Church in China has survived to this day, must certainly be partly due to the inspired preaching of this extraordinary young man.

Whatever Elizabeth's personal feeling about John Sung, Dr. Stanley Carson, her long-time friend and missionary associate, told me that he thought the greatest contribution Will Brewster made to China, might well be bringing to Hinghwa and to a

Christian experience the boy, who later became the father of John Sung. Because he was Chinese, he was able to mediate to his countrymen a faith, free from the stigma of race and nationality, vital enough to withstand the testing to come.

* * *

The shock of leaving China was greater than Elizabeth admitted. This was evident from her preoccupation that first summer with a memorial stone for her family's burial plot in Ohio. Before coming to us, she had visited London, Ohio, and the cemetery there.

"Oh, Eva, you can't imagine how it hurt me to see that burial plot. All those wonderful people who had contributed so much to Ohio in civic life, in church, in music and in teaching! There was no marker for the family; some of the graves had a first-name marker only, others none at all. So far as the present generation is concerned, those people never lived. I want a stone put there with the Fisher name on it, and an inscription telling who is buried in the plot, and why they should be remembered. George and Mary are taking care of it. I have given them money."

Day-after-day she dwelt on this grief. I was dismayed because it was so unlike her. When we visited those graves in 1936, she had displayed no such emotion. She was as sure now, as then, that we would know each other in Heaven. Why then this new grief? Doubly strange was her desire to be buried there, instead of near her husband in Troy.

"No one knows us in Troy," she told me "There is just room enough for me to be buried with my family in London, if a tree on the lot is removed. Dorothy Fisher has consented, so it can be arranged."

If she had died in China, she would have lived in the memory of her "children" at least, for decades. Her birthday would have been observed, her grave visited and cared for. In that London cemetery she saw herself forgotten like the others buried there, and so she wanted a stone!

In China, she might even be written into the family records of some who loved her like a mother. In America, few families keep such records. Among the people I love here in Wisconsin, is a transplanted Chinese family, whose members grieve for their lost records more than for any other possession. Their library had preserved, intact, those records for more than a thousand years. This in itself is a form of earthly immortality. Apparently, Elizabeth craved both kinds.

One day as I listened to her I was reminded of the Bible passage which asks, "Which of you, if his son asked for bread, would give him a stone?"

"Well, I reasoned, "Mother is asking for a stone, which I don't think is much of a memorial to anyone so wonderful. I'll be like the Chinese and write down her story, so that her children's children will know all about her."

This story began that day.

When word finally came that the memorial stone had been erected, she was curiously content. It seemed to me that her pride in family, the most obvious of her small sins, had at last been laid. Perhaps it wasn't pride at all, but an unconscious rebellion against the ancient dictum: "their place shall know them no more." She never went back to that London cemetery. Even if she had, her failing eyesight would have prevented her from seeing how curtailed were her loving descriptions of her family.

"It would take a stone as big as a house to cut all that writing," the stonecutter had protested. As a result the stone in Oakhill Cemetery, London, Ohio, lists only Elizabeth's immediate family buried there.

FISHER
William H R. Fisher, Son of Isaac Byers Fisher and
Elizabeth Jefferson, Radiant Evangelist 1836–1876

Mary Jane, Beloved Wife of William H. R.
Daughter of Walter Watson Minshall and Maria Heath
Gentle and loving always 1835–1927

Adeline, Daughter of Wm. H.R. and Mary Jane Fisher
Sweet Singer 1860–1872

Carrie Annette, Daughter of Wm. H.R. and Mary Jane Fisher
Brilliant Scholar and Loved Teacher 1864–1886

So Elizabeth provided a record in stone of those nearest to her. She had suffered many frustrations while assembling the Brewster and Fisher family trees because of burned records and of incomplete recording of names of wives. She made sure that so long as the stone stood, anyone looking for such information would find it preserved. This much she could do for her beloved family.[1]

While Elizabeth waited expectantly to join Will in Heaven, their works continued to bear fruit, once quite literally. One summer while Elizabeth was with us at the farm, Harold and his family came to visit. Mail, from Montclair, New Jersey, informed them that a box of fresh lychees had arrived and had been refrigerated for Elizabeth by a thoughtful neighbor. This was not the first time we had heard about that shipment of lychee trees Will had made so long ago.

It was Edward Brewster who came across an article about some orchards in Florida that were putting a delicious new fruit on the market, called the Brewster lychee. Writing for information, he was delighted to receive, not only a courteous and interested letter, but a brochure from the orchard owner, Mr. William H. Grove, giving a history of the "Brewster lychee," so called, because the first grafts were brought to this country at the beginning of the century by a missionary from China named Brewster! There was also a snapshot of the owner standing beside one of the beautiful evergreen trees. His orchards are at Laurel, Florida. Others are located elsewhere in the state.

Every year we take special interest in the Florida weather reports, hoping the lychee orchards will survive frost and hurricane until we can all get down there to see them! After all, they are a living memorial to Father Brewster. We also hope this delicious fruit will soon be

1 I wondered at the time why Elizabeth's name was not cut into the stone. No one, including Elizabeth, ever thought of removing the tree from the burial plot. For these reasons she is buried near Will and Raymond at Troy, Ohio. I am sure she does not mind, busy as she is in her five-storey house, caring for her family!

available in northern markets. Because it is so perishable, it now must come airmail by special order. We were amused when Chinese friends told us that in the year 900 A.D., a special pony express was arranged to speed the luscious fruit from the Hinghwa orchards to the distant northern capital, where the favorite concubine of the emperor waited their arrival with eager appetite.

All of us were particularly grateful to Mr. Groves, when Marybelle, daughter of Harold and Dorothy Brewster, was married. He sent a box of the beautiful green foliage of her grandfather's lychee trees to add to her wedding flowers. So Will and Elizabeth continue to bless their children. The good deeds of the parents may also visit their children until the tenth generation it would seem!

Elizabeth's last summer with us was difficult. She obviously felt herself to be on the wrong side of all the oceans. Karis and Frank Manton, after a year's furlough, were planning their return to Burma where they had served the Anglo-Indian Church for many years. Mary and George Hollister, unable to return to China, had preceded them to Rangoon, and were already established in the work of church and school. Harold and Dorothy Brewster were scheduled to tour the Orient, inspecting the medical work of the Methodist Church.

Elizabeth found it hard to be left behind. To make matters worse, my husband and I were very busy on the farm. He was working overtime trying to make up for the falling prices of broiler chickens, by increasing production. As a result, I saw very little of him. Since I was with Elizabeth all day, and saw him so little, we used to get up early to have an hour alone together for prayers and planning. Other summers, Elizabeth sensed our need of this time together and never came down until she smelled coffee. That last summer, we found it necessary to get up earlier and earlier to finish our prayers before we heard her on the stairs. Often my husband would be closing the book or saying "Amen" as she peered in the door.

One day in August, I knew her health was failing. She had been telling me about the lepers, whose care had been so large a part of her Hinghwa years.

"It was rumored that the Communist government had a plan to

collect all the lepers and transport them to a small island, where they promised some sort of shelter would be provided. These poor people were terrified, beseeching me to intercede for them. They feared it was just a plan to dispose of them permanently.

"If you leave us now, Mrs. Brewster, who will care for us? Who will care what happens to us? Our families will not be able to get food to us out there across the water. We shall starve to death."

Then, without explanation, she slid into the story of Will's year in Singapore and his conversation with the Bishop.

"Will, you ought to have a wife."

I smiled as she started on this well-loved story, repeated so often during our conversations. But this time, instead of going on to the happy ending, she kept repeating,

"Will, you ought to have a wife!"

Sweat broke out on my own forehead as I listened to her. At last she said sadly,

"Can't get across. Can't get across," and stopped talking. Her fingers kept tracing a pattern on the table, so I knew she wasn't seriously ill. Nevertheless, we watched for evidence of a stroke. Except for diminishing awareness, she went around as usual.

Toward the end of August, she became as joyously excited as a child. Harold was going to stop for her on his way home from a western conference. Together they would fly to New York, where she would visit briefly, before going to Williamsburg, Ohio, where she would spend the winter with Helen and Edward. She loved most to be at the Montclair home of the Harold Brewster's, for through it flowed a constant stream of people from all over the world. This was what Elizabeth loved. She asked me to give her a permanent, even showing me how to do it, for I had never even had one myself. She talked about the weather and planned what to wear.

My husband, our son Bill and I accompanied them to Truax Field. It was a hot, sunny afternoon. Elizabeth was charming in thin blue wool with white accessories. She was herself again, happy and alert, eager to be going someplace more exciting than the lonely farm. We sat quietly in the waiting room, holding hands, while the men talked of Harold's recent trip to Africa. Suddenly, giving my hand a little squeeze, Elizabeth said,

"You know nothing can ever separate us, don't you dear?" I squeezed her hand but could say nothing. I knew that she was speaking to me for the last time, telling me that we should not meet on earth again, assuring me that sometime, somewhere we should meet again, and until that time came, prayer would be the bond between us. And so it has been.

Later from the observation platform, we watched them fly away.

"There goes mother. We'll never see her again."

It was my husband speaking. He, too, was feeling bereft. So long as she was alive, we felt somehow young and protected. If, indeed, we were never to see her again on earth, which of her children could take her place?

"There will never again be a Mother Brewster!" I thought, as we drove back to the farm she had named Fairfield, after the Connecticut homestead of the Brewster ancestor who settled there.

Through that sunny September and into a radiant October, my husband and I rested. We cancelled the fall consignment of broiler chicks, and took a few weeks of vacation. For the first time, we visited some of the historic spots of Wisconsin—Wade House at Greenbush and Villa Louis at Prairie du Chien on the Mississippi. How my husband enjoyed those houses that preserve so true a picture of pioneer America. Since American history was almost a passion with him, we had to resign ourselves to stopping at every historic marker so that he could read what happened at the spot. One day, we drove over Wild Cat Mountain, the highest place we had seen in the State. For a long time we stood there, looking through the haze into the lovely valley, and were reluctant to leave. "Reminds me of Hinghwa valley from Si-Ga-Boi, the mountain summer home," he said, as we drove away.

We haven't had such an autumn since. Wisconsin is always beautiful, sometimes lush green from spring until November. That year October burned with color unequalled in my memory. Finally, I got out my drawing paper and pastels.

"I just have to see if I can get some of this beauty onto paper," I told my husband, who was always pleased when I dabbled with color or words on paper. But I am no artist, and the magic of the hills and cornfields continued to elude my childlike efforts.

On a bright Monday morning, we finished our devotions, as was our custom, with the Lord's Prayer. As often happened, one of us said, "forgive, us our debts" and the other "forgive us our trespasses." With sudden impulse, I spoke,

"From now on let's always say "sins." Forgive us our sins as we forgive those who sin against us. That means so much more than debts or trespasses. One makes me think of money and the other of grass. Sins have to do with me and God."

My husband marked the place for the next morning, put the book on the shelf, smiled at me and went out to the barn. I didn't know if he had heard me or not. Often, his thoughts sped to the current political crisis, as soon as we finished prayers. This morning he was unusually thoughtful. When he had finished reading the lesson for the day he had turned back several pages to read aloud with deep feeling:

"The pain of penitence takes the place of outward punishment, so that the outward punishment can be lifted from the soul without loss or degradation to the soul. It is an operation without anesthetics. A sharp pain of penitence goes through you, then you look up into that dear Face that bends over you, and you know that the operation is successful. You walk forth from that operating room free from a cancerous 'I' and now free to live with an 'I,' that is Christ-centered and therefore contributive."[2]

"Someday he will tell me why those words struck so deep," I thought, watching through the window as he walked to the barn. Then I turned to the rapture of color which lay like still-fire across our farm. The sunburned hill to the east wore its encircling oaks like a ruddy scarf whose gay ends, knotted under the chin, escaped in clumps of glowing sumac to border the golden cornfield sloping toward our house.

"It will never be so beautiful again. I'll wash this morning, but I'll

---

2 E. Stanley Jones, *Growing Spiritually,* p.21

finish my picture this afternoon," I promised myself.

Instantly an inner voice commanded, "Wash this morning, but sit with Fran while he works this afternoon."

Although, astonished by the vividness of the command, I remonstrated.

"Sit in the barnyard on a day like this? I'll wash clothes this morning, yes, but I'm going to work on picture this afternoon. Tomorrow it will probably rain and all the foliage will fall."

So I hurried through my Monday chores. All afternoon I reveled in color, my joy occasionally disturbed by the lonely tapping of my husband's hammer from the other side of the barn. Late in the afternoon, he came up to see how the picture was progressing. He nodded, approvingly.

"October Hill. That's what we should call our farm. This is the way I like it best—the grain in, the corn ripe, the alfalfa still green. I think that tree is too far this way, though." He loved his land with a fervor known only to those who find their heart's desire late in life, and granted no one artistic license with it. It was a secret grief with him, I knew, that I did not fully share this love. I resented the work the farm required of him, because I was sure it was too much for a man in his fifties not accustomed to hard, physical labor. Besides, I liked people too much to be isolated from them.

My husband was pleased when I put the drawing away and walked back to the barnyard with him. Sitting on a pile of lumber, I watched as he sawed, fitted, and nailed together some new equipment for the broiler barn. I noted, with pleasure, what a satisfying picture he made, too, in his faded yellow sweatshirt and bleached blue overalls against the soft rosy-red of the barn.

A flock of big lambs joined us, nibbling at the sparse alfalfa which had straggled in from the adjoining pasture; I held out my hands to them, murmuring words of affection. They were our pets, deserted by their mothers, bottle-fed by us until they could fend for themselves. Now they roamed the farm in a close fraternity, like children orphaned by war

"There are only nine lambs! Where is the tenth one, Fran?" I cried, anxiously. My husband straightened up slowly to count them. There were only nine lambs, but I was more worried about him than the missing lamb, when he answered casually,

"We'll look for it tomorrow. It may be with the ewes. I hope it hasn't found its way out to the alfalfa field."

He really was tired! Ordinarily he went at once to look for a missing member of his flock. Just a few weeks earlier, coming in to supper, he called me to the door.

"Do you hear Queenie baaing?"

I listened. "Well, I do hear an ewe baaing, but I wouldn't know if it's Queenie," I laughed.

"It's Queenie. She hasn't been acting right, lately. She's down and calling me for help."

Knowing that an animal "down" is sick and helpless, I did not protest, though supper waited. Later, I watched as they came in through the chilly twilight together. In the old metal wheelbarrow, her spindly forelegs dangling on either side of the wheel, rode the old ewe. She might be sick and helpless, but her nose was high in the air. No wonder Fran called her "Queenie." He, poor dear, was bent awkwardly low over the hand-shafts, to keep the barrow level enough so that the old girl would not slide out into the dust on her haughty nose.

"Well, I never saw the likes of that! He certainly loves those sheep," I laughed to myself.

***

As I had predicted, the weather broke in the night. Tuesday morning, I stood at a hospital window watching a cold autumn storm beat the leaves from the trees. Sadly, I mused, I had chosen the wrong picture. The trees would burn over the hill again; the sumac would twist a gay fringe around the ripe corn. It was my husband who never again would stand in tired yellow and faded blue against the rose-red of the barn. "Terminal," was the hospital's description of the heart attack that had stricken him in the night.

The sweetest hours of our lives were left to us. In the morning, at our usual prayer time, I leaned close, repeating softly familiar psalms and prayers. Opening his eyes, he found me, and laboriously joined in when he could. When we came to the prayer of our Lord, he took the lead. "Forgive us our sins as we forgive those who sin against us," I heard.

"You remembered, darling!" I marveled

"Of course, I remembered. I'll always remember," he answered.

There was time for holding his hand to my cheek; time to kiss his fingers, now so rough and stained. There was time for prayer, and this time, when that inner Voice commanded, compassionately, "Pray now, or foolish one, you will reproach yourself the rest of your life for leaving this undone, I did. So numbly, mechanically, I prayed and sent out requests for prayer for my husband about to die.

Once as I bent over him, he reached up and began to massage the back of my neck, a loving ministry he used whenever I was too tired or worried. In the late afternoon, he begged suddenly,

"Do you forgive me?"

Bewildered, living only in the precious present, I cried, "Forgive you! For what, darling?" Then with a flash of unusual grace, I prayed,

"Do you forgive me?"

How many times I have been grateful for that God-sent humility. Surely, the cruelest sting of death must be the recollection of sins for which, too late, we long to hear the words of absolution. Now, as I watched, aghast, I saw a cloud of remembrance darken his eyes. In this his moment of truth, he found much to forgive as well as much to be forgiven. Like a jig-saw puzzle that has been too rudely jolted, I saw our lives together break apart, our sins against each other standing out from the happy years. Then the darkness melted, dispelled completely by love.

"I forgive you, my wife, my sweetheart. I forgive you everything. I forgive everybody everything." He was reaching out to encompass all those in our land and abroad who so often had outraged his sense of right and duty, who had endangered the principles of Christianity and democracy for which he had so willingly offered himself in two wars and the peace between.

"I love you. I send my love to everyone. I love Sara. I pray Julie will grow into a good and beautiful woman." Sara was three years old and Julie two months old, our first grandchildren.

Our son, Tony, father of those two little girls, was with him at the end. He said his father was groping through the 23rd psalm when death came. I knew he was calling, with faith, into the twilight, for his own Good Shepherd to come and help him out of a pasture grown lonely and cold. And I know that Help came; it came for me, too.

As his Chinese fortune had said, on a day in autumn the little bird became a phoenix, their symbol of immortality, flying happy and free where it had never been able to go before. Heaven itself opens to love and forgiveness.

As for me, I have a tryst with my husband in the Lord's Prayer. Ever since that October day, I have prayed, "Forgive us our sins, as we forgive those who sin against us," and always, wherever I am, I hear him saying those words.

From Germany came a letter of consolation and tribute from which I am proud to quote:

"Thank you so much for your letter of November 7th, but what a sad message it contained. Mr. Brewster is no longer among the living. Please accept our heartfelt sympathy. When we saw the photo in the newspaper clipping, his presence was vividly with us. That was the way we saw him, handing down decisions in his military office, that was the way we saw him at home, with you. Then, too, we remembered that lovely Advent evening you spent with us in our parish hall when you greeted us with the unforgettable words:

'I am one of those fortunate people who have three homelands. The first is America, the second, China, and now the third is Germany.'

"How much those words helped us; how good they sounded against the background of those days! No other representative of the Occupation had spoken thus to us. That was because you and your husband spoke and acted out of Christian living. In him, we saw quite clearly what a Christian can make of an official army position, for certainly, he was a reconciling power between your people and ours. I have often reminded my congregation of those words you spoke that night, and I will do so again on its anniversary in December. Then I must also break the sorrowful news of Mr. Brewster's death to my people, and I know your thoughts will be present with us."

The Advent evening referred to above was one of innumerable parties we attended that year, if those sad and Spartan occasions could be called parties. On the Advent evening referred to, we arrived late to find the parish hall packed with people sitting at tables waiting for us. We were ushered up to the head table where Mr. Kelber, the talented and enthusiastic Lutheran pastor of the community, awaited us. As soon as we were seated, he was on his feet making a welcoming address.

My husband began at once to scribble something on an envelope which he pushed across the table to me. Before I had finished reading it, I heard Mr. Kelber say my name, and all the people began applauding politely. I looked at my husband, and he was beaming with pride and applauding with the rest. He could speak no German, and therefore, had an exaggerated opinion of my conversational ability. However, I could see no way out. With the help of the minister's charming daughter, I made the shortest speech of my life and apparently the most memorable. It went something like this:

"My husband scribbled this note while Mr. Kelber was speaking just now. It says, "Darling, I forgot to tell you that I promised Mr. Kelber that you would talk to his congregation in German about China tonight." You women, at least, will understand that I shall have something to say on the way home tonight." At this, laughter broke out all over the hall. I was delighted, for laughter was scarce that heartbreaking year. Greatly encouraged, I went on. "I can't tell you about China tonight, but sometime when I have had a chance to prepare, I shall be glad to. This evening I shall only say that we are among those fortunate people who have three homelands. The first is America, the second, China, and now the third is Germany. Thank you for making us feel at home, and for inviting us here tonight."

When Elizabeth received news of Francis' death she was with the Edward Brewsters in Williamsburg, Ohio. She had just said goodbye to the Mantons and to the Harold Brewsters. So many farewells had added to the confusion that we had noticed in the summer, and it was with great difficulty that they made her understand that it was Francis who had died. Her letter to me was almost illegible, but several poignant lines were clear:

> Dear Eva:
>
> I can hardly believe Fran has gone. He was so well and strong last summer. If I could help you, I would come to you, but I should only be in the way now. I know Fran was ready, for I used to see you at prayers together. I wanted to join you, but I could never get there on time. I got up earlier every day, but when I got downstairs, Fran was always closing the book or saying Amen.

How glad I am that she forgave us, too. When she flew away that day, she had said,

"Nothing will ever separate us," and she had meant it.

She lived long enough to learn, through Dorothy Brewster's fascinating letters, that she and Will were not forgotten in the Orient. Dorothy wrote that in Singapore enlarged photographs of Elizabeth and Will occupied a place of honor in the Chinese Methodist Church, where one of their Hinghwa protégées was pastor.

From Sarawak, Borneo, Dorothy wrote of the wonderfully happy Christmas spent at the Hinghwa Colony Will had established in 1911. Many of the original group and their children gathered around Harold and herself with grins of delight, to express their loving gratitude for the new way of life, and even wealth, made possible for them by Will's concern.

She and Harold went up the jungle river to visit the Dyak longhouses. The Dyaks are the stately original inhabitants of the island who have been good neighbors to the Chinese colonists. They came to honor Elizabeth when she visited Sarawak in 1938, and are vitally interested in the "Strong Jesus religion" of their Chinese friends. As a result of the visit, Harold selected their jungle land as one place that needed a hospital.

Three years later the Methodist Church made that hospital possible. Harold took a leave of absence from his desk in New York, and with the capable assistance of Dorothy and Richard Blakney, now a son-in-law, Christ Hospital, with its four Matthew, Mark, Luke and John wards was built. Kapit must be a delightful place, for Harold and Dorothy left their hearts there, and long to go back to work with those charming jungle people.

* * *

There must have been bells ringing and trumpets blowing in Heaven on the 18th of March, 1955, for that day E1izabeh died. I felt no sorrow. Something akin to exultation accompanies every thought of her. After all, our "child of the King" had gone home!

For her funeral service the minister read the magnificent Bible passages that had determined her life.

Therefore the Lord waits to be gracious to you,
And therefore he will rise to have pity upon you;
For the Lord is a God of justice.
Happy are all those who wait for him!
O people in Zion, who dwell at Jerusalem,
No more will you weep;
He will be gracious to you at the sound of your crying;
As soon as he hears, he will answer you.
Even though the Lord may have given you
Bread in short measure and water in scanty allowance,
Your teacher will no more hide himself,
But your eyes will behold your teacher,
And when you turn to right or to left,
Your ears will hear a voice behind you saying,
"This is the way; walk in it.'

Sitting there, listening, I recalled the poverty of her childhood; the dreams and ambitions she had surrendered to do God's will; and how, truly, He had come to live with her and be gracious to her. He had led her out from that obscure Ohio village and used her greatly in China, so that in that land, in Singapore, Borneo, and here at home, people rise up to bless her. Hers was a joyous life. It has been said that those who give everything to God, get God in return. This was the secret of Elizabeth's life, which she eagerly sought to share with others. Like her father, she knew God, walked as He directed, and at the end of life on earth knew no regrets.

The minister read on,

"And I, brethren, when I came to you, came not with excellency of speech or wisdom, declaring unto you the wisdom of God. For I am determined to know nothing among you, save Jesus Christ, and Him crucified."

I thought of Will looking over into Hinghwa, accepting those words as his life motto, and of Elizabeth's joyful acquiescence in his choice. I remembered the temptations to use their friendship with the people and their knowledge of the province to make themselves wealthy through affiliations with business firms eager to enter that vast untouched market. It was the age old choice, God or Mammon, and they chose God.

I remembered, too, Elizabeth's indignant refusal to accept the protection of gunboats in days of peril. Nothing but Christ, even Him crucified. This had been her advice to one of the grandchildren asking in bewilderment, "What is the matter? Everything is so dark today; where shall we look for help?"

"Nothing is the matter," was Elizabeth's stalwart reply. "Keep your eye on Christ and follow Him and everything will be right, whatever happens." She saw the joy that is set before those who follow Him, and was undismayed. In Him she had lived and died.

I smiled when I heard the lovely words:

"Eye hath not seen, nor ear heard, neither hath it entered into the heart of man the wonders that God hath prepared for them that love Him," for I saw our son, Bill, deep in conversation with his grandmother. They were discussing Heaven. She couldn't tell him whether Heaven is a place or a state of being, she only knew it, and that it is marvelous beyond comprehension. She expected to find Will again and all the other people she loved.

She did not look for streets of gold, nor try to picture what it would be like.

"I bank on the promise of Jesus Christ, who has never failed me, that I shall be where He is. For the rest I can wait."

And then the language changed from the majestic King James English to the poignant words of her Chinese children:

We call her mother, this little lady,
Who came to us from far shores long ago.
We are her people now, and she is one of us
For she has been with us in weal and woe;
To outcaste, orphan, leper she is mother,
The friendless and the poor her kindness know;
Herself has ministered to our misfortunes,
Herself was tireless when our hopes ebbed low;
Her heart is wide, all need and care embracing,
Her daily acts of grace Her spirit show
She is our mother; our faith and hope and wisdom
To her unwearied loving heart we owe.
Oh, mother heart, how rare is such devotion!
Our gratitude and praise we must bestow.

There was no political expediency, no hope of private gain in Elizabeth's tour abroad. The people knew it and judged America accordingly—the Beautiful Country they used to call us. How could anyone grieve over a life so well spent, or doubt its joyful continuance in Heaven? The tears we shed were only from gratitude for the priceless dower she left us—her shining faith. She made it easy for us to believe in God and His goodness.

This, then, is the story of my mother-in-law, Elizabeth Fisher Brewster. Ages have kaleidoscoped since I began it. Now that it is finished, I am wondering if it contains any message for the world today.

As Will and Elizabeth feared long ago, there was not time enough to change China's millions from the inside out before the coming of national stature. To be sure, thousands turned somewhere along the road of life to find God waiting with love and forgiveness to claim them as sons. For decades these men and women witnessed to their faith by being clean and temperate in their homes and in their lives, by educating their children, by being honest in their dealings with all men, by being loving and kind, in service to others. In the midst of a corrupt society, they stood out. For the love of God and through Him, they were free, they were different.

Today, if one dare believe books and articles written by apparently responsible people, many of these virtues have been successfully imposed on the masses of both China and Russia by fear of death and pride in country. Even if morality cannot be legislated, it seems it can be imposed. I recall it was men with lashes who built the Chinese wall.

If these reports are true, these people who neither recognize God nor their need of Him, may be closer to Him than we think. Perhaps they are waiting for us to show them how allegiance to God is higher than allegiance to country. I quote from Elizabeth:

"Nearly every day brings news of some one of our Christian trained young men going into the army.

"This I do not criticize, if they go for love of country with conviction as to how to save China, and ready to live and even to die for her. I'll even say, 'God bless you. Go ahead. But be sure self is not first. God, country, family, self should be the order of every man's devotion.'"

As Christians, we have to answer Jesus' question, "What do ye more than these?"

One hundred years ago, Lord Elgin, speaking to his English countrymen doing business in Shanghai, outlined the fateful position in which we find ourselves today:

"When the barriers which prevent free access to the country shall have been removed (he referred to China), Christian civilization of the West will find itself face to face not with barbarism, but with an ancient civilization in many respects effete and imperfect, but in others not without claims to our sympathy and respect. In the rivalry which will then ensue, Christian civilization will have to win its way among a skeptical and ingenious people, by making it manifest that a faith which reaches to Heaven furnishes better guarantees for public and private morality than one which does not rise above the earth."

It seems to me, this is a greater challenge than placing a man on the moon, if there must be a choice. Surely, this is the time to abandon the selfish sins and pleasures which disfigure us and go to seek our Father to do Him honor and obedience. Certainly it is the proud tradition, not only of Elizabeth and her children, but of all God's people to witness to the truth that only through Him can men be truly free, even in America.

Starting where we are then, let us accept this challenge, in which every one of us must share, and with Elizabeth, pray in penitence and promise:

"May everything we do, and everything we say, living, and dying, be to the glory of Thy name. Amen"

A Chinese Tale

(as told to Elizabeth's children)

In the days when the Ming Dynasty was declining, a pirate by the name of Nicholas Iquan controlled the China seas. He was partly Chinese, but in his pursuit of wealth was as likely to attack Ming Dynasty ships on government business as he was the rich merchant ships of the Dutch, Portuguese and Japanese. He surrounded himself by armed guards, the most spectacular of which were some three hundred tall, handsome Africans whom the Portuguese had landed at their port city of Macao. When this splendid contingent escaped, Nicholas Iquan engaged their services, clothing them in brilliantly colored, beautiful silks. To this day, the Chinese refer to those days as the "time of the black pirates," for villages along the coast were frequently attacked, plundered and destroyed by Iquan, his fellow pirates, and the resplendent black bodyguard.

During one such raid, the women and children fled inland, leaving the men to defend their homes, if possible. Sometime later a woman carrying a beautiful baby boy returned to what was left of her village, inquiring of survivors and for her husband. They told her they thought he had been carried off by the pirates, perhaps to be sold, perhaps to be released in a city far to the south. Like many another woman, she slaved and starved through the years in order to support her adored son, always reminding him of the father who might just possibly be alive somewhere.

As the boy grew older, heedless of his mother's anxious advice, he began to keep bad company. It was not long before his face began to change, reflecting the dissipation and evil habits in which he engaged. One good impulse remained in him, however. From childhood he had promised his mother that, when he grew up, he would go to seek his father in the great cities to the south. The day came when he said to her, "I am ready now, to go look for my father. But how shall I recognize him? Has he any distinguishing marks, scars or habits that you remember?"

After considering the question, his mother shook her head.

"Nothing at all that I remember, except that when you were a baby everyone said you looked just like your father. Perhaps something of the resemblance remains. Take a mirror along, and when you arrive in a city, sit at the busiest spot, and look into the mirror. Everyone who passes, will want to know what you are doing. Tell them you are looking for your father, whom you are said to resemble. Ask every man to look into the mirror with you. If you find one who resembles you, question him. He might well be your father."

So the boy left home. After months of working his way down the coast he came at last to a very great city. As was his custom, he sat down at the busiest intersection and, taking out his polished brass mirror, buffed it with his sleeve, and looked at himself. Even his mother would have had difficulty recognizing him, so greatly had weariness, hunger, and boredom added to its disfiguration. But men did stop to question him, and look, out of curiosity, into his mirror, and pass on. One day, as a group of sympathetic people stood around him, a man with a very kind face, stopped to watch and listen. With a glad cry he exclaimed,

"I am your father!" The bystanders moved aside to let him look into the mirror with the boy, but all of them said, "There is no resemblance at all!" In spite of them the stranger insisted.

The boy shook his head. "My mother said I looked like my father. All these people agree, I do not look like you at all."

The man would not be dissuaded. "Look, my son, I am your father, but if you will not believe it, will you accept me as a friend? You need food and clothing. Come, stay with me awhile until you are strong enough to make the journey home. Then we will both go to find your mother. I thought you were dead, otherwise I should have sought you years ago."

The boy was glad for a home, although he felt somewhat ill at ease with his new friend. Gradually he found himself responding to kindness, and began to abandon his old ways, replacing them with the habits and attitudes of the man who claimed to be his father. The impulse which had sent him abroad kept him restless, however. The day came when he insisted he must be on his way.

His friend sighed. "If you could only believe that I am your father! May I ask how you propose to look for him this time?"

"I have no new plan. I will polish my mirror and go sit in the city streets. Surely, if my father is there, he will someday pass my way."

His friend stood watching him polish the brass disk wondering how he could persuade the boy to accept their kinship. As he watched, he realized how the boy had changed since coming to live with him. Stepping behind him, he asked,

"How is the mirror coming? Is it bright enough now?"

"Almost," replied the lad, holding it up for his friend to see. Then seeing the reflection beside his own in the mirror, he cried in glad recognition,

"Father! You are my father. What has happened? Now I look like YOU!"

Index

A

Advent in Germany, 299, 301
Agricultural mission, 120
Air raids, 219
Alone in China, 235, 239
Amahs, 113, 158, 191
American imperialism, 270
American travelers, 209, 210
Amoy, China, 227
Ancestors, 103, 104
Anglo Chinese College, 179
Anniversary in Hinghwa, 157, 220
Anti American sentiments, 264, 271, 276, 277
Apple, Miss Blanche, 231
Arrival in Foochow, 35, 37, 179
Arrival in Hinghwa, 80
Arthur H. Smith, 143
A Siang, 88, 228
Automobile accident, 221
Autumn in Wisconsin, 294, 297

B

Baltimore, Maryland, 30, 61, 62
Bandits, 47, 187, 208, 209, 228
Bayreuth painting, 247, 248, 250
Bean curd, 108
Berlin Crossroads, Ohio, 12
Bethel, Ohio, 3
Between Midnight and Morning, 238, 239
Bible reading, 145
Bible teacher, 141
Bible School for Women, 37
Bible women, 170, 172
Birthday, 230, 231, 232, 233
Birthday service, 230
Bishop William X. Ninde, 80
Bishop Thoburn, 72
Bishop Wiley, 41, 42
Black Market, 246, 247
Black Pirates, 139
Blanche Apple, Miss, 231
Blind students, 94, 96, 236, 237
Blind women's story
  in Foochow, 191, 194
  in Yellowstone, 169, 170
Boats, 109
Bomb shelters, 219, 230
Bombings, 220
Borneo colony, 117, 118, 120, 215 216, 301
Boxer Rebellion. See Boxer Uprising
Boxer Uprising, 125, 141
Boxers, the, 47, 135
"Brawn without brain", 107, 108
Brewster, Dorothy, 208, 234, 301
Brewster, Eva, 179, 245, 246, 250, 290
Brewster, Fisher, 254
Brewster, Francis, 87, 88, 179, 199, 213, 219, 227, 246, 251, 252, 298
Brewster, Harold, 208, 214, 215, 221, 234, 242
Brewster, Karis, 201, 218, 219
Brewster, Mary, 88, 242
Brewster, Raymond, 153, 254
Brewster, Rebecca, 212
Brewster, William Nesbitt, 63, 64, 72, 78, 99, 100, 101, 112, 116, 136, 158, 289
Brewster homestead, 21, 212
Brewster lychee, 291, 292
Brown, Cora, 172
Bridge of Ten Thousand Ages, 40, 123
Buckeyes, 3

Budget in Manhasset, 202, 203
Buddhism, 102, 103, 127
Building projects, 67, 68, 113, 225, 226, 255
Burial ground in Foochow, 206
Burial plot in London, Ohio, 289, 291
Burma visit, 218

C

Canton Revolutionists, 188, 189
Carlton Lacy, 269
Carol singing, 192
Carrie Jewel, 33, 37, 56
Celibacy, 116, 117
Censure, 111, 112, 117
Central Conference, 220
Chapel for lepers, 90, 91
Chau sia, China, 260
Chiang Kai shek, 205, 207, 255, 263
Children, 88, 115, 116, 153, 155, 158, 218, 230, 254
China, 100, 103, 112, 123, 129, 207, 254, 264, 283, 305
Chinese Christians, 135, 136, 140, 144, 285
Chinese diet, 110, 120
Chinese language, 43, 44, 81, 89
Chinese names, 42, 43
Chinese proverb, 106
Chinese tale, 309, 311
Cholera, 52, 53, 53, 55
Christ Hospital, Borneo, 302
Christian community, 101, 144, 145
Christian Educational Association citation, 233, 234
Christianity, 104, 142, 143, 144, 148
Christmas, 184, 186, 192, 193, 194, 201, 205, 250
Christmas matinee, 202
Christmas presents, 184, 186
Church attendance, 274
Church in Manhasset, 205
Church of Christ, 227
Church of Heavenly Peace, 74
Church membership, 105
Church reform, 152, 153, 271, 272
Church services in Germany, 250
Church subscriptions, 231
Churches, 101, 145
Cigarettes, 246
Cincinnati, Ohio, 63
Citizen of Heaven, 227
City life in Hinghwa, 100, 101, 108
Civil war, 169, 174, 178, 263
Clothing, 228
Coats, 190, 191, 193
Cole, W.B., 232
Commitment, 111, 112, 169, 220
Communism, 103, 189, 207, 264
Communist armies, 255
Communist Revolution, 52
Communist take over, 266, 269, 270, 272, 275, 281, 284, 306
Companionship, 28
Confucian philosophy, 102, 103, 127
Constitutional government, 142
Converts, 46, 106, 107, 127, 145, 159
Cora Brown, 172
Correspondence, 98, 147, 246
See also Letters from Elizabeth
Corruption, 104, 130, 284
Cory, Kathryn, Dr., 53
"Cost of Christian Conquest, The", 144
Cost of war time living, 226, 227, 231, 238
Cottage for blind boys, 93
Country day schools, 44
Country village travels, 44, 46, 47, 105, 106, 107
Courtship, 180
Cows, 109, 110, 243, 244, 245
Cradle scythe, 110, 111
Curio dealer's story, 195, 197
Currency, 151, 152
Currency reform, 247
Current events digest, 141
Customs, 106

D

Dairies, 110
Date sandwiches, 214
Death of Elizabeth, 302
Death of Elizabeth's children, 254, 299, 301
Death of father, 12, 13, 21
Death of husband, 158, 159, 169
Death of mother, 63
Death of sisters, 12
Democrary, 148, 151
Deng gang, China, 260
Denunciation, 284
Depression, 199, 203, 208
Digest of current events, 141
Dinner conversations, 116
Discrimination, 272
Discussion group, 140
Dr. Fisher, 235
Dr. J. A. Otte, 86, 97
Dr. Kathryn Cory, 53
Doctors, 86
Dong Buo, 206, 207
Donkeys, 108, 237
Door to door salesmen, 202
Dorothy Brewster, 208, 234, 301
Dragons, 101, 195
Duai Muoi, 191, 193
Dyaks, 215, 301, 302
Dysentery, 56

E

Earl of Minshall, 19
Educational equality, 51
Educational reform, 130, 134, 142
Elections, 152
Elgin, Lord, 305, 306
Emperor of China, 103, 130, 134, 147
Empress Dowager, 130, 135, 136, 147
English language, 39
Ethel Wallace, 159
Eva Brewster, 179, 245, 246, 250, 290
Evacuation appeals, 232, 233, 264, 270
Evangelistic campaigns, 172
See also Revivals
Evolution of New China, 80
Executions, 280, 281
Exit permits, 264, 265, 266, 271, 276
Export/import business, 186, 188, 189
Eyesight, 146, 147, 239

F

Faith, 70, 251
Faith healing, 146
Families, 103, 104
Famille rose, 183
Family burial plot, 289, 291
Family records, 210, 211, 291
Family reunion, 211, 213, 245
Family traditions, 214
Farewell feast, 279
Farewell gifts, 190, 282
Farewell tea, 222, 223
Farming, 113, 120
Fear, 238
Feuds, 139, 140
Financial chaos, 255, 257
Financial retaliation, 278
Fisher Brewster, 254
Fisher, Dr., 235
Fisher, Mary Jane, 2, 12, 15, 16, 63
Fisher, William Henry Raper, 1, 2, 4, 8, 12, 13
Flour mill, 111
Flower Mountain, 125
Flowers, 121
Foochow, China, 28, 37 39, 52, 124, 126, 176, 275
Foochow Consul, 138, 139
Foochow valley, 40
Food distribution, 231 232
Foot binding, 46, 48, 49, 90, 150
Foreign influence, 106, 125
Foreign takeover, 129
Foreigners, hostility toward, 135,139, 284
See also Anti American sentiments
Forgiveness, 283, 284, 298

Formosa, 238
Francis Brewster, 87, 88, 179, 199, 213, 219, 227, 246, 251 252, 298
Frank Manton, 201, 218
Friend of the bandits, 209, 210
Fruit, 121
Fruit trees, 121
Fukien Christian Educational Association citation, 233–234
Fukien Province, China, 89, 232, 239
Funding, 93, 98, 144, 273
Funeral service, 302, 303
Furlough, 235

G

General Conference, 210, 220
George Hollister, 264, 265, 271, 276, 277, 282
Gifts, 184
Ginger jar, 200
Girl's school in Foochow, 37, 39, 44, 46
Girl's school in Hinghwa, 93
Golden Candlesticks. See Six Golden Candlesticks
Government, 131, 142
Grandchildren, 68, 183, 208, 230, 299
Grandmother, 11
Great Wall of China, 147, 148
Ground beef, 204
Guests, 184
Guidance, 176, 178, 205

H

Haitan island, 48, 49
Harold Brewster, 208, 214, 215, 221, 234, 242
Hartford, Mabel, 67, 71
Head Boss, 258, 259, 262
Health and Child Care Center, 258
Health crisis, 56, 57, 58, 59
Heaven's Well, 82
Hinghwa, China, 73, 74, 77, 137
Hinghwa colony. See Borneo colony
Hinghwa Conference, 152
Hinghwa Orphanage, 93
Hollister, George, 264, 265, 271, 276, 277, 282
Home in Hinghwa, 78, 79, 81 82, 84, 85, 88, 109, 286
Home Missionary Society, 128
Horse chestnuts, 3
Horses, 108
Hostility toward foreigners, 135, 139
Hua Nan College for women, 51
Hua Sang, 125
Hua Sang Massacre, 125, 127, 128
Huang, Joseph, 280
Hunting, 247, 248
Hwa Nan College, 51

I

Ice cream remedy, 282
Illness, 86, 87
Imperial army mutiny, 147
Import/export company, 186, 188, 189
Independent Siberian Republic, 189
Industrial school, 113
Inflation, 226, 227, 231, 238, 243, 255
Inns, 117
Interview with Elizabeth, 283
Invitation to China, 28, 29

J

Jackson, Dr., 22, 26
Japan, 56, 103, 128, 142, 186, 207
Japanese encroachment, 129, 214, 218, 224, 232
Jesus, story of, 66
Jewel, Carrie, 33, 37, 56
John Sung, 146, 286, 289
Joseph Huang, 280
Journey to China, 30, 31, 33

Journey to Foochow, 33, 35
Journey to Hinghwa, 79, 80, 180

K

Karis Brewster, 201, 218, 219
Kathleen Apperson Phillips, 68
Kathryn Cory, Dr., 53
Kerosene, 109
Kitchen in Manhasset, 200, 201
Korea, 128, 271, 276
Kucheng, China, 65, 67, 215, 227, 234
Kuliang, China, 67

L

Lacy, Carlton, 269
Ladder episode, 228, 229
Land distribution program, 277, 278
Lanterns, 109
Last days in Germany, 252, 253
Last years in China, 186, 189, 190
Last year in U.S., 292, 294, 301, 302
Laundry, 202, 222, 223
Learning Christ Prayer, 253
Leaving China, 194, 197, 239, 279 281, 289
Leaving Hinghwa, 138, 139, 140
Lectures. See Speaking engagements
Lepers, 91, 214
Leper colonies, 90, 92, 215
Letters from Elizabeth, 204, 205, 207, 214, 215, 219, 220, 224, 226, 227, 229, 230, 236, 238, 239, 243, 275
Levies, 174
Likin, 149
Literary work, 273, 274
Literati, 140, 141, 148
Lo cho, China, 261
London, Ohio, 12, 13, 16, 17
Long Tom, 184, 186
Longans, 121
Looting, 137, 140, 148, 176
Lord Elgin's message, 305, 306
Lord's Prayer, 295, 298, 299
Love, 58, 181
Lychees, 121, 291, 292
Lydia Trimble, Miss, 159

M

Mabel Hartford, 67, 71, 125, 126
Maddaus, Reverend Oscar, 205
Malay Peninsula colony. See Borneo colony
Manchu dynasty, 47, 130
Manhasset, New York, 200
Manhasset High School, 205
Manton, Frank, 201, 218
March on Hinghwa, 150, 151
Marriage, 74, 75, 180
Mary Brewster, 88, 95, 242
Mary Jane Fisher, 2, 12, 15, 16, 63
Matsu islands, 57
Meals, 116, 203, 204
Memorial service, 159
Memorial stone, 290, 291
Merchant houses, 61
Methodist church, 1, 3, 208, 227
Methodist Overseas Relief, 243
Methodist Rest Home, 34
Midway, Ohio, 1, 12
Migration, 117, 118
Military governor, Germany, 245
Milk, 109, 110
Ming bowls, 197, 199, 203
Minshall, Mary Jane. See Fisher, Mary Jane
Minshall castle, 19
Mission study group, 22
Missionaries, 22, 80, 101, 106, 227, 272
Missionary housing, 117
Missionary work, 88–89, 97, 104, 111
Modernization, 206, 207
See also Reform
Moral regeneration, 285
Morrison, Robert, 81

Mount Pleasant, Ohio, 8, 12
Move to Hinghwa, 82–83
Move to Vinton County, 4–7
Murray, Aunt Sally, 212, 213
Music, 50, 66, 94, 173, 236
Music lessons, 18
Musical instruments, 94
Mutiny, 147

N

Nathan Sites, 58 59, 73, 77
National Socialism, 285
Nationalists, 188, 189, 255, 263
Nativity pageant, 192
Neutral ground, 175
New China, 205
New Year, 190
New Year's celebrations, 84, 93
New York, 199
New York dinner, 225
Night watchmen, 149

O

Occupational training, 94, 95
October Hill, 296
Old lady's message, 285
Open Door policy, 142
Opium, 130
Opium War, 39
Orphanage in Hinghwa, 93, 272
Orphanage in Yellowstone, 169, 170, 242, 243
See also Rebecca McCabe Orphanage
Orphans, 92, 93, 94, 96, 175, 262
Oscar Maddaus, Reverend, 205
Otte, Dr. J. A. , 86 97
Owen, Seaman, Sir, 238

P

Pack mules, 108, 237
Pagoda Anchorage, China, 35, 208
Pastor Jackson, Dr., 22, 26
Paul Wright, 208
Pauline Westcott, 231
Pearl Harbor, 226
Peco butter, 214
Peking, China, 136, 146, 152
Penitence, 295
People's Army, 174, 175, 176
Persecution, 266
Phillips, Kathleen Apperson, 68
Phoenix, 200
Physicians, 86
Plantation, 243
See also Agricultural mission
Plumb family, 67, 71
Political affiliation, 213, 245
Political reform, 131, 132, 133, 142, 147, 207
Political unrest, 174, 189, 255, 257
Porcelain, 151, 195, 197, 199 200, 202, 203, 206, 247
Post war era, 246, 247, 250, 254
Prayer meetings, 2
Prayers, 23, 27, 100, 104
President Roosevelt, 213, 224
Prodigal Son, 24
Proposal of marriage, 73–74
Provincial governers, 136
Public health programs, 242, 262

Q

Quaker teachings, 23
Quan Yin statue, 195, 196, 203
Queues, 149, 150

R

Rangoon, Burma, 218, 219
Raymond Brewster, 153, 254
Reading, 141, 145
Rebecca Brewster, 212
Rebecca McCabe Orphanage, 244, 261, 262
Reclamation project, 245
See also Plantation
Recovery from cholera, 55–57

Recruitment of students, 46
Reform, 134, 135, 142, 147, 152, 205, 284
See also Modernization
Refuge, 230
Refugees, 175, 251
Regency, 147
Rejang delta, Borneo, 119
Relationship between Eva and Elizabeth, 180, 182, 186, 204, 205, 210, 225, 238
Religions, 101, 102
Religious studies, 3, 27, 100
Religious turmoil, 145
Remembrance, 301, 303, 305, 306
Resignations, 111, 112
Resistance bands, 174
Return to Foochow, 64–65, 67, 181
Return to Hinghwa, 128, 129, 218, 219, 223
Return to Ohio, 59
Return to the Republic of China, 241, 242, 243
Return to Wisconsin, 240
Reverend Oscar Maddaus, 205
Revival meetings, 2, 46, 55
Revival song, 172, 174
"Revivalist, The," 140, 141
Revolution, 147, 148, 150, 174
Revolutionists, 188
Richmond Hospital, China, 241
River of Heaven, 57
Roads, 205, 206, 220, 228
Robert Morrison, 81
Roses, 121
Rubber planter's son, 216, 217
Rural reconstruction, 258, 259, 262
Russia, 189

S

Sacrifice, 60, 61, 62
Salaries, 116, 235, 272
Sally Murray, Aunt, 212, 213
Sampans, 109
Sarawak, Borneo, 119, 215, 301
Scalp ringworm, 96, 244
Scare devils, 102
School for Boys, 39, 97
School for Girls. See Girl's school
School for the Blind, 170
Scioto Trail, 5
Seaman, Sir Owen, 238
Secret societies, 129, 135, 147
Separation, 152, 154, 157
Serpent's eggs, 120
Shanghai bank incident, 186, 188
Shanghai International Settlement, 123
Sharp Peak, China, 56, 58, 138
Shepherdess Mother, 178
Sienyu Hospital, 236
Siong ceh Sung. See John Sung
Shipping business, 184
See also Export/import business
Siberian Republic, 189
Siblings, 2, 16
Sien Yu valley, 89
Si ga boi hill, 229
Sikh police, 123
Silver knives, 207
Singing, 236
Sites, Nathan, 58, 59, 73, 77
Six Golden Candlesticks, 81, 97
Smallpox, 87
Smith, Arthur H., 143
Social unrest, 127, 128
Socialists, 284
Sowing beside all waters, 257, 263
Spanish Civil War, 284
Speaking engagements, 59, 60, 62, 63, 100, 216
Spirits, 101, 103, 104
Spiritual armor, 30, 58, 229
Spiritual crisis and revelation, 21, 23, 24, 25, 26, 27
Spread of Christianity, 144
Star, 43
Starvation, 262

Stock market crash, 189
Storm at sea, 70–71
Story of Jesus, 66
Strawberries, 120
Strawberry jam, 157 158
Students, 44, 96, 97, 105
Sui Dong, 159
Sun Yat sen, 130, 152, 188
Sung, John, 146, 286, 289
Sung bowls, 197, 199, 203
Superstitions, 78, 101, 102
Surrender, 242
Sweet potatoes, 113, 115

T

Talkie True, 195, 196, 206
Taoism, 102, 103
Taoist priests, 101
Taxation, 128, 130, 174
Teaching, 25, 65, 97–98, 205
Temple of Heaven, 104
Temples, 101
Territorial governments, 187
Testimonials, 98, 225
Theft, 85–86
Theological schools, 46, 105
Thoburn, Bishop, 72
Three Religions Society, 107
Tigers, 181
Tithing, 231
Tomatoes, 120
Tornado shelter, 70
Translations, 147
Transportation, 108, 109, 205, 220, 234
Travel, 187, 208, 209, 228
Trimble, Miss Lydia, 159
Trip to China, 30, 31, 33
Trip to Foochow, 33, 35
Trip to Hinghwa, 79, 80, 180
Typhoons, 68–70

U

Union Hospital, 235
Uprisings, 125, 186
U.S. policy toward China, 263, 264

V

Vegetables, 120, 121
Vegetarians sect, 127
Village woman's blessing, 181
Vinton County, 4
Vision for China, 100, 112, 143, 144, 152, 225
Visits from Elizabeth, 180, 182 183, 184, 210, 213, 221, 222, 234
Visits to village churches, 267, 268

W

W.B. Cole, 232
Wallace, Ethel, 159
War with Japan, 127, 128
Warlord Era, 124, 140
Warlords, 187, 188
Water travel, 109
Weaving project, 111
Wedding, 74–75
Westcott, Pauline, 231
Wesley Foundation, 216
Westernization, 130, 134, 143
Wildcat episode, 208
Wiley, Bishop, 41, 42
William Nesbitt Brewster, 63, 64, 72, 78, 99, 100 101, 112, 136, 158, 289
William Henry Raper Fisher, 1, 2, 4, 8, 12, 13
Wisconsin farm, 227, 237
Wisconsin vacation, 294
Women's Annual Conference, 50, 51
Women's Foreign Mission Society, 67
World War I, 169
World War II, 226, 227, 230, 232, 238, 239

Wright, Paul, 208

Y

Yellow Peril, The, 143
Yellowstone, China, 169, 176, 244
Yellowstone Orphanage, 169, 170, 242
See also Rebecca McCabe Orphanage
Yuan Shi Kai, 152

Z

Zane's Trace, 6

Lightning Source UK Ltd.
Milton Keynes UK
UKHW010609040722
405338UK00001B/9

9 781732 437302